IMAGE OF THE BEAST

Glenn Morrick

WESTBOW
PRESS®
A DIVISION OF THOMAS NELSON
& ZONDERVAN

WestBow Press books may be ordered through booksellers or by contacting:

WestBow Press
A Division of Thomas Nelson & Zondervan
1663 Liberty Drive
Bloomington, IN 47403
www.westbowpress.com
1 (866) 928-1240

ISBN: 978-1-9736-3286-3 (sc)
ISBN: 978-1-9736-3287-0 (hc)
ISBN: 978-1-9736-3288-7 (e)

Library of Congress Control Number: 2018907704

Print information available on the last page.

WestBow Press rev. date: 11/20/2018

Contents

Introduction

The Bible is the word of God. This also identifies Jesus as the word and express image of God. It is the purpose of this book to reveal that the Bible was written so that all can understand the purity and simplicity of its words. All that is necessary is to believe these words. The greatest hindrance to believing and then understanding the Bible is the cross. Not that there *was* a cross, but the *message* of the cross. For unless with all your heart you desire such a God, this book is foolishness. The greater the knowledge of the Lord, the greater the joy.

CHAPTER 1

IMAGE OF THE BEAST

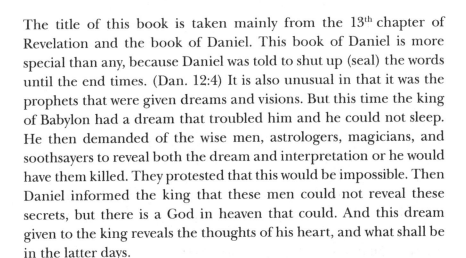

The title of this book is taken mainly from the 13th chapter of Revelation and the book of Daniel. This book of Daniel is more special than any, because Daniel was told to shut up (seal) the words until the end times. (Dan. 12:4) It is also unusual in that it was the prophets that were given dreams and visions. But this time the king of Babylon had a dream that troubled him and he could not sleep. He then demanded of the wise men, astrologers, magicians, and soothsayers to reveal both the dream and interpretation or he would have them killed. They protested that this would be impossible. Then Daniel informed the king that these men could not reveal these secrets, but there is a God in heaven that could. And this dream given to the king reveals the thoughts of his heart, and what shall be in the latter days.

The Lord then revealed to Daniel the dream and interpretation. The king saw a great image. This great image whose brightness was excellent stood before him, and the form of it was terrible. The head was of gold, its breast and arms of silver, its belly and thighs of bronze, its legs of iron and its feet of iron and clay. (Dan. 2:31-33)

Daniel informed the king that Babylon was the first kingdom, to be followed by these others. In fact, he told the king that he was this head of gold. (Daniel 2:38) This unusual statement is given so that special insight can be gained, by asking the Lord "Why is this wording so?" This will be explored after the accuracy of this prophesy is revealed. This prophesy and interpretation was correct in every detail. So much so, that secularists insist the book of Daniel was written after the fact. The order of nations was Babylonian, Medo-Persian, Grecian, then followed by the Roman Empire that was in place during the time of the birth of Christ, his death and resurrection, and his ascension into the heavens. This beast continues to the feet, with the ten toes world that will be in place when Jesus will return from the heavens with the saints to do away with the world's kingdoms, while establishing his everlasting kingdom.

As to answer this statement to the king. "This dream was given to the king to reveal to him what shall be in the latter days, and the thoughts of his heart." Daniel revealed to the king that this stone cut without hands will destroy this kingdom of the beast, and God will establish his everlasting kingdom that will stand forever. Daniel had told the king he was this head of gold. In the very next chapter, the king of Babylon had a golden image seventy-five feet high by nine feet wide built of which all of his kingdom must bow down to and worship. This, shortly after the king had fallen down and worshiped Daniel, stating Daniel's God was God over all gods. So, we know the thoughts of the king, as his heart ignored the complete ending and destruction of the beast. But most importantly, ignoring God's purpose and will, somehow rejecting the actual presence and purpose of God.

Not going into great detail analyzing the king, we will examine God's word. The 14th chapter of Isaiah speaks of these very end times. Satan is called Lucifer, son of the morning. But what is significant is Isaiah 14:4, "Thou shall take up this proverb against the king of Babylon, and say, 'How hath the oppressor ceased! The golden city ceased!'" Satan is called the king of Babylon.

This also speaks of the demise of him who knows the Lord and his purpose, but has rejected both, saying "I will be like the Most High". Also Satan is prophetically called, in Ezek. 28:1-19, the prince of Tyre. This chapter also proclaims his beauty, wisdom and brightness, extending to the end of his world when he will almost destroy it. There are many more scriptures that coordinate and affirm the absolute reliability of the Bible and that answer the question as to who or what is mystery Babylon.

Rev.18:1-4 "I saw another angel come down from heaven, having great power, and the earth was made bright with his glory. - And he called mightily with a strong voice, saying, 'Babylon the great is fallen, is fallen, and is become the habitation of demons, and the hold of every foul spirit, and the cage of every unclean and hateful bird. - For all the nations have drunk of the wine of the wrath of her fornication. And the kings of the earth have committed fornication with her, and the merchants of the earth are grown rich through the abundance of her delicacies.' - And I heard another voice from heaven saying, 'Come out of her, my people.'" This scripture is specifically speaking of the last days. Actually Babylon is this world, which Christians are in but not of (this will be made clear later.) Described as a habitation of demons, this is also speaking of the time of the last worldwide government. Daniel and Jesus spoke of this; if the Lord would delay his coming, there would be no flesh saved alive. This habitation of demons corresponds also with Dan. 2:43 "They shall mingle themselves with the seed of man; but they will not adhere one to another."

MADNESS

Bible prophesy extends beyond what will come to pass, to identifying the creator. Any reading of prophesy will neither contradict itself nor another prophesy in the Bible. The continuation of this prophesy will be when Jesus returns from the heavens to establish his everlasting kingdom. This from the end time world kingdom of the beast of which Christ returns to. What we have is an unbroken continuation to verify the reliability of the word of God.

This world that Jesus returns to will have been divided into ten sections. It is at this last kingdom of feet with ten toes that Jesus returns from the heavens with the saints to establish his everlasting kingdom. This all done by a stone cut out of the mountain without hands. This is all recorded in Dan. 2:31-35 and Rev. 19:14-15.

This identical time frame of earth's history is described in the 13th chapter of Revelation. Except there are ten horns, with ten crowns. Rev. 13:1,3-4,11-14. "And I saw the beast rise out of the sea having ten horns (toes) - and all the world worshiped the dragon and beast. - And another beast coming up out of the earth causes them to worship the first beast before him, whose deadly wound was healed, and to make an image to the beast that had the wound to the head, and did live." And then in verse 15 it is stated this beast has power to give life unto this image of the beast, that the image of the beast should both speak, and cause as many as would not worship the image of the beast should be killed.

Jesus spoke of this very time, saying "For then shall be great tribulation, such as was not since the beginning of the world to this time, no, nor ever shall be. And except those days should be shortened, there would be no flesh be saved, but for the elect's sake those days shall be shortened." (Matt. 24:21-22) Daniel also addresses this time. Dan. 12:1-3 "And at that time shall Michael stand up, the great prince who stands up for the children of your people, and there shall be a time of trouble, such as never was since there was a nation even to that time; and at that time will thy people be delivered, every one that shall be found written in the book. - And many of those who sleep in the dust of the earth shall awake, some to everlasting life, and some to shame and everlasting contempt. - And they that be wise shall shine like the brightness of the firmament; and they that turn many to righteousness, as the stars forever and ever."

Chapter 2

Another Image

It is quite clear that this beast in whom this image is of is a continuation of this world's nations, until a final unity, or one world government will come to be. All but a few, as this world will be of the beast, or their names would be written in the Lamb's book of life. None of the nations or individuals will be neutral or non-committal. Satan being the head is made quite clear. 2nd Cor. 4:3-4 "But if our gospel be hidden it is hidden to them who are lost, - Whom the god of this world (age) has blinded the minds of them who believe not, lest the light of the glorious gospel of Christ, who is the image of God, should shine unto them."

Now what has been introduced is another image; the image of God. Clarified as the "express image of God" (Hebrews 1:3), it is this light that cannot be seen because they believe not. "Believing not" is rejecting what was told or revealed. It is then, after rejecting what they have received, that their minds are blinded to the glorious gospel. The Lord is a God of justice, and justice will not condemn anyone for not receiving what was not revealed.

In order to be blinded to anything, it must be clearly presented or visible. There must be a *knowing* rejection, and in this case a rejection of an absolute truth. What presents itself is a blindness that is willingly self-imposed. Actually, much more than that. There is a full rejection of what God created man to be.

The Lord created man for a wondrous eternity, which man in his present state is incapable of even conceiving. This cannot be taken away. But it can be rejected. And in order to be rejected there must be not only the rejection of his Son who is the door, but there must be the acceptance of another in his place who is opposite in every way. This image that this world will make themselves of, is described as a liar with no truth in him. This is proclaimed by the Lord who is the way, the truth, and the life.

THY WORD IS TRUTH

Hopefully this narrative will not be received as a book explaining prophesies just for the purpose of revealing what will come to pass. Prophesy is supernatural verification of absolute truths. As will soon be evident, there is a purpose in allowing prophesies to interpret themselves. At this time, what will be addressed is the third image in the very first chapter of the Bible. And what will be applied here will be called the law of non-contradiction. This applies to all prophesy and scripture. This is based on a simple standard verified by fulfilled prophesy. God is the Alpha and Omega, the Beginning and the End. And he is incapable of error or deception, as he is the Word of Truth. What is demanded of all of us is to search the scriptures to see if these things are so.

The key to understanding prophesy is to embrace the non-contradiction of the Bible. God cannot and will not give contrary statements. And then, to concentrate on what *seems* out of place, because of the assurance that there is nothing out of place in the Word of God. It is then, with this assurance, that a full understanding can be more clearly seen. There is a realization that there is some special insight for believers. Much like when Jesus explained the meaning of a parable. He then said "He who has ears to hear, let him hear. - And the disciples asked, 'Why do you speak to them in parables?' - He answered, 'Because it is given unto you to know the mysteries of the kingdom of heaven, but to them it is not given.'" (Matt. 13:9-11) Only those who are assured that he who is speaking is of truth could believe his words. And to them are given words that pertain to them, because of their belief.

The Old Testament is written in Hebrew, and the New Testament in Greek. Obviously, the translations into other languages are not perfect. Prayer, common sense and a good concordance helps overcome most problems. The Bible presents continual verification of moral and prophetic standards and truths, so that any errors in translations can easily be overcome. There is also an advantage that can be gained in understanding these words by inquiring of the author, and not man. John 14:26 "But the Comforter, who is the Holy Spirit, whom the Father will send in my name, he will teach you all things, and bring all things to remembrance, whatever I said to you."

NON-CONTRADICTION

With this standard of non-contradiction, we will examine what is the most important prophetic statement in the Bible. It is given in the context of the very creation of man, being the sole purpose for man's creation. This also involves an image. Unfortunately, this is not taken as a prophetic statement. But a statement of fact; which it is. This was the sixth day of creation. Genesis 1:26-27 "And God said, 'Let us make man in our image after our likeness; and let them have dominion over the fish of the sea, and over the fowl of the air, and over the cattle, and over all the earth, and over all creeping thing that creeps on the earth.' - So God created man in his own image, in the image of God created he him. Male and female created he them."

This is a clear statement that God created man in his image, after his likeness. As God is spirit and no man can comprehend he who is omnipresent (all present), the Hebrew word for image (tseh-lem) is an unused root. Shade, phantom, resemblance. And the word likeness (dem-outh) model, shape. There is no physical comparison of image or likeness. And as the Lord is completely void of any sin or unrighteousness, this would further eliminate any comparison of God and man. There are none righteous, no not one. Our greatest righteousness are as filthy rags. There are none that doeth good, no not one, etc.

There is something else that does not take much thought with Christians. The reason they are Christians is because of their full awareness of their need of a Savior. Then, with this same awareness, that the word of God is completely reliable. The answer is quite clear. The Lord Jesus as Savior took the sins of those who believe on him. Then these words "So, God created man in his own image", has to be something else. Because if we were in the image of God we could not sin, nor would we need a savior. The Lord said "let us create man in our image". This "us" and "our" includes the Godhead; Father, Son and Holy Spirit. Then chapter 2 tells the creation story again, stating God formed man out of the dust of the ground and breathed into his nostrils the breath of life; and man became a living soul.

Christians are told this is a combining of the first chapter of the creation story to make it easy to understand. Those who reject the Bible point out the many discrepancies that make this to be the same story. Those who believe, do so because of the gospel of Christ. The gospel states Jesus is the word, truth, life and way. John 1:1-4 "In the beginning was the Word, and the Word was with God, and the Word was God. – The same was in the beginning with God. - All things were made by him; and without him was not anything made that was made. - In him was life; and the life was the light of men." If Jesus is truth then one or both of these narratives are wrong. But if he is truth then both are true. This brings about a great mystery. Not only with the creation story, but all of the Bible.

Some scriptures will be given without explaining in great detail how these are both true. Jesus explained this to Nicodemus, and he didn't even ask. In the third chapter of John, verse 16 "God so loved the world that he gave his only begotten Son, that whosoever believes in him shall not perish, but have everlasting life." Now Nicodemus came to Jesus at night. John 3:2 "'We know, Rabbi, you are a teacher come from God; for no man can do these miracles you do except God be with him.' – Jesus answered, 'Except a man be born again he cannot see the kingdom of God.' – Nicodemus asked. 'How can this be?' – Jesus said, 'Unless a man be born of water and of the Spirit he cannot enter the Kingdom of God. – That what is born of the flesh is flesh; and that what is born of the Spirit is Spirit.'"

You must be born again to see the kingdom of heaven, but to enter the kingdom of heaven you must be born of the water and of the Spirit. When are you born of the water? Your physical birth. When are you fully born of the Spirit? At the rapture of gathering of the Saints to meet the Lord in the air. How do we know this is a Spiritual birth? 1st Cor. 15:51-53 "I show you a great mystery; we shall not all sleep, but we shall be changed. – In a moment, in the twinkling of an eye, at the last trump. We shall be raised incorruptible. – For this corruption must put on incorruption, and this mortal must put on immortality."

Many more scriptures will be given later, keeping in mind that your body made from the dust returns to the dust but your created spirit is eternal. And with these scriptures just given, these eternal spirits that were created before the foundation of the earth in Revelation 13:8 already have their names written in the book of life. Yet this birth will not happen until 6,000 years after the forming of the first man from the dust of the ground. There is a fantastic, beautiful chain of events called the mystery of God that this writer can barely reveal. As the more that the Lord reveals, the more the realization of how much is missed.

There must be a complete assurance of the reliability of the word of God, expanding to the Law of non-contradiction, letting the Bible make clarity, drawing us closer to understanding this and other mysteries. What will be addressed is for the purpose of our growth, or continued maturity in the Lord. As for man being made in God's image being actual, it is so, along with our names written in the book of life of the Lamb slain from the foundation of the world. With God being spirit, and man flesh, this causes a contrast that cannot be breached while occupying this present body. Jesus himself addressed this very subject.

CHAPTER 3

CHOOSING OUR FATHER

So we are speaking of two births. Our physical birth and life that lasts for only a season, in which we have no say as to whom our father will be. Then our second birth, in which we make the final decision, and this will be for eternity. The Father not only gave his only begotten Son, that whosoever believes in him shall have everlasting life; but also reveals who that life will be with. Along with the knowledge that the Son is the express image of the Father. He who has seen the Son has seen the Father. Those who reject what or who God has created them to be, do so with open eyes and are without excuse.

Interestingly the Lord said "Let *us* make man in *our* image after *our* likeness". This second birth is involving Father, Son, and Holy Spirit. Each has a part in this endeavor. Yes, all three are involved in this second birth in which we decide to whom we are to be born of. This choice to choose our Father, and what we will be, is beyond comprehension. And though we do not know *what* we will be, we know it *will* be.

GOD DECLARES THE END FROM THE BEGINNING

The Lord makes prophetic pronouncements in which there can be no doubt his words are true, and God's truth has a purpose. Words without truth have no purpose. Isaiah 46:10,11 "I am God, declaring the end from the beginning, and from ancient times the things that are not yet done, saying, My counsel shall stand, and I will do all my pleasure; - ... I have spoken it, I will also bring it to pass; I have purposed it, I will also do it." Anything stated in the word of God is as though it has happened.

As God created man in his image, no one can hinder this from coming to be except the very one who rejects what they were created to be. This absolute justice of God is revealed in the 13th chapter of Revelation. This has been occurring from the dawn of time, then clearly revealed when most of the world becomes the image of the beast; except for those who have the seal of God. Anyone whose name is in the Lamb's book of life will be killed. This will be a universal single-minded purpose. In fact, it is the only purpose for the beast. It is very clear that only Christians will be killed. And it seems beheading will be the mode of execution.

This mindless rejection of what God created man to be, followed by the complete submission to the beast in order to eradicate every one that would with joy and anticipation be looking for the coming of the Lord from the heavens with his army of saints. *This* is the time that those demons spoke of when they encountered Jesus, and said. "What have we to do with thee, Jesus the Son of God? Are you come to torment us before the time?" (Matt. 8:29)

This is what Satan and one third of God's angels have also done; rejected what they were created to be. Heb.1:14 "Are they not all ministering spirits, sent forth to minister for them who shall be heirs of salvation?" These angels were not only in the presence of God, but rejoiced while witnessing the creation. Job 38:7 - "When the morning stars sang together, and all the sons of God shouted for joy." (Also Ezekiel 28:13-14)

Just as Satan and one third of the angels rejected the very purpose for their creation, so will man reject the Son who is the express image of the Father. The Lord calls them "My little flock." In the 13th chapter of Revelation there is revealed a world of mankind that will not only reject the image God created them to be, but by willfully rejecting the purpose for their creation, become of a different image that will bring about a strange and sick perversion and bondage of indescribable evil and terror.

THE GATHERING

This is a mystery because those who die in Christ are immediately in his presence. 2nd Cor. 5:6,8 - "While we are at home in the body, we are absent from the Lord. - We are willing to be absent from the body, and to be present with the Lord." However, it is clear that the dead who are in the presence of the Lord will be changed along with the living, both to be raised incorruptible. Both to be changed. This is not to be taken lightly. The difference is the change that takes place resulting in our incorruption, at this designated time. "We know not what we will be, but when he shall appear, we shall be like him. For we shall see him as he is." This event will happen at a specific future time shortly before the Lord returns from the heavens. And he will return with these resurrected saints. It is at this time that it will be known what God has prepared for those who love him (1st Cor. 2:9). All believers are born again. But the actual birth of truly being the incorruptible image of God will be when we see him as he is, when the believers meet the Lord in the air. Only incorruption can recognize incorruption.

And this same event is recorded in 1st Thess. 4:13-17 "I would not have you to be ignorant, brethren, concerning them who are asleep, that you sorrow not, even as others who have no hope. - For if we believe that Jesus died and rose again, even so them who also sleep in Jesus will God bring with him. - For this we say to you by the word of the Lord, that we who are alive and remain unto the coming of the Lord shall not precede them who are asleep. - For the Lord Himself shall descend from heaven with a shout, with the voice of the archangel, and the trump of God; and the dead in Christ shall rise first. - Then we who are alive, and do remain, shall be caught up together to meet the Lord in the air; and we shall ever be with the Lord."

Because it is widely taught that man is in the image of God, and because the word of God clearly states this to be so, one more scripture will be given (many more could). The purpose is to better understand prophesy; to obtain a greater understanding of what the spirit of prophesy is. "The spirit of prophesy is the testimony of Jesus." (Revelation 19:10.) Prophesy, the word, and Jesus cannot be separated. They are one and the same.

Romans 8:23,29 "And not only they, but ourselves also, who have the first fruits of the Spirit, even we ourselves groan within ourselves, waiting for the adoption, that is the redemption of our body. - For whom he did foreknow, he also did predestinate to be conformed to the image of his Son, that he might be the first born among many brethren."

This clearly states that God, who knows what will be before it happens, does foreknow whoever is predestined to be conformed to the image of his Son. One whole book of the Bible, containing 42 chapters, was written about Job - the most righteous man on the earth. And when his eyes were opened that he could truly see the Lord, he abhorred himself and repented in dust and ashes. If he were already in the image of God, he would have beheld the beauty of the Lord, unable to contain himself with unspeakable joy and praise.

The amazing thing is that Job knew his Savior lived, and knew he would see him in the latter days. Job 19:25-27 "I know my redeemer lives, and that he shall stand at the latter days upon the earth. - And though after my skin worms destroy this body, yet in my flesh shall I see God. - Whom I shall see for myself, and my eyes shall behold him and not another, though my heart be consumed within me." Then Job is given further words of insight and prophesy. Job 19:28-29 "But ye should say, Why persecute we him, seeing the root of the matter is found in me? - Be ye afraid of the sword, for wrath brings the punishment of the sword, that you might know there is a judgment."

Job had understanding to the extent that he asked why God would punish our redeemer, seeing as the root of the matter was found in himself. This was a clear reference of Job's savior taking the punishment for Job, or taking the sins that are Job's. It then extended to the punishment by the sword that brings judgment. This judgment brought about by this same savior as he returns from the heavens with the saints who are now in his image, to judge the nations. Rev. 19:13-16 "And he was clothed with a vesture dipped in blood; and his name is called the Word of God. - And the armies that were in heaven followed him upon white horses, clothed in fine linen, white and clean. - And out of his mouth goes a sharp sword, that with it he should smite the nations, and he shall rule them with a rod of iron; and he treads the winepress of the fierceness and wrath of Almighty God."

It is difficult for us in the flesh to have an understanding of what we will be. In fact, we cannot know what we will be, nor has it entered into our heart. But what has been made abundantly clear is that only those who love truth can spend eternity with Truth. 1st Cor. 13:12 "For now we see in a mirror darkly; but then, face to face. Now I know in part, but then I shall know even as I am known."

WISDOM CORRUPTED BY REASON OF BEAUTY

We will address the importance of these words spoken on the sixth day of creation, along with the reliability and assurance of seemingly unconnected information that actually addresses the same event. Revealing a corruption of wisdom brought about by a beauty that is not earned, the 28th chapter of Ezekiel and 14th chapter of Isaiah give a description of an angel (Satan) created to be a ministering spirit unto mankind. This description given of Satan's beauty is used with heavenly comparisons. It is as though this beauty was the very image of God. But as for this beauty of Satan, he was created so by God. He had no part in becoming this visual beauty.

In fact, because of this undeserved beauty his wisdom was corrupted. Ezek.28:17 "Your heart was lifted up because of your beauty, you have corrupted your wisdom by reason of your brightness." Isaiah 14 expands on this corruption of his wisdom. 14:13-14 "You have said in your heart, I will ascend into heaven, I will exalt my throne above the stars of God. - I will be like the Most High." It is clear that this beauty was such that he actually believed that he would exalt his throne above the stars of God. This brings up a question… how was it that he obtained this throne?

It would appear one third of the angels preferred to follow this beauty of Satan rather than to be ministering spirits to heirs of salvation, as they saw no beauty in the blood of the Lamb.

As Satan states, he will exalt his throne above the stars of heaven. Rev.12:3-4 "And there appeared another wonder in heaven. A great red dragon having seven heads and ten horns, and seven crowns upon his head. - And his tail drew the third part of the stars of heaven and did cast them to the earth." This, along with Rev. 8:12 that speaks of the third part of the stars being darkened, would all appear to be Satan being cast down from the heavens. Rev. 12:9 "That great dragon was cast out, that old serpent, called the Devil and Satan who deceived the whole world, and his angels were cast out with him." These scriptures will be repeated when making more clarity.

Every word of the Lord is given for man's benefit, there are no exceptions. As for the ability of man to be born in God's image, it is clearly defined by Jesus to Nicodemus. There must be a second birth, in which believers are covered by the blood of the Lamb of God. 1st Cor. 1:18 "The preaching of the cross is to them that perish foolishness; but to us who are saved it is the power of God." The believers are covered by the blood of the Son, which washes away all sin. Jesus returns from the heavens with a vesture dipped in blood; the same blood that washed the garments, being the covering or clothing of the armies that follow the Lord to the earth, white and clean.

Two thirds of the angels, and God's little flock, have no need for anyone to explain what beauty is. Nor is it necessary to explain the beauty of the justice of God, allowing mankind to choose the desires of their heart. This will be revealed with unmistakable clarity in the final chapter of this world; to be followed by a new heaven and new earth, and Jerusalem. The knowledge and understanding of this grace is incumbent upon accepting and wanting what the Lord wants for man. The only thing necessary to *receive* this beauty beyond description is to *recognize* this is as beauty beyond description.

CHAPTER 4

SCIENCE

Just as the Judeo-Christian Bible is truth, science is based on truth. Man has established laws of science based on theories. These theories must pass a test of time and authenticity before being accepted as a Law of science. Were any error to be found, it would lose its definition as a law.

THERMODYNAMICS AND BIOGENESIS

The very first law of science is the Law of Thermodynamics. It states that matter can be neither created nor destroyed. As matter *is* present, both organic and inorganic, this leaves only one possibility: there must be a creator God. The fact that there is life is addressed by another law that also requires a creator God: the Law of Biogenesis. This states life can only come from life, and after its kind. The conclusion is that this creator God must be a living God that creates life that in turn produce life after their kind.

THE SECOND LAW OF THERMODYNAMICS, OR LAW OF ENTROPY

Everything deteriorates or runs down. This law of science is perhaps the most observable: simple logic and common sense dictates that for anything to deteriorate, it was better at some time. There must be some intelligent supernatural creator, since there would be less order now than when this supposedly miraculous, disorganized Big Bang occurred about 14 billion years ago. The second law of thermodynamics clearly dictates that time is an enemy of the Evolutionary and Big Bang theories. It is amazing that by adding billions of years to something that cannot possibly exist, suddenly it's reasonable. Before continuing, there will be this continual reminder. There are no atheists. Only *professing* atheists. If the creator God of the Bible did not clearly reveal himself to all of mankind, he would not be a God of justice. And the Bible clearly speaks of justice and judgment.

This brings about a reasonable question. Why would not the God of justice reveal himself in such a manner that none would possibly reject his purpose for their creation? Angels were created to be ministering spirits to the heirs of salvation. And man, the heirs of salvation, were created to be in the image of God. The answer is, the Lord God has clearly revealed himself and his purpose for both man and angels. In fact, to such an extent that the ultimate justice is being played out before both. And this justice is that we choose exactly the desires of our heart.

HIGGS

As each year of scientific breakthroughs reveals a greater understanding of the amazing complexity, order, miniaturization and design of all matter, and then life itself, a new theory from secular scientists must be formulated that will silence the growing evidence that increasingly brings a greater separation between the secular scientists and science. (Secular scientists only separate themselves from science pertaining to creation and the creator.)

In an effort to make legitimate the twin theories of the Big Bang and Evolution -- theories that contradict all laws of science -- this has begun with the combined effort of many nations. And the United States of America appears to be the major contributor. The purpose of this multibillion dollar venture is the search for this mysterious Higgs Boson particle. The wording is, "we are looking for the secret of the universe". And what is the secret of the universe?

This secret is, something is holding everything together. And without this one thing there would be nothing. Absolutely nothing. These are the combined words of particle scientists around the world. This reasoning is coming from experimental and proven science. What will be reviewed here can easily be understood by all. It only gets complicated when that which is reasonable is purposely made confusing in order to mask or hide logic and truth that reveals the creator God.

A more extensive, but not a complete, description will be given later concerning the explanation, or understanding concerning the search for this particle that holds the secret of the universe, which makes matter possible. Efforts to verify its existence and then perhaps gain knowledge as to its secrets is the goal at Fermilab, just outside of Chicago. This along with the newly built, and much larger International Hadron Collider in Switzerland, at the costs of billions.

BORN TO BE BORN AGAIN

The pleasant surprise is that when describing this mysterious, as yet undiscovered particle that must be present for anything to exist, they are using the exact words of the Bible while describing what has to be happening in order for there to be anything. Which also applies to the awareness that there is anything. Gen. 1:1 "In the beginning God created the heavens and the earth". John 1:1-3 "In the beginning was the Word, and the Word was with God, and the Word was God. - All things were made by him, and without him was not anything made." The first chapters of Colossians and Hebrews reveal Jesus as creator, and by him all things consist and exist, and without him nothing exists. Then in Acts of the Apostles there is more affirmation along with a personal component and relationship that does not require a degree in particle science, nor billions of dollars. Acts 17:27-28 "That they should seek the Lord, if perhaps they might feel after him, and find him, though he is not far from every one of us. - For in him we live and move and have our being. For we are also his offspring."

Then thousands of years after these words were written, scientists from several countries spend billions to find whom the Judeo-Christian Bible identifies as Jesus the Son of God. Who not only created all things, but sustains and upholds everything he created.

And then reassures us he can easily be found, as he is near to every one of us. And this at no cost to us

It would appear the secular world is giving up; this particle, called the Higgs particle, is better known as the God particle. No, Satan is not giving up, but is moving into the next chapter of his aspirations. This is described in Isaiah 14:13-14 "For you have said in your heart, 'I will ascend into heaven, I will exalt my throne above the stars of God. I will sit also upon the mount of the congregation, in the sides of the north. - I will ascend above the heights of the clouds. I will be like the Most High.'"

Lucifer appears to be successful in this world, and then proves there are no atheists. Rev. 13:8 "All that dwell upon the earth shall worship him, whose names are not written in the book of life of the Lamb slain from the foundation of the world." This in a world that has already affirmed that Satan is the god of. But that does not complete his aspirations. And that is to be worshiped as God, whom he must replace as omnipresent, creator, and sustainer of all things. This he cannot obtain, and he is well aware of it. The Lord would have fallen man take a hard look at whom they are imitating. And most importantly, in whose image they are becoming.

This we know: Satan wants to be worshiped because of what is recorded in the Gospels. In Luke 4:1-14, Jesus was led by the Spirit into the wilderness and tested by the devil for 40 days. Verses 5-8 "And the devil, taking him into a high mountain, showed him all the kingdoms of the world in a moment of time. And said to Jesus, 'All this authority will I give you, and the glory of them; for it is delivered unto me, and to whomsoever I will, I give it.'" As Jesus did not rebuke or correct him concerning his authority to give the world's kingdoms and their glory to whoever he willed, this affirms Satan is the god of this world. The Lord did not make him so. But man, in rejecting God and his word, has chosen another who is contrary in every way. When truth is rejected, it is rejected for a lie. Please keep in mind that Jesus and Christians are not of this world. John 17:15-16 "I pray not that you should take them out of the world, but you should keep them from the evil. - For they are not of the world, even as I am not of the world."

Lucifer's goal is to be God, and worshiped as such by mankind. However, those he desires most to worship him refuse to do so. And those who eagerly follow him or his example, he has the greater contempt for (as he has contempt for all of mankind). But he knows the word of God is just that. The word of God. Whatever the Lord proclaims, it will be. That assurance leaves only one possibility for him not to be cast into the pit when Jesus returns from the heavens with the Saints. (Rev. 19:14) The very next event after the Lord returns from the heavens is the casting of Satan into the pit for 1,000 years. Rev. 20:1-2 "And I saw an angel come down from heaven, having a great chain in his hand. - And he laid hold on the dragon, that old serpent who is the Devil and Satan, and bound him a thousand years."

There is a sure way that Satan knows he will not be cast into the pit. And that is if God's word were altered in any way. It is a sad commentary, but Satan has more belief and assurance in the word of God then Christians do. Zechariah 12:10 "In the spirit of grace and of supplications they shall look upon me whom they have pierced, and they shall mourn for him, as one mourns for his only son, and shall be in bitterness for him, as one has bitterness for his first born." This is when the Lord will return from the heavens to be greeted by believing Jews in Israel. Were there not to be any Israelites to greet Jesus as the prophet proclaims, neither would Rev. 20:2 follow: "And he laid hold on the dragon and bound him one thousand years." This immediately follows Jesus' return from the heavens.

Only if there was an absolute assurance that God's word is completely accurate, would it even enter into the mind of Satan that the only way to alter the outcome would be to alter what was stated to be. He has a problem, however. Knowing the reliability and assurance of God's word, there is that same assurance; these events cannot be altered. It is being assumed here that Dragon has been giving up on altering scriptures, in light of his inability of stopping Israel from becoming a nation - exactly as the prophet stated would be. (Ezek. 37:1-14) And then the constant unsuccessful effort to drive her out after these scriptures were fulfilled on May 14, 1948.

This leaves but one option for that Dragon. And Jesus spoke of this specific time in Matt. 24:22, "Were I to delay my coming there would be no flesh saved alive." And when he is cast out of heaven to the earth, it is then when the awareness of his inability to achieve his goal of becoming God is much more than unattainable; it has cost him dearly. It is then that not only the Jews, but all of mankind whom God created must be destroyed. Rev. 12:12 "Rejoice, ye heavens, and you that dwell in them. Woe to the inhabitants of the earth and the sea. For the Devil is come down to you, having great wrath, because he knows he has but a short time."

PURPOSE

Satan is defined as the god of this world. This is man's temporary home, and we are assured all of the world, except those whose names are written in the Lamb's book of life, will worship the dragon. And in a mad rage they will then hunt down and kill Christians. (Rev. 13) As this is so stated, it will so be. This makes it prudent to examine the heart of that old serpent, of whom it seems quite clear most will follow. For in so doing, there is the examining of your own heart.

Why did an all knowing and loving God create the Devil? This should be asked of God, as a child would ask their father to understand his words. And not as an accusation, but with the assurance there is an answer, knowing there is a purpose for all the Lord does and says. Just as in examining the intricacies of all of life, the more that is revealed, the greater the realization that man will never even begin to grasp the full enormity and complexity of life. But what *can* be easily grasped is that not only man, but all of creation is fearfully and wonderfully made. Satan was created for the day of evil. It is easier to long for and seek the good when evil is present.

As wonderfully as man is made for this short time in this body of flesh, we are assured we cannot even conceive what we will be. The Apostle Paul revealed that while in this body, how little we really know of what we will be. That is when we become as God is. 1st Cor.13:12 "Now we see in a mirror darkly, but then, face to face, now I know in part, but then shall I know even as I am known." This continues to 1st John 3:1-2 "The world knows us not. - We are the children of God, and it does not appear what we will be. But we know that when he shall appear, we shall be like him, as we shall see him as he is." The only way the children of God will be able to see the Lord as he is will be when we are changed to be as he is. This is when the believers are caught up to meet the Lord in the air. First the dead in Christ, then the living. In a moment – in the twinkling of an eye.

Jesus told Nicodemus of this time. "Nicodemus, unless a man be born again he cannot *see* the kingdom of God." Then he said.

"Except a man be born of water and of the Spirit he cannot *enter into* the kingdom of God." The Lord is making two statements. You must be born again to see the kingdom of God, and then be born of the water and the Spirit to enter the kingdom of God. You must first be able to see the kingdom of God. How can one enter when they cannot see the way? The disciples said to Jesus, "We know not the way". Of which Jesus said. "I am the way, the truth, and life." And if what they are seeing they do not desire, would they not cease to look upon the way to enter the kingdom of God? It is foolishness to even ask that question, as they are rejecting the very word of God.

TRUTH AND COMMON SENSE

How is it possible that in knowing these things, sinful and prideful man could believe they are even now created in the image of God? Rather, we *will be* created in the image of God at the fullness of time, when we are caught up to meet the Lord in the air. If man was created in the image of God there would be no need or reason for a Savior. This is not rocket science, but common sense. Jesus clearly explained this to Nicodemus. You must first be born again to see the kingdom of God. (Believe and receive Jesus, who is the express image of God.) John 10:7 "I am the door of the sheep." The Son of God is the door, or entrance to the kingdom of God. The door that is the entrance when the church is caught up to meet the Lord in the air. John 3:3-5 "Except a man be born again he cannot *see* the kingdom of God. - Except a man be born of water and of the Spirit, he cannot *enter* the kingdom of God". Before this final event, Christians are in the world, but not of the world.

It is at this time they will be taken out of this world. But not before. In John 17:14-15, Jesus is praying, "I have given them thy word, and the world has hated them, because they are not of the world, even as I am not of the world. - I pray not that you should take them out of the world, but you should keep them from the evil."

Many scriptures are given here to reveal that God is God. And man is not. And many, many more could be given. This book's title is "The Image of the Beast". It would be appropriate to review what the Lord has to say concerning the god of this world (the beast.) The Lord gave him beauty beyond comprehension. Because of this beauty (which he did nothing to bring about), he deemed himself to be in the image of God. And then pride brought him to elevating himself above God. Anyone that can visualize himself to be as God has positioned themselves to elevate themselves above the Lord. Satan said "I will be above the stars of God."

The 14th Chapter of Isaiah and 28th chapter of Ezekiel reveal what brought on the corruption and evil that overcame the god of this world. It was the brightness of his beauty, and pride. And then he deceived himself into believing he was in the image of God. Ezek. 28:17 "Thine heart was lifted up because of thy beauty, you have corrupted thy wisdom because of thy brightness."

TRUE BEAUTY

The Word and words of God are even more wondrous, intricate and beautiful than this physical body that we abide in for a season. This also holds with the beauty that describes Lucifer. This is a concept that is parroted by man. A picture is worth a thousand words. But can a picture describe love, faith, forgiveness, or even describe itself?

How many people would describe the presence of a beaten figure on a cross as beautiful? 1st Cor. 1:18 "The preaching of the cross is to them that perish foolishness, but unto us who are saved it is the power of God." The Bible and Jesus, the Son of God, are both described as the word of God. This leaves us with the assurance that it is the word of God that defines beauty and truth. Would it not be prudent to examine the word of God with the assurance that there are no contradictions? And because God is truth, logic, and common sense? The word of God, then, is perfect beauty.

Satan was visually beautiful, and this beauty lifted up his heart to corrupt his wisdom. He became who Jesus described as "a liar with no truth in him". Does this not make him void of all beauty?

Much time has been spent here examining if man is in the image of God. Reason and common sense alone tell us that if we were to believe this to be so – that we are the image of God – our conduct would mirror the conduct of the Shirley MacLaine's of the world. Those who shout to the world "I am God." But this is not so, as Christians are sure of one thing. God is God, and man is not. Perhaps it would be more prudent to use as an example the one whom the Lord calls the god of this world. As the MacLaine's come and go with regularity.

Are we then mirroring the god of this world when we convince ourselves we are created in the image of God? This when the word of God clearly states there is none righteous. No, not one. There is no one that does good. Isaiah 64:6 "We are all as an unclean thing, and all our greatest righteousness are as filthy rags."

THE GOD OF THIS WORLD

We are assured Satan is the god of this world (God has not made him so, but man). By rejecting He who is Truth, fallen man has embraced he who has no truth in him. 2nd Cor. 4:3-4 "But if our gospel be hidden, it is hidden to them that are lost. - In whom the god of this world has blinded the minds of those who believe not, lest the light of the glorious gospel of Christ, who is the image of God, should shine unto them." Most reading these words assume Satan blinds only the minds of non-Christians. There is much more involved. There can be, and are, legitimate disagreements concerning the meaning of scriptural passages. However, there is one thing there can be no disagreement on. The God of the Judeo-Christian Bible is truth. He will not – nor can he – contradict himself, and is incapable of error.

NON-CONTRADICTION

At this time, we will examine more fully this scripture that was given on the sixth day of creation. This scripture is not what would be called controversial, and is accepted to mean what it states. Man is created in the image of God. Gen. 1:27 "So God created man in his own image, in the image of God created he him. Male and female created he them." Bible believing Christians affirm this must be so, because the Lord in his word makes a clear statement that he did just that. This on the sixth day of creation, when only Adam was created. Then, the rest of the Bible gives us constant reminders that man is everything *but* in the image of God. The argument often given is: "But after men and women were made in the image of God, they fell." Regardless that only Adam was present when the word of God said "God made man in his image, in the image of God created he them. Male and female created he them". If any were in the image of God, they would be incapable of any lies or sin. They could not fall. And because it was stated that man and woman were created in his image before Eve came to be from Adam's rib, this reveals an interesting truth. It is a statement that reveals truths and realities that are difficult to fully grasp. If this were not so, we have a complete contradiction.

If someone really believed God is truth and is incapable of deceiving or of uttering falsehoods, there would be no hesitation in accepting that the Lord is revealing something very special to those whom the world rejects. Matt. 13:10-11 "The disciples came to Jesus and asked, 'Why do you speak to them in parables?' - He answered, 'Because it is given unto you to know the mysteries of the kingdom of heaven, but to them it is not given.'"

These are not words to be taken lightly, or ignored. First of all, the Lord is God, period. Satan is the god of this world only. And that is because this world has rejected the Word of God. The Lord, as a God of justice, will not judge anyone of rejecting him until they have rejected the express image of himself, his Son, along with not believing his written word as truth. They have rejected the one whose image man was created to be of in exchange for another image, who is the complete opposite in every way. Jesus defined him as "A liar with no truth in him."

DECLARING THE END FROM THE BEGINNING

The scriptures verifying that man is not in the image of God are endless. In fact, this awareness that man is a sinner is what brings man to the knowledge that he *needs* a savior. Isaiah 46:9-10 "I am God... - Declaring the end from the beginning". These words are an affirmation that only God knows the end from the beginning. This is what defines prophesy; the foretelling with complete accuracy of what will be. Rev. 22:13 "I am Alpha and Omega, the beginning and the end, the first and the last." With these words, understanding rushes in that this is a statement of fact as the Father, Son and Holy Spirit have indeed created man in the image of God long before their actual birth. It is then it becomes abundantly clear this is a prophetic statement, as all prophesy of God is spoken with the assurance that it has been accomplished. This reveals, again, that the Lord is Alpha and Omega.

The Lord is declaring what man was created to be from the very beginning. And it will be as so proclaimed. This is clearly a prophetic pronouncement of fact given 6,000 years ago. But man is given the freedom to reject what God has created him to be. Jesus himself affirmed this 2,000 years ago when he told Nicodemus, a leader of the Jews, “You must be born again”. The Holy Spirit must quicken our spirit. You cannot change prophesy, but can only take your name out of the book of life after it was put in.

CHAPTER 5

THE ALPHA AND OMEGA

When just married as a young man and not yet farming, this hunger to know the Lord stirred within me. Having a Bible and attending many diverse churches, and also knowing there was a creator God, I begin my search for God. Being well aware of the diversity and contrary beliefs of Christianity, I was also aware of it being far more reliable having two books (the Old and New Testaments) covering thousands of years.

Immediately, however, problems arose. The very first chapter of the Bible stated God created the heavens, earth and all there is in six days. And all this took place about six thousand years ago. Being a science buff, I was convinced this could not be. And none of the churches I attended even addressed this. Billy Graham said "I cannot prove what the Bible states, but accept by faith that it is true". Regardless of the evidence? For me this is an insurmountable problem. As in my mind, that kind of faith is gullibility. How can you search out that which is not trustworthy, especially in the very first chapter?

Common sense reveals that you put your faith in someone that has a reputation of impeccable standards of truth and reliability. Even at that young age, I knew enough of science to know that there had to be a creator God. So Evolution and the Big Bang theory did not impress me, as both were at complete odds with the laws of science. But one thing that was an insurmountable problem was starlight and time. I knew light travels at 186,200 miles per second. And the estimated distance of the farthest visible star is about 13,000,000,000 light years away. That means it takes 13 billion years for the light from this star to reach the earth. These stars could not be seen if creation was less than 13 billion years ago.

If the Judeo-Christian Bible started out with a glaring scientific error in the very first chapter, this stopped my reading. Several times I would start reading but could not continue because of starlight and time. At this time I was told by a Christian friend who, like Billy Graham, accepted the Bible by faith, to start in the New Testament. Reading in Matthew, there was a continual reference to the prophetic events that authenticated these words as true. And so many references of the coming Messiah. No man can foretell these events with such unfailing accuracy but God. It was only a few days later that I became a Christian. This, with a special joy of assurance knowing every word of God is true. And there is a special blessing for those who search out apparent errors. For that is when special insight and mysteries are revealed.

As stated, the greatest hindrance to accepting the Bible as the word of God was starlight and time. But I had completely forgotten a program that was on channel 21 in Madison shortly after being married. This was the explaining of Dr. Albert Einstein's theory of relativity. Now this TV narrator was not arguing for the six-day creation, about six thousand years ago. This scientist defined it quite well, and apparently did not realize the enormity of what he was presenting. This is how he explained relativity and time. This was almost identical to Russell Humphreys, a creation scientist, in his booklet Starlight and Time which was written thirty-nine years later, in which he clearly authenticated the Bible.

BEYOND TIME

In Revelation 1:8 God defines himself. "I am Alpha and Omega, the beginning and the ending, saith the Lord, which is, and which was, and which is to come, the Almighty." This is difficult to impossible to understand until Albert Einstein's Theory of Relativity. Which is also difficult to understand, but is proven to be correct and completely accepted by all scientists.

1955 WISCONSIN PUBLIC TELEVISION

This is how this scientist explained Dr. Einstein's theory of relativity (which, again, is identical to Dr. Humphreys). At this present time, all of the universe is expanding at a steady rate. The speed of light is 186,200 miles per second. This is the ultimate speed. And as will be explained, when this speed is exceeded there is a time warp.

If you were able to witness a spaceship or a planet and its occupants that were expanding away from your position in your time; that is, if you could see the occupants on a screen, you would notice almost immediately that everything in their world would began speeding up at an accelerated speed. And then in a flash, everything would disappear as the total speed of light was reached. Were you able to observe them for any length of time in your timeframe, you would notice they would age at an accelerated rate. And the farther out they go in this expanding universe, their whole life would pass in but a moment. If it were possible to continue observing this spaceship there would be the passing of many generations, with each generation passing with a greater speed.

Dr. Humphreys states if they knew the exact rate of this expansion along with the size of the universe immediately after creation, it could be figured out exactly when the creation occurred. But with the information they have even now, it comes to but a few thousand years. Star Trek and other science fiction movies have employed this time travel in many of their programs.

This brings up a question. Why does not all of academia apologize to the Christian community for their years of ridicule of the Judeo-Christian Bible and those that believed in its words? Would they not be thankful and ecstatic, as there being a creator God would also mean there is a redeemer God? But there is no apology from them, as they continue as before. This reveals another truth of the Bible: spiritual blindness.

SPIRITUAL BLINDNESS

We have two problems in this understanding of this time warp because of speed. (Gravity also has an effect on time, as gravity slows down time.) Why is there not great excitement and thankfulness with the added realization of a creator God? And the second amazement is the Christians and Seminaries that have compromised the word of God to gain favor with the world. As they have compromised biblical truth, they too will not admit to being in error. Then they become a greater adversary of the Bible than the world. And in the last few years the churches and Christians that believe in the six-day creation that happened about six thousand years ago are diminishing. And this, as each new scientific discovery reveals there must be a Creator God. Most all of the public is aware of the concept of time travel. But why is it that few of our Seminaries actually believe the whole word of God? This is why life as a Christian is exciting beyond belief. The excitement comes as the mission field increases.

1st Cor. 2:11-12, 14-16 "What man knows the things of man, save the spirit of man that is in him? Even so the things of God knows no man, but the Spirit of God. - Now we have not received the spirit of the world, but the spirit that is of God, that we might know the things that are freely given to us of God. - But the natural man receives not the things of the Spirit of God; for they are foolishness unto him, neither can he know them, because they are spiritually discerned. - But he that is spiritual judges all things, yet he himself is judged of no man. - For who has known the mind of the Lord, that he may instruct him? But we have the mind of Christ." This is not saying Christians have perfect knowledge. Only that they believe and know that there *is* perfect knowledge, and this is Christ Jesus, the Word of God.

WORSHIP

Worship is the ultimate form of adoration and love. The Lord would have that those who worship him want more than anything to be in his presence and to be as he is. Not because of what is received in the flesh, but to know the Lord. Because they are seeking the heart of God, to see him as he is. Yes, the Lord would have such to worship him. Contrast that with the event of the mob calling for his crucifixion that only a few days before would have had Jesus to be their King.

The heart of God is not hidden, but clearly recognizable in his Son. Fulfilled prophesy and miracles authenticate to the mind that the Bible is the word of God. But it is the heart of man that the Lord desires. The heart reveals who we are, and also our desires. That is why the preaching of the cross is foolishness to them that perish. But to us who are saved it is the power of God. This power was made weakness, for those seeking the heart of God.

This writer was overwhelmed with the constant prophesies written hundreds of years before. Prophesies that precisely proclaimed the coming birth and place of birth of the promised Jewish Messiah, along with the words he would speak, miracles he would do, and his purpose for coming. This, along with being born of a virgin, as truly man and truly God. Isaiah 7:14 & 9:6. "His name shall be called God with us. - His name shall be called Almighty God, The Everlasting Father." And then his death, burial, resurrection, and promised return.

THE ENORMITY OF GOD

It was these prophetic truths, that were so overwhelming, that immediately exposed what was later found to be obvious deception concerning creation. This is designed deception with an agenda, being different than misunderstandings of what the Bible reveals. Deception is self-imposed. Rather like birds of a feather flocking together, those who are deceived know of whom they are joining themselves with. This adds more fuel to silence that which offends and exposes them.

The purpose of the scriptures is to reveal the heart of man, and the choices to be made according to the desires of their heart. These words of the Lord, in which he said "My little flock" have great significance and meaning to those who are not of this world and seek the wisdom that comes of the Lord. This is revealed at a climactic time shortly before Jesus' promised return from the heavens. Rev. 13:8 "And all that dwell on the earth will worship him, whose names are not written in the book of life of the Lamb slain from the foundation of the earth." We are given but a glimpse of the enormity of God in these few words. Even before there was a creation there was a book written, called the Lamb's book of life. Mankind born of Adam and Eve, not yet created, not yet born, had their names written in a book that assures eternal life to them. And what is more amazing is all of those yet to be born were created with the free will to reject Him. The Lord knows who they will be without controlling their choices.

Man cannot comprehend the enormity of God, just as he cannot comprehend the love of God. There will never, for all eternity, be a time that man can completely comprehend this love of God. But there will be an unbelievable comprehension when we see the Lord as he is, and as we become as he is. This will be but the beginning of an eternity of beholding the beauty of the Lord, with ever-increasing inquiring to know of him.

None of this would be possible were man to believe he is in the image of God; as there would be no need of a Savior. The third chapter of Philippians reveals this with clarity. Phil. 3:9,11-13,20-21 "The righteousness which is of God by faith... If by any means I might attain unto the resurrection of the dead... Not as though I have already attained, either were already perfect, but I follow after... Forgetting those things are behind, and reaching forth unto those things which are before... For our citizenship is in heaven, from which also we look for the Savior, the Lord Jesus Christ, - Who shall change our lowly body, that it may be fashioned like his glorious body, according to the working by which he is able even to subdue all things to himself."

This writer does not state that these Christians who align with the world that rejects the recent creation are not Christians. Christians are just that *because* we are aware of our shortcomings, and that none of us are good. (The more one believes the Bible, the more one is aware of their shortcomings.) It is, rather, meant to bring about an honest assessment of believing the Bible or not. It is not perfect understanding and knowing of the Bible that is in question, but rejection of the Word of God, the Son of God.

We have in the last book of the word of God a clear understanding that you are either of the Lord, or you are not. There are no grey areas. Jesus is the express image of God. Heb. 1:3 "Who, being the brightness of his glory, and the express image of his person..." The Lord is a just God who will not hinder anyone from entering into his kingdom without full knowledge that they are rejecting him. This assurance of rejection can only be verified by the acceptance of one who is completely contrary in every way. Jesus is the way, the truth, and life. Satan is a liar, with no truth in him. And he is death.

Much time has been spent on being in the image of God. This is not to be taken lightly or as a casual insignificant occurrence. As previously mentioned, Job, the most righteous man on earth, stated that he had heard of God. But then when he saw the Lord for the first time, he said "I abhor myself, and repent in dust and ashes." But when Job shall see the Lord in his resurrected body, he will be unwilling to take his eyes off of him. The reason is that he will have a new body, completely cleansed and changed. David spoke of this change and the resulting consequences of it. Psalm 27:4 "…and that I may dwell in the house of the Lord all the days of my life, to behold the beauty of the Lord..." Phil. 3:21 "Who will change our lowly body, that it may be fashioned like his glorious body…" The references which affirm what the Bible states are endless. We, in this body of flesh, cannot even conceive what we will be.

We are assured that Job will see the Lord in his resurrected body. Job 19:25-27 "For I know my redeemer lives, and that he shall stand at the latter day upon the earth, - And though after my skin worms destroy this body, yet in my flesh shall I see God. - Whom I shall see for myself, and my eyes shall behold, and not another."

When Christians state they were created in God's image, this is not offensive – as most are making a stand against the evolutionary theory of man evolving from apes, and those denying the creator. They are also recognizing that man is a special creation who was given an eternal spirit. Man was created to be in the image of God, separate from beasts or animals. Ecclesiastes 3:21 "Who knows the spirit of man that goes upward, and the spirit of the beast that that goes downward to the earth?"

It is this same spirit that is the essence of man, which is the candle of God. Proverbs 20:27 "The spirit of man is the candle of the Lord, searching all the inwards parts." It is during this short time, while occupying this body of flesh, that searches and choices are being made as to whose image to be of. Those who choose the Lord are those born of the Holy Spirit. Then these candles will enter God's Kingdom completely washed, burning brightly for all of eternity. Daniel 12:2-3 "And many of those who sleep in the dust of the earth shall awake, some to everlasting life, and some to shame and everlasting contempt. - And they that be wise shall shine like the firmament, and they that turn many to righteousness, as the stars forever and ever."

Not all will burn brightly, as they will be as the god of this world, desiring a different brightness. A brightness of self. A pride escalating to a process of trying to bring God down to man's level. Much like the poor deluded souls as the Shirley MacLaines of this world, as they cry out for all to hear: "I am God." The god of this world proclaims the same, demanding worship as God while inhabiting the body of man whom he is set out to destroy.

This is recorded in Isaiah 14:12-17 in which Satan, who weakened the nations, is cut down. After stating he will be like God, then acclaiming to rise above God; resulting in being cast down to the earth because of the pride of his brightness. He then will make the world to tremble, making a wilderness of it. "And were Jesus to delay his return there would be no flesh saved." (Matt. 24:22)

CHAPTER 6

EVOLUTION AND SCIENCE

"Satan is a liar, with no truth in him." This scriptural reference has been, and will continually be stated all through this book, as a reminder that as the god of this world, those of this world will bear his image. (A precursor of the time Jesus spoke of.) Matt. 24:21 "Then shall be great tribulation, such as was not since the beginning of the world to this time, no, nor ever shall be." And Jesus is the way, the truth, the life, and the very word of God. Satan, as the god of this world, blinds the minds of those who believe not. Truth is being replaced with lies and falsehoods. These falsehoods exclusively pertain to the words of life. 2nd Cor. 4:4 "In whom the god of this age has blinded the minds of them who believe not, lest the glorious gospel of Christ, who is the image of God, should shine unto them."

It would be expedient to understand exactly what is stated here. These are not just hollow words, but words of life involving the gospel of Christ. Without these there can be no new birth. Precisely what does it mean, "to those who believe not"? We are assured the demons also believe. James 2:19-20 "You believe there is one God; you do well. The demons also believe and tremble. - Do you not know, vain man, that faith without works is dead."

Satan blinds the minds of those who believe not. As James recorded: The demons believe. But he continues with: Faith without works is dead. As we are assured, Jesus is truth and Satan is a liar with no truth in him. With this same assurance, there are two contrary definitions of faith which define belief in Jesus as Lord and Savior. It is often stated: if you have to have proof, where then is your faith? This is usually stated concerning any effort to expose evolution, and extends to endless false doctrines and beliefs. All this for the sake of unity. A unity of the world, designed to weaken and destroy the word of truth.

The biblical definition of faith is based on truth. How is it possible to have faith in a persistent liar or one who is unreliable? The statement "Satan blinds the minds of those who believe not" obviously is speaking of the Word of God, that being he who is defined as truth, and his words. The very first chapter of the gospel of John reveals quite clearly that Jesus is the creator of all there is. Those, then, who believe not these words that God created all there is? It is their minds that are blinded.

Believers in God include demons, along with all of man. (Demons, being spirits, have a far greater knowledge of the Lord, and are terrified of Jesus.) Satan, as the god of this world, has convinced the world that faith in the creator God is blind unsubstantiated belief in God's word. Never question words that appear to contradict other scriptures. This creates a bad habit of never questioning or communicating with your Lord for clarity. The Lord said "Let us reason together". Is it reasonable to have faith in a persistent liar? Or one who rejects any inquiring of his words? Faith is earned by consistent reliability. Faith in God is faith in absolute truth and righteousness. Not ours, but the Lord's.

EVOLUTION

Evolution contradicts the very laws of science it claims to use to support its theory. The first and second Laws of Thermodynamics state matter can't be created. Then, states all matter deteriorates. This is also the Law of Entropy, of which an interesting ploy was used by evolutionists: time. Time is the enemy of evolution. Plain common sense reveals that if everything is running down, it cannot be evolving upward. It had to have been created; and in better condition at the time it was created. But by inserting billions of years, this law of entropy magically reverses itself.

There has been a new element that scientists have discovered, affirming this law of entropy. For years it has been taught that evolution is the result of the mutation of living matter to improve its original state. But what has been discovered is that all mutations, which are a loss of information, are harmful. New information is never added. How do we know this? Science comes to the rescue in the form of DNA.

BLINDING OF THE MINDS

Add more time, like 13 billion plus years. Then miraculously, entropy and mutations do not occur. But the opposite happens. How is it possible that educators would even suggest this, as they have to know this to be an absurd impossibility? It must be noted that the only perversion of science is pertaining to creation and life itself. This reveals a specific agenda. There is no hiding of this agenda, with those who masquerade as scientific leaders. A specific truth being perverted or hidden always reveals who is involved. Science is based on truth, and all Laws of Science must be without contradiction or error, or they are just theories. There is an absurd but absolute standard or rule established by our science community in which any theory involving any supernatural creation will not be considered. All theories pertaining to the beginning of our universe and life itself must be based on natural selection. (Natural selection cannot occur from nothing.) Then rules of man disallowed whatever would be unacceptable to them, this being that there could be a creator God. In not allowing the only possible solution for this world and life, then calling it science, in a search for truth? No, the objectivity of science has been compromised and lost. Thus, it loses all credibility. This, then, is no longer science.

The very first law of science states matter cannot be created. And then the Law of Biogenesis states life only comes from life, and after its kind. This leaves only one possibility. As matter is here, it had to be made so by a Creator God. True science not only affirms the Creator God, but also that all life must come from a life giver who is a living God. These are based on Laws of science.

Science not only affirms the Bible, but by scientists abandoning their objectivity and reason it affirms that there is indeed a god of this world who blinds the minds of those who believe not. It is not that difficult to understand what is not believed. It is truth. A very specific and special truth. Truth that brings eternal life.

What has just been stated is not hidden from our scientific world, but has been *found* by them. What is unacceptable is the creator God. This is what allows the god of this word to blind their minds. Those that reject, therefore believing not. 2 Cor. 4:4 "...lest the glorious gospel of Christ, who is the image of God, should shine upon them." This also affirms what was written 2,000 years ago. As the Lord stated this to be, by the god of this world. This blindness and the cause of it was revealed in the Garden of Eden. Eve believed Satan, and not God. Thus, it is man who has established Satan as the god of this world.

CHAPTER 7

SECULAR WORLD

Let us continue with the affirmation of the law of entropy, in which all matter deteriorates. Science came to discover that all of living matter is not only complex, but is wonderfully designed with intricately encoded, intelligently designed blueprinted information. This is called DNA. What would be humorous, were not the consequences so permanent and life altering, is that this discovery reveals with clarity the unfathomable abilities and presence of the Creator God and what can only be defined as his hand on all creation. With the central concern focused on mankind, who was created for one purpose only: to be in his image.

We are told by the word of God, that "It has not even entered into the heart of man what God has prepared for them who love him." This means we do not know what we will be, period. Otherwise these prophetic truths would be just empty words, with no meaning, with the nullifying of what will be so; and believing it has already been done. Yes, Jesus said you must be born again to *see* the Kingdom of God. That whom you see is Jesus. And you must be born of the Spirit to *enter* the Kingdom of God. It is then we will know what we will be, and see the Lord in a fullness beyond our present comprehension. This will occur at the rapture of the church, when the dead and living will receive their new bodies. This includes the dead who are presently with the Lord.

We do know the least will be the greatest. Jesus came not to be served, but to serve. John gave a brief description of what he saw. "He saw no temple, as the Lord God Almighty and the Lamb are the temple of it. And the city had no need of the sun nor moon to shine in it, for the glory of God did light it. And the Lamb of God is the lamp of it." (Rev.21:22-23)

This would explain why man cannot conceive what God has prepared for them who love him. There is no mention in the Bible of the future glory or an indescribable beauty of man. But man will be constantly clothed in the light of God and the Lamb. This completely contrasts with Lucifer and his beauty, which corrupted him. Ezek. 28:17 "Your heart was lifted up because of your beauty, you have corrupted your wisdom by reason of your brightness." Satan's brightness was self-illumination. Whereas the light from God illuminates all it touches. The beauty of man will be a reflection of the Lord and the absolute awareness of it. Thus, pride will not exist. Nor can it be with the Lord, as all that there is will be illuminated by him. This is the ultimate servant, and cannot now be fully understood.

We are assured that "It has not even entered into the heart of man what God has prepared for them that love him. But God has revealed them unto us by his Spirit; for the Spirit searches all things, yea the deep things of God." (1st Cor. 2:9-10.) This would appear to be another contrary statement in the Bible, a Bible that cannot contradict itself. So how can something be revealed that has not even entered the heart?

THE SPIRIT OF MAN RECEIVES INSTRUCTIONS

There is no way this or any other writer can convey the fullness of the spirit of man, much less the Holy Spirit. Also, science has no way to examine or to study it. Our modern science therefore examines and studies the brain, believing it evolved into awareness and intelligence. It is interesting that all ancient and present backward cultures have a strong awareness of a spirit of man separate from the flesh.

Our advanced secular societies spend endless time, finances and efforts to convince mankind that there is no creator God or spirit. They are gaining control of our educational systems and children. There is not an effort to eradicate religion in general, but Christianity is found offensive. Why? What is so offensive about a God that so loves the world that he sent his only begotten Son to take away their sins? All that is necessary is to believe that there *is* such a God, for our children to be raised with moral standards, and believing that such a God is absolute light and truth in all things.

This nation is continually decrying the out-of-control children in our schools. Why not follow the example of schools that successfully incorporate these Christian teachings? Their success is well observed, but denied by our secular society. This is a direct result of accepting a lie; for what purpose? The Lord always has a small remnant that retain this light from the Holy Spirit. Darkness cannot overcome this light. This special light offends. However, it cannot be put out, only rejected. This is not a nullifying of the Holy Spirit, but clearly reveals another spirit that wars against the Spirit of God and those who receive this special light. This forces all of man to choose. And no matter how apparently successful our secular humanists are, there are still no atheists. Only professing atheists, who have chosen who to be of. Not because they have the better argument, but because the truth is unacceptable.

Just being aware you were created logically implies a purpose, and God created you for a purpose. All are aware of this. Anything that is created or made by man has a purpose. From a house, plow or tractor, or even paintings or art. It is not being unkind to expose deception and deceivers. And what we have witnessed and is taking place would be called childish behavior. But because of the evil intent, this childish behavior is of those who parrot that which is spoon fed to them. This is much more than childish; it is the ultimate evil because of who they target: the children. We are called to be watchmen on the wall.

There is a responsibility that is extended to all of mankind, and that is to point out to our children good and evil. And not make excuses for evil, or even what is happening all too often: calling evil good and good evil. This is not just for children, but for all of mankind. This will be a continual battle as we are tried and tested. Not many years from now there will be no one that will even profess they are atheists. A just God would not condemn a man for eternity for rejecting what they were ignorant of. This leaves us with the question: Is there a clear message of what is being revealed? The answer appears to be a resounding yes. It would seem there is more than a revealing, but a clear understanding. Those increasingly being offended with God's chosen people, and the people that have chosen God, in the person of his Son, along with the word of God.

Much time has been spent revealing scriptures affirming that man is a living spirit whom God created to be in his image. Hopefully these scriptures reveal man as flesh. It is in this state of flesh that it is impossible to be in the image of God. When you are born again you see, in the person of Jesus, the Kingdom of God. Our hope and promise is entering the kingdom of God, at the gathering of the saints when the Lord returns from the heavens.

1st Cor. 15:42-50 "So is the resurrection of the dead. It is sown in corruption, it is raised in incorruption. - It is sown in dishonor, it is raised in glory. It is sown in weakness, it is raised in power. - It is sown a natural body; it is raised a spiritual body. There is a natural body, and there is a spiritual body. - And it is written, the first man, Adam, was made a living soul; the last Adam was made a life-giving spirit. – However, that was not first which is spiritual, but that what was natural, and afterward that which is spiritual. - The first man is of the earth, earthly, the second man is the Lord from heaven. - As it is earthly, such are they that are earthly; and as is the heavenly, such are they also that are heavenly. - And as we have borne the image of the earthly, we shall also bear the image of the heavenly. - Now I say brethren, that flesh and blood cannot inherit the Kingdom of God; neither does corruption inherit incorruption."

ALL ARE SINNERS

There has been much time spent revealing that man is not in the image of God. The Bible, from beginning to end, reveals that all are sinners in need of a savior. In fact, even before the creation of this world, there is a book of life. All will worship the dragon and the beast, except those whose names are written in the Lamb's book of life - this Lamb slain from the foundation of the earth. Jesus is the Alpha and Omega; the beginning and the end, and he knew the names of every man, woman, and child that would hunger to be in his presence for eternity even before the creation of this world.

Chapter 8

Spirits in a Prison of Death

The essence or the existence of man is a created spirit. A spirit occupying a flesh and blood body, which is a temporal home. Referred to as this "body of death" by the apostle Paul, "spirits in prison" by Peter, and "captives to be set free" by Jesus. This prison that man's eternal spirit must dwell in for his brief existence on this earth. This makes sense to those who know there is a just and loving God in this world in which there are terrible sufferings and injustices, but where man can be set free.

This prison in which the spirit of man abides is a body of flesh and its limitations. Possessing a fleshly computer, the brain - which is of unbelievable sophistication and complexity - is only a flesh and blood organ, mimicking awareness and reason. The spirit of man is limited by this computer to such a degree that we are told we cannot even comprehend the vastness of being freed from this prison. The spirit is the programmer as they both grow together, yet trapped by the limitations of their computers. Along with all of the body's functions, needs and desires. The Lord chose such a means to try the heart or spirit of man. And only Jesus can set the prisoners free.

Jesus was speaking to the Pharisees and telling them how they can be free. John 8:23-24, 31-34, 36. "Jesus said, 'You are from beneath, I am from above. You are of this world, I am not of this world. And you shall die in your sins, because you believe not that I Am. Ye shall die in your sins.' - Then said Jesus to those Jews that believed on him, 'If you continue in my word, then are you my disciples. - And you will know the truth and the truth will make you free.' – They answered him – 'We were never in bondage.' - Jesus answered them, 'Whosoever commits sin is the servant of sin. - If the Son, therefore, shall make you free, you shall be free indeed.'"

Peter wrote of this bondage as a prison, in which Christ preached to all of the earth's inhabitants before the flood in which all were in prison. Only eight souls escaped, revealing the cross before the flood. 1st Peter 3:18-20 "For Christ also has once suffered for sins, the just for the unjust, that he might bring us to God, being put to death in the flesh but made alive by the Spirit. - In whom also he went and preached to the spirits in prison. - Which were disobedient when the longsuffering of God waited in the days of Noah, while the ark was being prepared, wherein eight souls were saved."

How did Jesus preach to all this world? The Father, Son, and Holy Spirit are one. Job 32:8 "There is a spirit in man, and the inspiration of the Almighty gives them understanding." What is this understanding? Chapter 33 reveals what this understanding is and when it is given. Job 33:4 "The Spirit of God has made me, and the breath of the Almighty has given me life." This reveals Genesis 1, where the Godhead created the essence of man, his eternal spirit; and Genesis 2, where God in the person of Jesus breathed life to man formed out of the dust of the earth.

Then this book tells what this information is and when it is given. Not just to Job, but to all of mankind. Job 33:14-18 "God speaks once, yea twice, yet man perceives it not. – In a dream, in a vision of the night, when deep sleep falls upon a man, in slumbering upon the bed. – Then he opens the ears of men and seals their instructions. – That he may withdraw man for his purpose and hide pride from man. – He keeps back his soul from the pit, and his life from perishing by the sword."

It must be noted that the inspiration of the Almighty gives understanding to the spirit of man. Yet man does not perceive it. This is confusing and difficult to explain except as a guilty conscience when doing wrong, or the moving of compassion and justice, or the hardening of the heart. All peoples of the earth are aware that murder, stealing and sexual improprieties etc. are wrong. This the result of the Holy Spirit revealing this to the spirit of man. Yet man does not perceive it. Some are moved to model their life and actions as their conscience or heart moves them. As Job 33:17 states, "To withdraw the soul of man from his purpose." Others are moved by the flesh; their purpose or self-interests, and ignore this still quiet voice.

This explains why upon hearing the gospel of Christ, some are moved to tears of joy, barely able to believe that God could so love them. Others hearing the same gospel are unmoved. And still others are moved to rage.

What is taking place is the Holy Spirit revealing to all of mankind the will of their creator, along with his gentleness, love and servant heart. As Satan tempted Eve, there is another spirit involved. This spirit is completely contrary in every way to the spirit of God, bringing about this battle of choices. It would appear the Lord would have the advantage, with the Holy Spirit continually revealing himself to man. This is not a contest or game that the Lord is engaging in with Satan. Satan is also a created creature, whose fate is assured because he has rejected God's purpose for him. Satan is the god of this world because this world has chosen him as such. God is God, *period.* Those who have chosen Jesus are not of this world. Nor is Israel of this world. Leviticus 25:23 "The land shall not be sold forever: As the land is my land." As for man, the Lord is testing and refining him as pure gold and casting out the dross.

The Holy Spirit is a gentleman. He reveals, and does not control. Jesus told believers to pray to the Father, and when asking, ask in his name. Never was man to seek out, inquire of, or ask angels to intervene, or to ask them for anything. Angels are ministering spirit to the heirs of Salvation. They minister only as the Lord directs. The calling on or praying to angels or any dead is strictly forbidden.

Leviticus 19:31 "Regard not them that have familiar spirits, neither seek after wizards, to be defiled by them. I am the Lord your God." Do not seek these spirits by yourself or by a witch, medium, or any other means. This could lead to an unclean spirit sharing your body of flesh. These spirits do not regard your earthly home as a prison, but an opportunity to control, howbeit in a very small kingdom. These spirits will be anything but a gentleman, like the Holy Spirit that guides. As they are all but gentle, and as lying spirits will answer to any name.

Paul defines this prison that the spirit of man occupies for a season, and the seemingly impossible task of man making the right choices. He defines this dilemma in Romans 7:18-23. "For I know that in me, in my flesh, dwells no good thing. For to will is present in me, but how to perform that what is good I find not. - For the good that I would, I do not; but the evil which I would not, that I do. Now if I do that which I would not, it is no longer I that do it, but sin that dwells in me. - I then find a law that when I would do good, evil is present with me. - For I delight in the law of God after the inward man. - But I see another law in my members, warring against the law of my mind, and bring me into captivity to the law of sin which is my members. - Wretched man that I am! Who will deliver me from the body of this death? - I thank God through Jesus Christ, our Lord. So that with the mind I myself serve the law of God, but with the flesh the law of sin."

Paul defines this body in which he is a prisoner, in which there appears to be no hope. And as he describes no hope at all in this body of sin and death, he thanks God for providing a way to be set free. This freedom is paid for with a terrible price. A price that no man can pay. This was provided before the very creation of the earth. That being the cross, which is foolishness to those who are lost. But to those seeking to be freed from this prison of death, it is the power of God.

The prophet Isaiah also wrote of this coming Messiah. And the freeing from this same prison of darkness by simply opening the blind eyes. Isaiah 42:7 "To open the blind eyes, to bring out the prisoners from the prison, and them that sit in darkness in the prison house."

Peter spoke of this world before the flood, in which Christ preached to these same spirits in prison (of which their very conduct brought about the flood). 2nd Peter 3:5 "And spared not the old world, but saved Noah, the eighth person, a preacher of righteousness, bringing in a flood upon the world of the ungodly."

ABSOLUTE RIGHTEOUSNESS

There must be an awareness that without the cleansing blood of the Lamb of God, not one person could enter the Kingdom of God. Scriptures constantly remind man that none can enter into life without a complete cleansing, and that sinful man is incapable of accomplishing this. In fact, one whole book of the Bible is about the most righteous man in all the earth – a man by the name of Job. Job knew his redeemer lives, and he would see him with his own eyes, long after his death, in his resurrected body. (Job 19:25-27) So what was God's purpose in allowing Satan to try Job? The answer is in the last very last chapter of Job, in which God opened the eyes of this man. A man whose righteousness far exceeded any on the earth.

Job 1:8 "The Lord stated to Satan. "Have you considered my servant Job? There is none like him in all the earth. A perfect and upright man, one that fears God and shuns evil." Then Satan, the god of this world, set about to have Job curse God. Job was then tried and tested as no man had ever been. Then the Lord himself addresses Job in chapters 38 to 41. It was after this, that Job made a thought provoking statement. Job 42:3-6 "Who is he that hides council without knowledge? Therefore have I uttered that which I understood not; things too wonderful for me, which I knew not. - Hear, I beseech thee, and I will speak; I will demand of thee, and declare thou unto me. - I have heard of thee by the hearing of the ear, but now my eye sees you. - Wherefore I abhor myself, and repent in dust and ashes."

CHAPTER 9

JOB'S EYES OPENED

As the Lord revealed the establishment and wonders of his creation, Job remained silent as it became quite clear there was a great separation between man and God. It was then that Job made a statement that would seem strange to most. But not from someone who was in the presence of God, as was Job. What were the things too wonderful for him, and things he knew not, which he then uttered after seeing the Lord? This knowledge causing Job to abhor himself and repent in dust and ashes… why would this knowledge be too wonderful for him, and also bring about such self-abasement to a perfect and upright man, who feared God and shunned evil?

As it was God who opened Job's eyes, we are assured these are the most knowledgeable and wonderful words to be revealed to all of mankind; and the most needful. These words are hidden from the children of pride. Their eyes are closed because they refuse to see, receive or ask. Job received knowledge along with this counsel from the Lord because he demanded truth from He who is Truth. You do not demand of God. What Job demanded of God were his words. Words that are truth. He demanded this for himself. This brings to mind the words of Job 32:8 and 33:17 "There is a spirit in man; and the inspiration of the Almighty gives them understanding. - That he may withdraw man from his purpose and hide pride from man."

The children of pride reject truth that would in any way hinder self-adoration. To receive deserved respect for well-doing is proper.

But it is an absolute necessity to expose the children of pride when it interferes in any way or diminishes the way of salvation. Or contributes to the degradation and violence that is increasing in this world at an ever-increasing rate. A blatant example of this blindness is that few recognize that the only place in the Middle East that Christians do not fear for their lives, and live in peace, is the tiny nation of Israel. God's word assures us that in the near future the degradation and violence will increase to such a level, that were Jesus to delay his coming there would be no flesh saved alive. (Matthew 24:22)

What did Job, the most righteous man on the earth, see? It is obvious he saw that God is God, and man is not. This not to be taken lightly. Both Isaiah and Ezekiel wrote of the father of pride. Ezek. 28 reveals a beauty that man cannot really comprehend. Beauty in which the devil had no part in, as he was created of God. Satan is no accident that happened to disrupt the purpose of God. He is the complete opposite from the Son of God. Jesus is the way, the truth, and life. Satan is death.

Then with unbelievable sadism and cruelty he targeted the most righteous man on the earth, for the sole purpose of Job cursing God to his face. Job 1:11 "Put forth your hand and touch all that he has and he will curse you to your face." Job 2:5 "Touch his bone and his flesh, and he will curse you to your face."

What is the significance of Job, or any man, cursing God to his face? These words are written for our benefit, and are an affirmation that God is God. You do not confront someone to their face who does not exist. This is the first step in rejecting God's sovereignty, or authority. As there are no atheists, the process has begun to fully change the truth of God for a lie. God created Satan for his purpose. Isaiah 45:7 "I form the light, I create darkness, I make peace, and create evil. I the Lord do all these things."

This is not a contest between God and Satan for the souls of man. The Lord is simply presenting what is completely the opposite of himself: Satan, and his angels that have rejected what God has created them to be. The Devil and demons are the result. With their final destination, the Lake of Fire. The same result awaits mankind who reject what they were created to be; in the image of God. The fire of God refines and makes pure, and it also destroys. There begins a process to reject that which is pure, and as there can be no doubt that this is a rejection of the Lord, there begins an alignment of themselves with he who has completely rejected God. A partial rejection of truth is a complete rejection of truth. There is then an acceptance of another.

This is revealed in whose definition of light we accept. Our adversary is clearly revealed as pure evil and darkness, with no light in him. We are told of the indescribable beauty of Satan. Then he, who has no light in him, transforms himself into an angel of light. 2nd Cor. 11:13-15 "For such are false apostles, deceitful workers, transforming themselves into the apostles of Christ. - And no marvel, for Satan himself is transformed into an angel of light. - Therefore, it is no great thing if his ministers also be transformed into ministers of righteousness, whose end shall be according to their works."

In the new heaven and earth there will be no need for the light of the sun, for the glory of God does light it, and the Lamb is the lamp of it. (Rev. 21:23) In God's eternal kingdom, resurrected man will have new eyes to see as never before. And not be bound by the limits of our earthly eyes, which can only perceive what is beauty and light.

There is a consistency exhibited in which the Lord often allows that old dragon to do what appears to be his will. The god of this world rejects the word of God, with the emphasis on self. This hatred exhibited by Satan toward man is merely the rejection of being, as he conceives, a servant for man. That is not the image which he wants for himself. Yet when the sons of God came to present themselves before the Lord, we are told Satan came among them. (Job 1:6) He is referred to as one of the sons of God. Then when God's only begotten Son came as a man - yet truly God - he came as one not to *be* served, but *to* serve. Matt. 20:28 "Even as the Son of man came not to be ministered unto, but to minister, and to give his life a ransom for many."

Satan, that old deceiver! By his standards, gods do not minister to lesser beings. It appears that his degrading of man before the Father reveals the sin that identifies Lucifer more than any; and that is pride. In his opinion, gods do not minister to lesser beings, neither do they die for them. Rather, *man* should die for their *masters*.

Satan cast out one third of the angels to kill the Christ child as soon as he was born. Then 2.000 years later, Satan and the rest of his angels will be cast out of heaven. Jesus, when speaking of the believers, called them "My little flock". Is this also his little flock? This is interesting.

This same pride has a familiar ring with our secular world. Except man goes farther, denying God's very existence. As there is a complete awareness of God among all of mankind, all those that profess to be atheists know this statement to be a lie. Rather it is a sick, perverted way to punish the Lord by diminishing the numbers that will follow him. For a person to state there is no God, he would have to be all knowing, therefore establishing himself as God. There is no limit of self-imposed delusion for the children of pride.

And the most amazing thing is, the more highly educated a person is the greater the tendency to profess atheism. The opposite should occur. What will be presented here is behavior that should be regarded as juvenile. But because of the eternal consequences resulting from this it is actually evil beyond description, because its main targets are children and young minds searching for truth.

Chapter 10

DNA and the God Particle

The greater the discoveries and understanding of science, particularly molecular science, the greater the affirmation of a Creator God. This is borne out in the discovery of DNA and the search for the Higgs Boson particle. These advancements of particle science reveal a world extremely vast and humbling in its complexity and wonder. This affirms three things. First, a creator God. Second, an apparently unexplainable rejection of the obvious. Two worlds at complete odds with each other. They see the same thing, but with different eyes. And the third, even with the revealing of the creator God with those with supposedly greater knowledge, there is no comprehension. More properly put, they are blinded... but not all of them. This also reveals that it is the heart of man that is chosen of God. John 15:16 "You have not chosen me, but I have chosen you, and ordained you." There will be an effort to make this clear.

The secular world continually states they are scientists, and that is the reason they reject any concept of God. "Because, you see, science reveals there is no God." This they proudly proclaim as factual; even though science itself rejects their claims. An example of this is the law of entropy. DNA extends to all of science, and now they have achieved their goal. And that is the theory of theories. The theory of everything. They have finally achieved their goal without even realizing it. Many have pointed this out to them, as they call this the God particle. And they are still blinded. And another thing which modern science can't ignore is an invisible source of unimaginable stabilizing power. Without this, all matter would explode and implode into nonexistence. The Atom bomb identified the principle of exploding, and the hydrogen bomb imploding. There were many scientists that warned against any development of nuclear weapons in the 1940's. They feared a chain reaction involving every atom in the universe, resulting in the complete annihilation of all there is.

THE GOD PARTICLE

Scientists built a huge Hadron collider in Switzerland to verify this Higgs particle that they insist must exist. Without this particle, these particle scientists insist this universe would be completely void. There would be absolutely nothing. How do you explain this presence that is involved in the very existence of all there is without revealing God? This is best explained by Him whom through all things consist and exist; and by whom we live, move and have our being. These very words were written 2,000 years ago in the Judeo-Christian Bible defining Jesus, the express image of the Father, being this invisible creative power which sustains and upholds all things.

Col. 1:16-17 "All things were created by him and for him. - And he is before all things, and by him all things consist." Heb. 1:3 "Being the brightness of his glory, and the express image of his person, and upholding all things by the word of his power." Acts 17:27-28 "That they should seek after the Lord if perhaps they might feel after him, and find him, though he is not very far from every one of us. - For in him we live, move and have our being."

These words written in the Judeo–Christian Bible define what these men of science would call the theory of everything, or the ultimate theory of everything. They are saying the same about this Higgs particle, of which nothing could exist except by its presence. The Bible stated the same thing 2,000 years ago. Except they are now spending billions of dollars to affirm this. And yet the Bible says: He is not far from every one of us.

And then we have in this same Bible these words written by Peter that mirror the fear of those scientists that the setting off of a nuclear bomb would start a chain reaction causing the complete destruction of the whole universe. 2nd Peter 3:10-12 "The Lord will come as a thief in the night, in which the heavens shall pass away with a great noise, and the elements shall melt with fervent heat; and the earth also, and the works that are in it shall be burnt up. - Seeing, then, that all these things shall be dissolved, what manner of persons ought you to be in all living and godliness, - Looking for and hastening unto the coming day of God, in which the heavens being on fire, shall be dissolved, and the elements shall melt with a fervent heat?" This is a prophetic pronouncement of the new heavens and earth that will replace this world.

This presence that sustains and upholds all things for a season, whom the Bible identifies as the Lord Jesus Christ, became man for a season. Our secular scientists have now spoken of these same things, apparently ignorant of these scriptural pronouncements. This power of creation had been revealed to them, but they refused the same truth and authority. Then a unified international search began to find this incomprehensible power and intelligence. This mysterious invisible undiscovered Higgs Boson particle, without which nothing, absolutely nothing, can exist. This is referred to as the God particle by some, but not by the secular world. What will be addressed here shortly is what molecular and particle science has revealed. A vastness that equals or exceeds our very universe, in a miniature world of wonder that will reveal the pride of man. What will be addressed here is an amazing statement that should change the Big Bang theory into revealing the hand of God.

With DNA that identifies the hand of the creator God, along with how the Lord has revealed himself in such a manner to these men of science they can no longer deny the word of God, the stage is being set for the final choice to be made as to whose image is desired. But first, a few logical conclusions that reveal how bankrupt these two theories always were, which have always revealed a blindness with an agenda. Or self-induced blindness from of a knowing rejection of truth, because of the unacceptability of this specific truth.

LOGICAL CONCLUSION

What has just been presented here is that DNA and then the Higgs, or God, particle cannot be regarded as just an amazing chain of coincidences. We have the same evidences proven to be correct by the detonation of the Hydrogen and Atomic bombs. That is: the presence of an incomprehensibly powerful force which is present in all the universe, and in all matter. Then an even greater presence in flesh that contains life. This life, extending to awareness, goes beyond what can be even conceived by man. (Man cannot comprehend or explain the thought processes, other than to attribute it to the brain which is only a computer of unbelievable sophistication.) Science is just now beginning to understand this.

There are two completely contrary beliefs that are presented from what is basically the same information. This does not include belief in God, as all know there is a creator God. Those of the one belief system seek to know this God who gave his Son to cleanse and purify man. The others, for varying reasons, reject the Lord. A lot of this difference involves control. But as we shall see, it is the ones that want to be free *from* the Lord who remain in bondage, and those who *receive* the Lord that are set free. This cannot be understood in its fullness apart from the cross. Not what man does for God, but what God did for man.

The Lord said. "Let us reason together." The very first thing that is being identified in this reasoning process is: the Lord himself desires to reason with man. But then, our educators decide or demand that the creator be excluded. What madness could cause this blindness? It would seem this rejection of light, preferring darkness, would be the first thing on the reasoning agenda.

We already know this is madness. There is only one possibility that makes sense. This is revealed in John 3:16 that "God so loved the world that he gave his only begotten Son." Just believing in his Son results in not perishing, but having everlasting life. Any reasoning reveals corrupt and deceptive minds, incapable of grasping truth; instead, pursuing and being a part of lies. And as God is God, it is the Lord that is allowing this deception for the purpose of verifying the choices being made. As the choices being made are so diametrically opposed to each other, there can be no confusion as to whose image has been chosen.

It is not only creation, but the cross that reveals God's love that the world rejects. In this also is the wisdom of God revealed, as it was given unto the Son to create all things, exposing those who reject he who created life and all there is. This blindness - or willing rejection - extends to control. But neither this blindness nor control involves atheism. The god of this world cannot blind the children of pride to the reality of a creator God. It is believed here that those in bondage to the god of this world have as much of an awareness, or even more, than many professing Christians. There should never even be a discussion as to the reality of God, only his words.

The word of God convicts and condemns all. When reasoning with the Lord, we are reminded of his Son, and the message of the cross. Reasonable people ask, what is so offensive about the cross? The obvious answer is the absolute necessity of Jesus shedding his blood for the sins of man. Why? Because it exposes the degradation and fallen state of man. To one, there is overwhelming gratitude and a thankfulness of such love - that he who is without sin would do such a thing for them.

But to another offense is taken, since what is desired is praise and adoration, not condemnation and truth. This is the heart of a world in which all things revolve around self. The Lord has revealed this pride in Lucifer, in whom this world has made him their god. These are the children of pride. "Rejoice, ye heavens and you that dwell in them. Woe to the inhabiters of the earth and of the sea! For the devil is come down to you, having great wrath, because he knows he has but a short time." (Rev. 12:12) At this time in the Lord's timetable there will be a finality of becoming in Satan's image, with the taking of his mark. And those doing so, with a total submission to this evil, will know terror as cannot be conceived.

CHAPTER 11

THE KINGDOM OF GOD

Jesus told Nicodemus "Unless you are born again, you cannot see the Kingdom of God." (John 3:3) and then in John 3:5 "Unless a man be born of water and of the Spirit, he cannot enter into the Kingdom of God." We will never, while in the flesh, understand the fullness of these words. We can comprehend that we see the Kingdom of God when we are born again through believing on the Lord Jesus. But what does this mean? That except we are born of the water and of the Spirit you cannot enter the Kingdom of God? As all natural births are of water, reason dictates the Lord is conveying a special water. This is revealed in the next chapter.

Jesus is speaking with an unusual woman, in that she engages in a conversation with the Lord as he asks her to give him water. (Having a conversation with the Lord concerning his word should be an everyday occurrence with all Christians.) Then Jesus said to her, "Whoever drinks of this water will thirst again. But whoever drinks of the water that I give him shall never thirst. The water I give him shall be a well of water springing up into everlasting life." Life is in the word. This is affirmed in John 1:1,4 "In the beginning was the Word, and the Word was with God, and the Word was God. - And in him was life."

As we combine these words that the Lord Jesus spoke to Nicodemus, "You must be born again to see the Kingdom of God", the drinking of the water of the word follows. And as flesh and blood cannot enter the Kingdom of God, the Kingdom is now seen but not entered into. Not until the gathering of the saints to meet the Lord in the air at his coming (the Rapture). The dead in Christ and living will receive their new bodies by the Holy Spirit. Then, with new eyes and bodies, they will enter the Kingdom of God. 1st John 3:2 "When he shall appear we shall be like him, for we shall see him as he is." It is important to remember the Lord said, "Let *us* make man in *our* image." The Holy Spirit is completing this birth for believers to be in the image of God, and forever be with the Lord.

This in itself brings about choices and self-evaluation. Why is there a desire to enter the Kingdom of Heaven? The answer to this will reveal your eternal home, and to whom you have chosen as your God. The Lord has created both angels and man for a purpose. Both were given a free will, and the right to reject or accept the Lord's purpose for their lives. Love defines God. And as God so loves the world, there is no distinction between those who receive this love. The distinction arises when this love is rejected or received. Those who receive this love are then no more of this world, and desire but one thing: to be eternally in the presence of he who loves them.

It has not even entered into the heart of man as to what the Lord has prepared for those who love him. There is only one thing we do know. The Lord has stated that those who receive this love will be changed, having a new body and heart. 1st Cor. 2:12 "We have not received the spirit of the world, but the Spirit who is of God, that we might know the things that are freely given to us of God." This desiring to know the things of God more than anything, reveals who will enter the Kingdom that God has prepared for them. It is precious beyond comprehension to those who want what the Lord wants for them. But it is foolishness to the children of pride, who desires what the god of this world wants. The desires of their fallen hearts.

KNOWING THERE IS A GOD, AND KNOWING GOD

There is a great difference between knowing God and knowing there is a God. All of mankind knows there is a God; a creator God. But God created man to know him through his Son, who is the express image of himself. This relationship when established between man and God through his Son is defined as a marriage, with Jesus as the groom and the believers as the bride. This goes far beyond simply knowing there is a God.

PROPHESY

Prophesy is historical evidence written even before it happens. This defines God as the Alpha and Omega, the beginning and the end. God is defined as God because he is not only all powerful and all present, but also all knowing, Man cannot even conceive of the depth of any of these three concepts. Nor the Trinity. How can it be that man has the freedom to reject or accept the Lord? And God knows exactly to what extent that will be, to the smallest detail. And yet the Lord does not control these decisions. This cannot be comprehended by man. And then in the fullness of time, God revealed himself in his Son. Man responded exactly as *prophetically foretold.*

Nostradamus (1503-1566) was a French physician. Some modern-day sensationalists attempt to pass him off as a prophet. But the proper word should be fortune teller, as the spirit of prophesy is the testimony of Jesus. And Nostradamus' writings neither testify of the Lord, nor are they the testimony of Jesus. He wrote a collection of predictions in rhymed quatrains, entitled Centuries. These quatrains were written in code. Normally when a code is broken all of the hidden messages in the quatrains would be revealed. But not so here, since each quatrain had its own individual code.

It requires a great amount of information to break a code, as it has a hidden message that is revealing something other than what it states. And as each quatrain has a different code you have to wait until some event takes place in order to identify it. When understanding Bible prophesy, there is no hidden code. Common sense, reason and being assured these words are true is the foundation for understanding biblical prophecy. Often events are recorded that appear unreasonable. It is then wise to inquire of the Lord. Isaiah 9:6 is prophesy concerning the coming Messiah that, when incorporated with Isaiah 7:14, clearly defines the birth of Jesus. Isaiah 9:6 says "A Child is born, a Son is given. His name shall be called The Mighty God, The Everlasting Father, The Prince of Peace." In Isaiah 7:14 we have "the virgin shall conceive and bear a son, and shall call his name Immanuel (God with us)". This is not an encoded difficult prophetic message. Many prophesies *are* difficult to understand. But they are not written in a different code for each prophesy. Often many prophesies are tied in with another, completing or complimenting each other. Also, as the spirit of prophesy is the testimony of Jesus, most are involved with the gospel message.

As to these encoded rhymes of Nostradamus? Their interpretation to these predictions extended to every country in the world, with no time frames, and most of all there is no need or purpose involved. This the complete opposite of the Judeo Christian Bible. This a clear attempt of man to diminish the prophetic word of God. Our warfare is spiritual, and it can be seen that sides are being taken.

This reveals the extent the world will go to in order to imitate truth for the purpose of perverting and destroying it. Because of the accuracy and reliability of biblical prophecy, man's attempts to foretell cannot be defined as prophesy. True prophesy is foretelling what will be, in conjunction with God's purpose. Most biblical scholars state the Bible is up to 20% prophesy. God is the author, and Jesus stated "Not one dot or comma shall pass till all be fulfilled." This would mean 100% of the Bible is prophesy. *All* the writers of the gospel were prophets. Rev. 19:10 "Worship God, for the testimony of Jesus is the spirit of prophesy." This is really not that difficult to understand. Biblical prophecy is the foretelling of future events for the purpose of authenticating the source and purpose of these special words of truth which are life, the testimony of Jesus, extending to believers testifying of Jesus.

THE WORLDWIDE FLOOD

There are about 250 stories from different nations telling of a worldwide flood in which all life was lost except those who entered into a boat. All the stories are about the same in which the world was destroyed by this flood, and only those animals and people who entered this boat survived. The Chinese story most closely mirrors the biblical story in that there was a man, his wife, their three sons and their wives. And as in all historical events, the Bible goes beyond simply the telling of this world changing event; it authenticates it.

CHAPTER 12

THE ENORMITY OF GOD

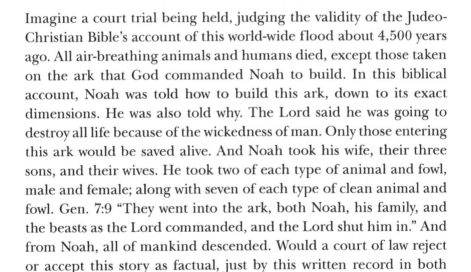

Imagine a court trial being held, judging the validity of the Judeo-Christian Bible's account of this world-wide flood about 4,500 years ago. All air-breathing animals and humans died, except those taken on the ark that God commanded Noah to build. In this biblical account, Noah was told how to build this ark, down to its exact dimensions. He was also told why. The Lord said he was going to destroy all life because of the wickedness of man. Only those entering this ark would be saved alive. And Noah took his wife, their three sons, and their wives. He took two of each type of animal and fowl, male and female; along with seven of each type of clean animal and fowl. Gen. 7:9 "They went into the ark, both Noah, his family, and the beasts as the Lord commanded, and the Lord shut him in." And from Noah, all of mankind descended. Would a court of law reject or accept this story as factual, just by this written record in both the Old and New Testament? What about a different trial with this evidence from another 250 nations having the same story; yes, with some differences, but the same story? Why do we not hear of this?

SCOFFERS IN THE LAST DAYS

Christians are confronted with a seemingly unreasonable and impossible task of bringing the light of the glorious gospel of Christ, who is the image of God, to these same ungodly people. As the Bible states, they are willingly ignorant of these things. 2nd Peter 3:3-7 "Knowing this first, that there shall come in the last days scoffers, walking after their own lusts, - And saying, Where is the promise of his coming? For since the fathers fell asleep, all things continue as from the beginning of the creation. - For this they are willingly ignorant of, that by the word of God the heavens were of old, and the earth standing out of the water and in the water, - By which the world that then was, being overflowed with water, perished. - But the heavens and earth which are now, by the same word are kept in store, reserved unto fire against the day of judgment and perdition of ungodly men."

As we are told, they are willingly ignorant of not only the flood and the biblical promise of the Lord's return, but also the creation. And most importantly, ignorant of the judgment of ungodly men. Thus, revealing a conscious effort to reject what has been revealed to them. This appears to be addressing professing atheists, because of the extent of these which are basic Christian teachings, and they will come at the last days. This is referring to the world. When God supernaturally intervenes when Israel is invaded toward the last days, we are assured all of the world will know the God of Israel is the Lord God.

UNDERSTANDING

What will be presented at this time is the heart of this book. This writer is not a professional writer but a farmer, who simply searches out the Bible and is assured that there is not one error. God demands that those who receive him must be convinced that truth defines God. Jesus is the Son of God, and his express image is truth and the word of truth. Man is terribly flawed, much like a newborn child. As children grow, their family life plays a large part in their development.

The Lord has a far greater system for all of mankind regardless of the influence of their parents or environment. This is revealed in Job 32:8 "There is a spirit in man, and the inspiration of the Almighty gives them understanding." These words are meaningless unless you are aware that the essence of man is his spirit that dwells for but a moment of time in this body of flesh. All primitive people of the world know this. What has taken place in modern educated societies that have gotten control of educating our children? There has been a concerted and successful effort to eliminate the awareness of the spirit of man. They have also been successful in making the Bible irrelevant. The very first and then second chapters of the Bible reveal this. We have two births, or creations, given. The first is the spirit of man, and the second the flesh from the dust of the ground which returns to the ground. Jesus reveals this to Nicodemus. Why is this so difficult to understand? Because few can understand that the Spirit of God is a still small voice. And this is why this Spirit that gives understanding is drowned out by the things of this world.

1st Cor. 2:9-10 "Eye has not seen, nor ear heard, neither has entered into the heart of man, the things that God has prepared for them that love him. But God has revealed them to us by his Spirit; for the Spirit searches all things, yea the deep things of God." We are told we do not know what God has prepared for us. But God has revealed them to us by his Spirit. This is not a contradiction, but a mystery for us to understand.

Our greatest blessing when reading the scripture is understanding. These "things that God has prepared for those that love him" which are not seen, heard or perceived is revealed to the spirit of all of mankind by his Spirit. This is the inspiration of the Almighty.

Job 32:8 "There is a spirit in man, and the inspiration of the Almighty gives them understanding." This writer looked up the word understanding in the original Hebrew language. The word is biyn (bene) Few words have such an extensive number of words that explain a single word. The first meaning given was "separate mentally", then – "attend, consider, be cunning, diligently, direct, discern, eloquent, feel, inform, instruct, have intelligence, know, look well to, perceive, be prudent, regard, skill, teach, think, make to, get, give, have understanding, view wisely, distinguish".

Job 33:14-18 "For God speaks once, yea twice, yet man perceives it not. - In a dream, in a vision of the night, when deep sleep falls upon men, in slumbering upon the bed; - Then he opens the ears of men and seals their instruction, - That he may withdraw man from his own purpose and hide pride from man. - He keeps back his soul from the pit, and his life from perishing from the sword."

Reading these scriptures verifies a just God and at the same time affirms the human brain as a computer. This computer is programmed by the spirit of man that abides there as a prisoner until released at death. (The complexity and wonder of the spirit of man is beyond this writer's ability to even begin to comprehend.) It would appear the inspiration of the Almighty (Holy Spirit) is programming man's spirit in the same manner as man's spirit is programming his brain.

When a computer is programmed by two programmers with two opposite agendas, this computer is corrupted and serves no useful purpose. When a computer has a virus, it must be found and destroyed. Great care must be taken as to what enters into computers that are manmade. How much more care should be taken with this computer which reflects or exposes the heart of our eternal spirit? This receives instructions from the Almighty. And what will be reviewed later is the danger of inviting in a programmer who has a completely different agenda than the Spirit of God.

These nighttime visitations of the Almighty (often identified as man's guilty conscience) should be enough to move the heart of man. And because the heart of man is fully set to do evil, there is a necessity to continually reveal that what is pure. As a reminder of what was revealed by the Holy Spirit, God sent his prophets, and then his Son. And then messengers to proclaim the words of his Son. All of this is documented in a book like no other - the Judeo-Christian Bible.

The truths of the Bible... being the word of God, or word of truth... are extensive, starting and ending with prophesy. The fulfilled coming of the Christ in exacting detail. His crucifixion and resurrection. And God's children Israel becoming one nation again after being divided into two nations, and then none. Then to become one united nation after over 2,600 years of being no nation. This happened as prophesied by the prophet Ezekiel, 37:1-22, and many more. This alone should be sufficient proof that this is indeed the word of God.

It is not necessary to present further authentication of the absolute reliability of the Bible, but the Lord presented documentation in this book that is beyond what man can grasp. He engraved in his book of life the most amazing chain of documentation. The scope and thoroughness of this alone leaves no doubt as to its authenticity in any court of law. The simplicity of what the Lord has done, along with being the Alpha and Omega, is complete assurance to all that the Bible, which is like no other book, is the word of God.

CONTINUING THE SEARCH

There are people who are interested in searching out their family tree. This is a tedious task, and the only acceptable information is the unbroken birth date and death of father or mother to birth of son or daughter to obtain accuracy. And once this documentation ends, the search ends. Along with any authenticity of genealogy.

Our creator has ingrained into mankind a hunger to know our fathers. And even a greater hunger to know our Creator Father. This is what separates man from animals.

Jesus tells those who believe on him, who are born again, how to pray. "When you pray, pray like this, 'Our Father who is in heaven.'" The prayer is to the Father, and his location. Prayer to your heavenly Father is wonderfully personal and intimate. There is an even greater intimacy when the Lord speaks to us. This he has done through his word. The fullness and extent of the Lord's words to believers grows as the intimacy of these words take root in the believers' hearts. It is when the believers enter the kingdom of God. And it will not be until the rapture that these words take on a reality of unbelievable proportions. The fullness of these words will then be understood: "God created man in his own image, in the image of God created he him; male and female created he them."

The Father is revealed through his Son. Hebrews 1:1-3 "God, who in sundry times and diverse manners spoke in times past unto the fathers by the prophets, - Has in these last days spoken unto us by his Son, whom he has appointed heir of all things, by whom also he made the worlds; - Who, being the brightness of his glory and the express image of his person, and upholding all things by the word of his power, when he had by himself purged our sins, sat down on the right hand of the Majesty on high."

These few words from Psalm 139 further reveal but a glimmer of the extent of the love that surrounds our creation. Psalm 139:1-8 "O Lord thou has searched me, and known me. - You know my downsitting and my uprising, you understand my thoughts afar off. - You compass my path and my lying down. You are acquainted with all my ways. - For there is not a word in my tongue, but thou O Lord, know it all together. - You have beset me behind and before, and laid your hand upon me. - Such knowledge is too wonderful for me, it is high, I cannot attain unto it. - Where can I go from your Spirit? Or where shall I flee from your presence? - If I ascend up to heaven, thou are there; If I make my bed in Sheol (hell), behold you are there."

CHOOSING GOD

The Lord has revealed and imbedded this knowledge of himself into the spirit of all of mankind. What has been quoted are but a few of the words of King David, who is defined as a man after the heart of God. The words of the Lord have also revealed to a degree the heart of fallen man in the fallen angel Lucifer, who was enamored by his own beauty. Then his wisdom was corrupted by reason of his brightness. When his heart was lifted up because of this beauty and wisdom, his wisdom became corrupted. All because he rejected the reason for which he was created.

The fall of Satan resulted in rejecting the Lord's purpose for him; to be a ministering spirit to those who shall be heirs of salvation. The fall of man also results in knowingly rejecting to be as the Lord created him to be, and choosing another. This is much like an artist who is in the midst of painting a beautiful picture, and then the picture itself decides how the artist must finish the portrait in order to obtain the picture's acceptance. A picture that would not even exist were it not for the artist! If man knew of the enormity of God, and the depravity of man, this analogy would be very reasonable.

We will receive from a gracious God the desires of our heart. Either what we want for ourselves, or what our Creator God wants for us. Who have we established as God? The god of this world, Satan, said in his heart "I will exalt my throne above the stars of heaven, I will be like the Most High." This identified the One he had rejected. And so, what are the desires of *our* hearts?

PROGRAMMED TO KNOW OUR FATHER

As the Lord has programmed into the heart of all of mankind to know their fathers, he has made it possible for anyone to search out their family tree to their very first Father (God). This special documentation starts at Mary, the mother of Jesus. But first there is the necessity of a new birth, as you must be born again to legally access your birth going back to the first Father. Of course it is an adoption, but just as legal. This was verified when Jesus called those who believed on him "brethren", and told all that believed on him to pray "our Father".

ADAM TO JESUS

In Matthew 1:17 the genealogy of Joseph, the husband of Mary, starts at Abraham. It travels to Isaac and then forward to each son all the way to Jacob, who begot Joseph, the husband of Mary. However, since Jesus was not born of Mary through Joseph, but rather through the Holy Spirit, *her* linage goes back to the Father of all. In Luke 3:23-38 the genealogy of Mary, who birthed Jesus, lists the names of the sons back to Abraham. It then continues back to the son of Shem, who was the son of Noah. From there it continues with this family tree unbroken, to Seth, the son of Adam, who was the son of God.

It is impossible for this documentation to have been accomplished other than being the word of God. Nor can this be fully grasped, because of the difficulty of the heart of man truly understanding the scope and enormity of our creator God.

SCOFFERS

2nd Peter 3:3-7 "In the last days scoffers will come, walking after their own lusts. – Saying, 'Where is the promise of his coming? For since the fathers fell asleep, all things continue as from the beginning of the creation.' - For this they are willingly ignorant of, that by the word of God the heavens were of old, and the earth standing out of the water and in the water. - By which the world that then was, being overflowed with water, perished."

It is quite telling that the scoffers mentioned by Peter are selectively ignorant. They pick and choose what they will accept or be willfully ignorant of. They cannot dispute the prophetic pronouncements, nor the reality of Jesus. Then they affirm his resurrection by stating "Where is his promised coming?" Willingly ignorant of means.

Purposely closing one's mind according to their discretions. The hundreds of fulfilled prophesies of Jesus' first coming contain a reliability of accuracy that is impossible to dispute. This, along with his seemingly endless recorded miracles and healings.

Not only is this so, but there is a joining together or combining of events separated by centuries that come together as one. By compiling these many events as one story having a purpose and direction, it exposes a reality of unity by which each event strengthens each other. This authenticates that the Lord indeed is the Alpha and Omega. These are the Lord's words that we are to reason together about. As we shall see, these events are continuing to this present day, and are accelerating as the day of the Lord's return draws near.

DELIVERANCE FROM THE BODY OF THIS DEATH

There is but one purpose for the creation of man. And this was established before this physical world or man was even created. The purpose is to fulfill what God already knows; the finished work by the Father, Son and Holy Spirit on those who become as they were created to be. That is, in God's image after his likeness. And there will be no error. How is it possible to grasp the enormity and depth of God?

Man can recognize a purity and righteousness that reflects God. This is clearly seen in Jesus, the heart and image of God. This mystery of mysteries that brings about absolute purity. The wise understand, as their hearts rejoice to know the heart of God. But other hearts reject He who is pure. Corruption is both offended and terrified of this incorruption. These are the same hearts who desired Barabbas, and cried out for the crucifixion of the Lamb of God. They have no desire to be washed clean if it means being exposed. Pride is a terrible hindrance to truth, and only the Lord can separate for eternity that what is contrary with a new heart.

This is the Lord's perfect justice; as would a just God condemn someone to spend eternity with someone whom they want no part of? Unfortunately, it is quite clear that many will be given the desires of their heart. The Bible defines these people as having a heart of stone, and they are completely aware of whom they are rejecting. Their number one priority is to have this world free from the Lamb of God with absolutely no reference to the Lord, as his purity exposes and reveals their failings.

LAODICEA

In the 2nd and 3rd chapter of Revelation we are given messages concerning the seven churches. It is the last church, Laodicea, which will be mentioned here because their fate will be identical to those who reject the Lord Jesus while professing to be Christian. The Lord makes it very clear that he is rejecting this church. Rev. 3:15-16 "I know thy works, that thou are neither cold nor hot. I would that you were cold or hot. - So then because you are lukewarm, and neither cold nor hot, I will spew you out of my mouth." It is not possible for believers to be anything but on fire when convicted by this amazing grace.

The church is built on the blood of the Martyrs. The greater the persecution and evil, the greater the hunger for righteousness and this pure love, and the conviction to stand against evil. With this comes an even greater desire to testify to all of what God has done for them. The greater the lies, the greater the hunger to proclaim truth. And as the proclaiming of this truth increases for the individuals, the greater is their capacity to receive more truth.

The enormity of this can never be understood by what the Bible calls the world. And the heart of the Laodiceans dominates all too much of the Christian churches. There is one thing that stands out with these churches. It is not the enemies of the Lord that they silence and vehemently oppose, but it is God's watchmen.

Jesus spoke of this very thing in Luke 11:33 "No man, when lighting a lamp, puts it in a secret place or under a basket; but on a lampstand, that they may see the light."

After speaking to the church of Laodicea, the Lord states in Rev. 3:19 "As many as I love, I rebuke and chasten; be zealous, therefore and repent."

CHAPTER 13

WATCHMEN ON THE WALL

Ezek. 3:17-21 "Son of man, I have made you a watchman unto the house of Israel. Therefore, hear the word at my mouth, and give them warning from me. - When I say to the wicked, 'Thou shall surly die'; and you give him not warning, nor speak to warn the wicked from his wicked way, to save his life, the same wicked man shall die in his iniquity. But his blood will I require at your hand. - Yet if you warn the wicked, and he turns not from his wickedness, nor from his wicked way, he will die in his iniquity. But you have delivered your soul.

"Again, when a righteous man does turn from his righteousness, and commits iniquity, and I lay a stumbling block before him, he shall die; because you have not given him warning, he shall die in his sin, and his righteousness which he has done shall not be remembered. But his blood will I require at your hand. Nevertheless, if you warn the righteous man, that the righteous man does not sin, he shall surely live, because he is warned. Also you have delivered your own soul."

Jesus himself reviewed the history of their fathers, and of the many that rejected these words of truth. Luke 11:47,49 "Ye build the sepulchers of the prophets, and your fathers killed them. - Therefore, said the wisdom of God, I will send them prophets and apostles, and some of them they shall they slay and persecute."

MESSAGE AND MESSENGERS

No Christian is ever offended by any scripture of honest rebuke. Quite the opposite, as their greatest fear is wrongly proclaiming the word of God; and they are eager and willing to discuss and reason together. Those who are offended are so because the word of God offends them, period. Being exposed as a sinner overrides any thankfulness that their sins are forgiven by the One who, even though he was without sin, became sin; *their* sin. This reveals two completely different hearts, who are both being tested and tried. This sacrifice of love is received with unspeakable joy by some. And by the others, this message and their messengers must be silenced.

The Bible reveals what may appear to be diverse ways this fallen spirit of mankind has rejected their creator. However, there is actually only one: Rejecting his word. This was first revealed in the Garden of Eden, when Eve rejected God's words and believed Satan, who is a liar with no truth in him. It does not require that much reasoning to understand this process is continuing and accelerating to this day.

FAITH

At a very young age there is a recognition of right and wrong, and this awareness increases with age. And so does the judging, as individuals establish their own standards. Then with the presence of Jesus 2,000 years ago, the Lord's absolute standards were revealed in his only begotten Son. It was then that the words of the prophet that said "Man's greatest righteousness are as filthy rags" could not be disputed. However, this recognition is received with a joy that cannot be described by those who believe this same Jesus takes all the sins of those who believe on him.

The prideful, however, are offended; as the preaching of the cross is foolishness to them that perish. And their darkened hearts are offended by he who is pure. An example will be given here that affirms this truth, and the search for and rejection of this special truth is an amazing motivator, and separates man as nothing else.

FROM ATHEISTS TO CREATIONISTS

A short article by Jerry Bergman, Ph.D. reveals a process that separates man. It involves a hunger for truth which will evolve into searching for the ultimate truth. Mr. Bergman always loved science and was a hands-on scientist. It was at Wayne State University that he earned his Bachelors, Master's, and Ph.D. degrees. This short article perhaps best explains seeking to understand truth and rejecting all contradictions. This always leads to the ultimate truth.

ACTS & FACTS FEB 2015

"I have always loved science, partially due to the influence of my atheist engineer father, who was heavily involved in research and development. At Wayne State University I was exposed to evolution and accepted this worldview, as did most of my peers. The atheist philosophy came with it. The University invited a number of speakers to lecture on religion, at least tangentially, all of whom were quite negative toward Christianity. One even stressed that since we have given Christianity 2,000 years to fix up the world, it is high time to try atheism.

"As I became more involved in the atheist's movement I got tired of hearing that all the problems of the world were the fault of Christianity, and if we got rid of all the Christians, the world would be a wonderful place. What especially bothered me was that my atheist peers were determined to suppress Christianity by any means, legal or illegal - first by banning it from the public square, then in the private domain. Atheists seem to feel the end justifies the means, so they ruthlessly sought to crush Christianity. I soon realized this goal was evil because in the end it always did more harm than good- and yet it is tried in so many places.

"As I studied evolution (the doorway to atheism) it eventually became apparent that the theory had many problems. The first example I researched in detail was the "vestigial organ" claim. There are over 1000 claimed vestigial organs. These are supposedly nonfunctional evolutional "leftovers" yet I found uses for all of them. I went on to study the fossil record, and then went on to examine the natural selection claim concluding that natural selection only explains the survival of the fittest.

"Sexual selection, instead of explaining sexual differences between males and females, actually serves to reduce deviation from the average. Research which documents this conclusion includes a computer program that combines the faces of many woman to produce the most beautiful women; ugliness is viewed as a deviation from this average and thus to be selected against.

"After exploring all of the major arguments for evolution, I eventually concluded that Darwinism has been falsified on the basis of science and realized that the evidence demands an intelligent creator.

"The biblical age question was more difficult to deal with. But in my mind, a major factor which supported a young creation was the profound evidence for genetic degradation. It is well documented that each new generation of humans adds about 100 to 150 mutations (genetic errors) per person, and an estimated 99.9 percent of these mutations are near neutral, harmful, or lethal. Consequently, there is no way life could have evolved 3.5 billion years ago and still be around today, because life would have become extinct long ago from genetic meltdown and cell catastrophe.

"Another important finding that supports the creation view was the discovery of soft tissue in dinosaur bones that were claimed to be 65 million years old. This is a problem because destructive forces such as cosmic rays would have destroyed soft tissue long ago.

"The evidence against Darwinism was a critical factor in my acceptance of creationism, which opened the door to my acceptance of Christianity, Biblical reliability, and a young earth creation world view. Like many scientists who came before me, I discovered that the evidence supports the truth of the Bible."

These observations by Jerry Bergman are confronted by all scientists. The conclusions reached should be the same by all of them, but is not. Most of these scientists are honorable men. So how can it be explained that truth is not only rejected, but there also exists a united and vindictive effort to suppress and malign Christianity and destroy it by any means?

To become consumed with an overwhelming vindictiveness against reason is completely irrational behavior, especially from ones whose life's calling is to for truth. What would cause a large percentage of these scientists to ignore the very laws of science that clearly reveal evolution is impossible? The law of entropy or 2nd Law of Thermodynamics revealed in genetic mutations have never been shown to be beneficial, but completely the opposite. All scientists know this. This will be addressed in more detail later

The latest Pew Research Center poll found that 65% of the public and 98% of scientists believe humans evolved over time. - Wisconsin State Journal, 2/13/2015.

PURPOSE

The complete opposite of evolution is occurring, as everything is becoming less stable. Jerry Bergman could just scratch the surface in this short article when revealing the bankrupt teaching of evolution. Evolution is based on mutations of DNA. Charles Darwin knew nothing of DNA, which is intelligently encoded information. But modern scientists *do* know. They also know that all mutations are a loss of information. There is never new information added.

It is difficult to impossible for 2% of the people to convince 98% that they are in error. Especially if an inordinate vindictiveness overcomes this 98%. They do not hear why they are in error, as these words stir up uncomfortable emotions in them. This is what must be addressed first: what is causing this erratic behavior? These scientists cannot see what is clearly revealed to them by their own laws of science. This brings about an even more telling behavior; an even greater insistence to belittle and silence any discussion or possibility of a creator God.

There is but one conclusion for this madness. It is spiritual. These same 98% of scientists have no disagreement with the 2% over even one law of science that does not directly reveal a Creator God. The spirit of man was created to be in the image of God, with the freedom to reject what they were created to be.

Science is based on truth, or all that is known to be true. There is no debate or problem between science and the Judeo-Christian Bible, in which there is a constant admonition to reject that what is false, and hunger after truth. All that is required is to accept what is already known to be true: with time, everything deteriorates. And with DNA this deterioration is observable. Also known is that there is never any new information added to DNA. Why is it necessary to have to point out that with the passage of time, evolution results in the elimination and deterioration of DNA to the point of eventually no useful information remaining? And as there never is any new information added, this always results in eventually no information at all. This is not that complicated.

Just having the ability to reason out the complexity and wonder of this encoded information that had to be created at a specific time in the not too distant past reveals not only consciousness, but an awareness of a Creator God.

If there is to be any debate as to what is happening, it should be about this strange behavior taking place in these men and women of science. Why this inordinate rejection and blindness to specific laws of science that reveal He who is the ultimate truth?

Science does not address or even comprehend this intellect with unlimited power that intelligently encoded information in all of life that produces after its kind. God created this life. All of this encoded information would be meaningless and would deteriorate immediately after its inception, were it not that it is living DNA in an environment conducive to life. Mankind does not even have a concept, let alone a theory, as to what life is, except to say it came into being from non-life. But that is also false and contrary to the laws of science that address this. For a man to profess he is a scientist and then pick and choose which laws of science to accept or reject automatically rejects him as a true scientist. Therefore, any man believing in evolution where life came from non-life is rejecting science itself.

What is dismissed or ignored is the most obvious, and that is life which is aware of the fact that they are alive, and conscious of themselves and the world around them. Man cannot even conceive the fullness of this.

However, this blindness is verified in their explanation of this strange logic. They state that up to 98% of this DNA is junk DNA, no longer needed. (At this present time there is a variation of the amount of junk DNA from these evolutionists from 92% to 98%) Apparently when junk DNA reaches 100% then man will have reached Godhood. Is it really necessary to point out that this leaves 0% of DNA - or a nothingness? And that the more intelligently encoded information is removed, the more efficient and intelligent and perfected one becomes, with never any new information added. (Since this was written many scientists have found much of this supposedly junk DNA is not junk, but has a specific purpose.)

What is being revealed is a gracious God who will not allow his ultimate truth to be perverted by outlandish nonsense, lies and contradictions. Those who reject the Lord do so with their eyes wide open. 2nd Cor. 4:3-4 "But if our gospel be hidden it is hidden to them that are lost, - In whom the god of this world has blinded the minds of them who believe not, lest the light of the glorious gospel of Christ, who is the image of God, should shine unto them."

What is being affirmed here is that there is a specific agenda for rejecting this special truth; a truth that defines Jesus. Their eyes are wide open. It is their minds that are blinded, as this special light is unacceptable.

Later on we will address DNA further, but to an abbreviated degree. As the focus here is revealing the ultimate truth; a truth that is not hidden. And any rejection of this truth that clearly identifies the Father and his Son, who is the heart of the Father, is with full knowledge of what or who they are rejecting. A just and loving Lord God will not allow those who are willingly ignorant to deceive with anything but blatant obvious errors. In fact, those seeking truth will also understand this deception and its evil agenda. Scientist Jerry Bergman recognized the evil of evolutionists designing falsification to deceive.

CHAPTER 14

MAN CREATED FOR A PURPOSE

Truth is not based on opinions of men or taking polls. In fact, the events that are taking place in this world reveal a prophetic timetable. As at this present time, 98% of highly educated men and women that are in the field of science – those that would appear to be the best qualified to correctly answer the question of a creator or evolution – state they believe man evolved. It is also from this same special, apparently open minded and inquisitive people that there is an insistence that biblical Christianity be silenced.

This raises a red flag. Reason would dictate that there is some type of outside influence that is active in the affairs of men, with the particular targeting and blinding the minds of those in the best position to further a certain agenda. It will not be long before none of whom the Bible calls "the world" will claim atheism. They will know there is one God, but not all will know him. Eph.6:12 "We wrestle not against flesh and blood, but principalities, against powers, against the rulers of darkness of this world, against spiritual wickedness in high places."

This wording "We wrestle not against flesh and blood", and then identifying it as spiritual wickedness in high places, reveals a spiritual warfare. This involves the spiritual world, which the Lord clearly warned man to not become involved with. This spiritual involvement was seen with Satan's temptation with Eve, and the actual intervention in Job's life, for the purpose that Job would curse God. And then the confusion of Satan when tempting Jesus in the wilderness. This confusion was brought about by rejecting God's purpose for his own creation. Then the ultimate blindness – that the creator would worship the created. Luke 4:5-7 "And the devil showed Jesus all the kingdoms of the world in a moment of time. - And said unto him, 'All this authority will I give you, and the glory of them. For that is given unto me, and to whomsoever I will, I give it. - If thou will worship me, all shall be yours.'"

Mankind that reject the purpose for their creation has also become confused. This confusion, or darkness to truth, expands to perversions of all spiritual and moral truths.

PROPHESY

The Bible reveals a vast difference between these two diverse and opposite standards and beliefs. The one is identified as a liar with no truth in him who is in darkness, with no light. The other, the Lord, is light and life. God spoke all things into existence. This includes Satan and all the angels. Reason dictates that God, who created all there is, had a purpose for his creation. This purpose of authenticity would naturally extend to his written word, identified as the Son of God, and God. Bible scholars estimate the Judeo-Christian Bible is about 25% prophetic with most of these prophesies authenticated, having been fulfilled. This leaves assurance of the reliability of the remaining prophesies.

The Bible extends this assurance of reliability to every word, extending the word of prophesy to 100%. Some of the last words to man given to John read, in Rev.1:1-3 "The Revelation of Jesus Christ, which God gave to him, to show unto his servants, things that must shortly come to pass, and he sent and signified by his angel unto his servant, John, - Who bore witness of the word of God, and of the testimony of Jesus Christ, and all of the things that he saw. - Blessed is he that reads, and they that hear the words of this prophesy, and keep those things which are written in it; for the time is at hand."

And then Rev. 19:10b gives the full meaning and purpose of prophesy. "Worship God; for the testimony of Jesus is the spirit of prophesy." As Jesus is truth, so is all of his word. (Not one of man's religions has a single authenticated fulfilled prophesy.)

PURPOSE, TRUTH AND JUSTICE

The truth of God is the Lord's justice. Perfect justice will not condemn a man for rejecting that which he has no knowledge of. Often, we will rightly hear man cry this out. "Would a just God condemn a man for eternity who has never even heard of salvation through Jesus? How about the countless millions in the remote areas of the world where the word was never preached? Or homes that curse or forbid even the mention of Christ's name?" And does the Lord even address this? The answer to that is yes. Constantly, and with such clarity that when brought before the judgment set of Christ, as all will be, not even one person can profess "I did not know".

PRISONERS

The Bible assures us that the Lord constantly reveals his purpose and person to all of mankind, with Jesus being the redeemer. But this, though clearly stated, cannot be fully comprehended. This is not double talk, as these words cannot be fully understood while prisoners in this body of death. Paul states in Romans 7:21-25 "I find then a law that, when I would do good, evil is present with me. - For I delight in the law of God after the inward man; - But I see another law in my members, warring against the law of my mind, and bringing me into captivity to the law of sin which is in my members. - Oh wretched man that I am! Who will deliver me from the body of this death? I thank God through Jesus Christ, our Lord. So then, with the mind I myself serve the law of God, but with the flesh, the law of sin."

Then Peter calls this body of death a prison, therefore adding a little more understanding. 1st Peter 3:18-19 "For Christ has once suffered for sins, the just for the unjust, that he might bring us to God, being put to death in the flesh but made alive by the Spirit, - By whom also he went and preached to the spirits in prison." The wording is quite clear that this prison is the body of this death.

Both of these scriptures reveal that flesh is sin and death. And Jesus revealed the same to Nicodemus in John 3:3b-4, "'Except a man be born again, he cannot see the kingdom of God.' Nicodemus then asked, 'How can a man be born again when he is old? Can he enter a second time into his mother's womb?'"

You must be born again to see the kingdom of God. Jesus said "To enter into the kingdom of God you must be born of water and of the Spirit. - That which is born of the flesh is flesh; and that which is born of the Spirit is spirit." (John 3:5-6) The Bible addresses this specific time and event when born again men and women will be free from the body of this death and sin, and be raised incorruptible (1st Cor. 15:51-57 and 1st Thes. 4:13-18). This event takes place at the time referred to as the gathering of the saints to meet the Lord in the air, when Jesus receives the believers.

It is then that more clarity and understanding is given concerning what takes place at this very event when they being changed, and why they will be changed; seeing the Lord as he is. And it is at that instant, when their spirit meets the Lord in the air, that they will receive their new incorruptible body. 1st John 3:2 "Beloved, now we are the children of God, and it does not yet appear what we will be, but we know that, when he shall appear, we shall be like him; for we shall see him as he is."

We are told we do not know what we will be until we meet him in the air. And then, having been completely cleansed and changed, we will see him as never before. The Lord tells us it has not even entered into the heart of man what the saints will be; until we see him as he is.

Continuing with this blindness that is caused by rejecting the light: This is a self-imposed blindness, by the rejection of what the Lord, through the Holy Spirit, has continually spoken to the spirit, or eternal essence, of man. There is a purpose for all of the word. What will be given is not that difficult to understand. And because it is given by God, every word is precious and of the utmost importance. Keep in mind what that old liar the serpent said to Eve to entice her to reject the word of God. Gen. 3:1-4 "Yea, hath God said you shall not eat of every tree of the garden?' - And the woman said unto the serpent, 'We may eat of the fruit of the trees of the garden, - But of the fruit of the tree in the midst of the garden God has said, You shall not eat of it, or touch it, lest you die.' - And the serpent said unto the woman, 'You shall not surely die.'"

The Lord put Adam in the Garden of Eden where there was no death and apparently no hurt. This garden would appear to be much like paradise, or the Kingdom of heaven as we envision it to be. Then with the introduction of sin, this brought separation and death. Man then had to be vacated from Eden. This was a separation where man no more had direct communication with God.

Gen. 3:8 "And they heard the voice of the Lord God walking in the garden in the cool of the day." (This wording "the voice of the Lord God walking" reveals a depth of communication that will probably be expanded to the smelling of colors, etc. This writer can but touch on the fullness of this narrative in the garden that helps man in his quest to return to God.) The tree of life that gives eternal life, if eaten, reveals Jesus' words of John 6:53 "Except you eat of flesh of the Son of man, and drink his blood, you have no life in you." And the angels of God guarding the way of life, and fallen angels revealed in Satan and his lies. No scripture is to be taken lightly. John 5:39 "Search the scriptures, for in them ye think you have eternal life; and they are they that testify of me."

Man had in the garden, as now, the freedom to choose to believe the Lord or reject these words of life. There are two things the Lord told Adam. Gen. 2:15-16 "And God took the man, and put him in the Garden of Eden to till (dress or take care of) it" as a gardener or servant. This is very much as God created angels to be ministering spirits, and commanded man to not eat only one fruit in the garden: The fruit of the knowledge of good and evil. Rejecting the word of God separated man from truth. But as the Bible continually reveals, truth has not separated Himself from man. There is an acute awareness of who is being rejected.

CHAPTER 15

GOD'S KINGDOM

The Spirit of the Almighty is continually speaking to all of mankind; even the deaf hear of the Lord's eternal Kingdom and how to enter. The scriptures clearly affirm this. Helen Keller was both blind and deaf from a small child. Years later, when she was able to communicate, she stated she always knew there was a God. She just didn't know his name.

Scripture also gives a clear understanding of the eternal torment in store for those who reject the way of salvation. And all that is required is to believe; and desire, more than anything, to be eternally in the Lord's presence.

We are told the heart cannot conceive what the Lord has prepared for those who love him. However, we are given insight.

Jesus stated "The first shall be last, and the last first." And in Luke 18:16 he says, "Permit little children to come unto me, and forbid them not; for of such is the kingdom of heaven." Also in Luke 7:28 "Among those born of women there in not a greater prophet than John the Baptist; but he that is least in the Kingdom of God is greater than he." The least would be the greatest? This world does not operate in that manner.

Luke 22:24-27 "There was a strife among them, as to who would be accounted the greatest. - And he (Jesus) said, 'The kings of the Gentiles exercise lordship over them; and they that exercise lordship over them are called benefactors. - But ye shall not be so, but he that is greatest among you, let him be as the younger; and he that is chief, as he that does serve. - Which is greater, he that is served, or him that serves? Is it not he who is served? But I am among you as one that serves.'"

This reality is seen when the people wanted to make Jesus king after the miracle of the feeding of the five thousand, plus women and children. In John 6:1-13, the Lord had blessed five barley loaves and two fishes. This multiplied to the feeding of the five thousand, of which twelve baskets of fragments were left after the people were filled. John 6:14-15 says "Then these men, after they had seen the miracle that Jesus did, said 'This is of a truth that prophet that should come into the world'. - And when Jesus perceived that they would come and take him by force, to make him a king, he departed again into a mountain himself alone."

Later these same people cried out with one voice to crucify him. Amazingly, the miracle of the multiplying of the bread and fishes was as nothing compared to what was to unfold. Because when Jesus - the Lamb of God and as a servant - gave his body as that true manna from heaven, it becomes life eternal to those who receive this true bread.

This does bring to question the difference between this world in which the greater exercise lordship over the least, and the Kingdom of God where the least will be the greatest. Pilate's words and the people's response are also telling. John 19:14 & Matt 27: 21-24. "And it was the preparation of the Passover, about the sixth hour, and he (Pilate) said to the Jews, 'Behold your King!' - But they cried out all the more, saying 'Away with him, away with him, crucify him!'"

What can be comprehended is a world where the greater have an eternity to strive to be the greatest. An example of this situation is given in Isaiah and Ezekiel. And interestingly, the setting is in the heavens. (As to what degree, it is not known here; as man has little knowledge of heaven.) As has been previously discussed, the Lord revealed an angel that rejected what God created him to be. This angel has been given many names. In Isaiah he is called Lucifer, son of the morning. And in Job he is called Satan. As one of the sons of God he had displayed great powers to destroy, keeping in mind that the Lord limited what he was allowed to do.

The 14th chapter of Isaiah and the 28th chapter of Ezekiel reveal the great beauty and power of this angel. It appears he had attained leadership because of his beauty and wisdom. He said in his heart "I will ascend into the heaven, I will exalt my throne above the stars of God. I will sit also upon the mount of the congregation, in the sides of the north. - I will ascend above the heights of the clouds; I will be like the most high." (Isaiah 14:13-14) And the Bible states in the very next verse "Yet you shall be brought down to hell, to the sides of the pit." Lucifer knew exactly what the result of his rebellion would be. As do demons, because when they encountered Jesus they cried out "Have you come to torment us before the time?" They were terrified of him. There is enough evidence to reveal that fallen angels were fully aware of eternal damnation. This awareness is also in the spirit of man, and it increases in intensity with each denial of the Lord.

CHAPTER 16

SPIRIT WORLD

There was an event that took place when Jesus came into the presence of people possessed by demons. He commanded the demons not to speak, because they correctly identified him. Is it because it was not yet his time? Or perhaps this reflects the Lord's displeasure in liars testifying of him? Maybe there is something that Jesus, as the son of man, was trying to reveal to man? Man is not in any way to communicate with this spirit world of demons, or the spirits of departed saints. You can contact *demons*, but cannot contact the spirit of the departed. And any apparently "successful" effort will result in the contacting of demons. Because, as lying spirits, they will answer to any name. Their deception, and ability to deceive, magnifies in those who ignore the Lord's admonitions.

WITCH OF ENDOR

There is recorded in the Bible an event that appears to contradict this statement that any effort to contact any spirit of the departed will result in contacting of lying spirits. It is of utmost importance to make a thorough study of scriptures that appear to contradict. This should then get your attention. Usually that is its purpose, as every appearance of contradiction then shows a greater assurance of reliability. And for that reason, there will be a brief look at this scripture concerning this man Saul, called of the Lord to be king.

But because of disobedience, he became an enemy of God. And as we search these scriptures, there is an awareness that God is never our enemy, and always reaches out his hand.

In 1st Samuel 28:1-25, it appears there is a contact being made between the living and the dead, by the efforts of man. This was strictly forbidden by the Lord. The severity of this practice and the dangers involved invoked the death penalty from the Lord. Ex. 22:18 "Thou shall not suffer a witch to live." Saul, as Israel's first King, had put those who were mediums and wizards out of the land. The Philistines came against Israel at that time; and Samuel, God's prophet who advised Saul, had just died.

Saul had no direction and did not know what to do, since the Lord had just rejected him from being King. This was because he had taken on himself to act in manners of authority that the Lord had not given to him. He had also ignored God's direct commandments. As he had severed all contact with God, he then searched out the witch of Endor to contact Samuel for advice. Saul disguised himself before visiting her, because she was aware that it was he who had put away all witches from the land.

1st Samuel 28:11-12 "Then said the woman, 'Whom shall I bring up unto you?' And he said, 'Bring me up Samuel'. - And when the woman saw Samuel she cried with a loud voice, saying 'Why have you deceived me? For you are Saul.'" When demon possessed people encountered Jesus, they spoke with a loud voice. (This reveals that it is not they, but the spirits speaking.) And they correctly identified the person, thus authenticating direct demonic involvement. And King Saul had asked her to bring up Samuel. The fact that she was surprised it was *actually Samuel that appeared* reveals this deception.

This is, then, no longer a medium contacting a departed spirit. As when a witch or medium contacts a spirit, the spirit speaks through the medium. As soon as the witch of Endor recognized Samuel and Saul, she was no longer involved. This absence of direct contact would negate any spiritual direction through mediums or wizards. This was now direct contact with Samuel… and a terrified Saul.

As there was no involvement with the witch, reason would affirm the Lord had involved himself in what would have been deception. It is unwise to limit God. We are commanded to try, or test, the spirits to see if they are of God. 1st Cor. Chapters 12, 13, and 14.

CHAPTER 17

THE LOVE AND GRACE OF GOD

Man cannot even conceive of the enormity of the Lord. Nor of his love or grace. Saul had rejected the word of God. Then Samuel told Saul that he had but one more day to live, as he and his two sons would die. He had one full day to reach out to the Lord's extended hand. This is offered to all. And unfortunately for most, their hardened hearts knowingly reject that what they know is true. (As God is truth, any rejection is rejection of truth.)

The extent to which the grace of God is continually given to all of mankind is such that not one individual can protest that perfect justice will not be administered. This is all based on the rejection or acceptance of Jesus Christ and His words. The Lord gives but two choices; and the choices are completely contrary one from another. The one being evil with no Love nor truth, based on lies. The other on He who visited this world for a season, whom man crucified. He then rose from the dead, and ascended up to the heavens. And promised to return in like manner.

GRACE

The amazing grace of God was briefly addressed before here. Written in most likely the oldest book of the Bible, these are the words of Elihu. Job 32:8 "There is a spirit in man, and the inspiration of the Almighty gives them understanding." This understanding is revealed in the next chapter. Job 33:14-18 "For God speaks once, yea twice; yet man perceives it not. - In a dream, in a vision of the night, when deep sleep falls upon men, in slumbering upon the bed; - Then he opens the ears of men, and seals their instructions, - That he may withdraw man from his purpose, and hide pride from man. - He keeps back his soul from the pit, and his life from perishing by the sword."

We are told in clearly defined words what these instructions are. The Lord hides pride from man that he may withdraw man from their purpose. This is done by revealing man's arrogance and pride. These things are revealed to the spirit of man by the Spirit of the Almighty in the night time, and they do not perceive it. The words 'observe' or 'regard' could have been used in place of "perceive it not". A combination of all three English words would probably best give the intent of the original Hebrew. Does this not mean they do not perceive or regard the depth of the consequences involved? They are completely cognizant of what has been stated, but dismiss its relevancy until an outside source becomes involved. This is similar to a brainwashed man committing an act that is planted in his mind, in response to a word or phrase previously encoded in his mind.

BODY SOUL AND SPIRIT

1st Thes. 5:23 "And the very God of peace sanctify you wholly: and I pray God your whole spirit and soul and body be preserved blameless unto the coming of our Lord Jesus." It is not necessary that man fully understand the workings of this spiritual battle that is going on. But we *are* told how to do battle against this enemy. Eph. 6:12-13a "For we wrestle not against flesh and blood, but against principalities, against powers, against the rulers of the darkness of this world, against spiritual wickedness in high places. – Wherefore, take on the whole armor of God…"

Common sense, with belief and trust in the Lord Jesus Christ. This, along with loving that which is good and hating what is evil, and taking on the armor of God. However, we are told of only two weapons in this battle. The most important part of this armor is the helmet of salvation. As without this salvation there will be no access to the sword of the Lord. Eph. 6:17 "And take the helmet of salvation, and the sword of the Spirit, which is the word of God." As it is believed here the word of God is given for our benefit, and not to ignore. Therefore, apparently, contrary scriptures would be of the most importance to understand. This solidifies biblical truths.

Gen.1:26-27 "And God said, 'Let us make man in our image, after our likeness'. - So God created man in his own image, in the image of God created he them. Male and female created he them." This creation is in the image of God, with God being both spirit and eternal. This is referring to the eternal part of man that must be born again of the Spirit of God.

Gen. 2:7 "And the Lord God formed man of the dust of the ground, and breathed into his nostrils the breath of life, and man became a living soul." As God created the spirit of man to be eternal, the physical temporal body was formed of the dust of the ground. This body will return to the dust from which it was formed. It is not difficult to understand that man is soul and spirit. What is difficult to comprehend is the spirit of man that is eternal, and his essence spending but a temporal time in this body of death.

There is an event that took place in the 2nd chapter of Genesis and played out in the 3rd chapter that parallels Eve's not regarding the gravity of God's words. The Lord spoke directly to Adam before the fall. Gen. 2:16 "And God commanded man, saying 'Of every tree of the garden you may freely eat. - But of the tree of the knowledge of good and evil, you shall not eat of, for the day you eat thereof you shall surely die.'" Satan then entered the picture. Knowing that Adam and Eve had been instructed of the Lord, he said to Eve in Gen. 3:1-5 "Yea, has God said you shall not eat of every tree of the garden?' - And Eve answered 'We may eat of all of the fruit of the garden. - But of the tree in the midst of the garden we may not eat or touch, lest we die.' - And the serpent said unto the woman 'You will not surely die. - For God does know that in the day you eat thereof, then your eyes will be opened, and you will be as God, knowing good and evil.'"

The story continues as Eve regards the word of God as little more than an effort to withhold from man his desires, finally being convinced by Satan that God's words are nothing more than a ploy to hinder man to be as God. What is thought-provoking is what happens after Adam and Eve believe the liar, and reject the Lord. The eyes of Adam and Eve were opened as they ate of the fruit of the tree of knowledge of good and evil. And they knew they were naked.

There is a common core among the most vocal professing atheists as to why they are atheists. They state Christianity interferes with their sexual morals. This is not atheism, but an open profession of a higher standard that offends them. It is also a childish attempt to make He who offends them to disappear by arrogantly stating, "I don't believe in him".

Gen.3:8-11 "And then they heard the voice of God walking in the garden in the cool of the day. Then the Lord called unto Adam 'Where are you?' And he said, 'I heard your voice in the garden, and I was afraid because I was naked, and hid myself.' (They heard the voice of God walking? As can be seen there is a greater depth of communication that is taking place in the garden.) And he said, 'Who told you that you were naked? Have you eaten of the tree I commanded you not to eat?'"

As this event is the fall of man, it is helpful to learn from this and not repeat or continue in this direction. First of all, the Lord spoke directly to Adam and Eve. This intimacy was severed when Eve rejected truth, and Adam followed. What must be understood is that man's conduct cannot alter or change in any way the Lord's nature any more than darkness can change light. God created man for a purpose. In his own image, after his likeness. God also created man as a free moral agent, with the right to choose or reject God. But man does not have the choice to establish his standards in the creator's creation. Not even man allows the inmates to set their own rules in the asylum. Nor are the criminal element allowed to establish their conduct to disrupt a normal society.

Gen.3:22 "And the Lord God said 'Behold, the man has become as one of us, to know good and evil; and now, lest he put forth his hand and take also of the tree of life, and eat, and live forever; - Therefore the Lord God sent him forth from the garden of Eden.'" There is a reason communists are professing atheists, with an inordinate hatred of Christianity. Mankind continually takes sides in a political standard that reflects what their heart, or spirit, has embraced. The Lord has established his standards of entrance into his kingdom. It is as a child; in which the least will be the greatest, etc. Man cannot grasp how this can be, other than there must be an established law of complete submission to absolute authority.

Communists and socialists, as professing atheists, reject their creator. Not because he does not exist, since they know he does. Rather, they find his laws and standards unacceptable. Very much like Satan finding God's laws and standards unacceptable, proclaiming himself to be like God. (Isaiah 14:14) These ungodly nations must first convince their subjects that there is no creator God in order for their subjects to accept their authority. (It is interesting that man esteems adoration and authority higher than wealth.) Such nations must rule by force to obtain order. A nation seeking justice obtains order by enforcing Godly laws. It is no accident that this nation has replaced God's truth and standards with their own. The start began with ungodly mindless evolution. This must start at a young age, and the younger the better to be successful.

Chapter 18

Seeking the Heart of God

All scripture is given of inspiration from God. Paul conveys these words as the law of God in Romans 7:16-17 "For we know the law is spiritual; but I am carnal, sold under sin." In the 7th and 8th chapters of Romans, Paul defines a clear knowledge of the vast difference between these two worlds, which man shares for a season. The flesh, which is carnal and temporal; and the eternal part of man, his spirit. Often referred to as "the heart of man seeking the heart of God", it is separate from physical desires.

David, like Paul, was such a man. 1st Sam. 13:14 "The Lord has sought a man after his own heart and commanded him (David) to be captain over his people." Now Samuel had just told Saul he had not kept the commandments of God, and therefore the Lord had chosen another.

As the book of Job explains, in the nighttime God reveals how he will save man from the pit; and then by whom: a Savior. Job 33:24 "Then he is gracious unto him, and says, 'Deliver him from going down to the pit. I have found a ransom.'" The Judeo-Christian Bible continues to state that this is an ongoing message to all of mankind during the nighttime. An explanation will be offered here as to how this can be; that is, knowing the Bible is the word of God and not being aware of any conscious confirmation. Some, when hearing the way of salvation, are absolutely sure that this is true. And others reject it with a seriousness and even vindictiveness that reveals a purpose for this rejection.

We have given as examples two Godly men, David and Paul; seeking the heart of God and knowing the heart of fallen man. The Lord seeks such as these to worship him and promised to send the Holy Spirit to permanently indwell believers.

COMFORTER

The Spirit of the Almighty is the Holy Spirit that Jesus said he would send to those who believe in him. John 16:7 "It is expedient for you that I go away, for if I go not away, the Comforter will not come unto you; but if I depart, I will send him unto you." In the next three verses, the Lord tells us the Holy Spirit will then reprove the world of sin, righteousness, and judgment. This is accelerating as the world enters into these final days, leading up to the presence of the Antichrist. Choices are being made, to both reprove the world that has rejected this light and choosing darkness.

This is the Holy Spirit, whom Jesus sent at the day of Pentecost after his crucifixion, of which he then spoke. John 14:17 "Even the Spirit of Truth, whom the world cannot receive, because it sees him not, nor knows him; But we know him, for he dwells with you, and shall be in you." These are the words of truth, whom those of the world will not receive because they are unacceptable.

GOSPEL IS HEARD BY ALL

Psalm 19:3 "There is no speech or language where their voice is not heard." Colossians 1:23 "If you continue in the faith grounded and settled, and be not moved away from the hope of the gospel, which you have heard, and which was preached to every creature under heaven…" Romans 2:14-15 "When the Gentiles, which have not the law, do by nature the things contained in the law, these, having not the law, are a law unto themselves. - Who show the work of the law written in their hearts, their conscience also bearing witness..." John 6:45 "It is written in the prophets, 'And they shall all be taught of God...'" And then Titus 2:11 "The grace of God that brings salvation has appeared to all men."

These scriptures state that all of mankind know the way of salvation. Would a God of justice condemn anyone for rejecting the way of salvation, without first revealing it in complete detail to all of mankind? And would he not also establish that those who rejected his way of salvation would not only reject this Savior, but choose another who is completely the opposite in every way? This is so that there can be no doubt of their rejection; this madness will increase until just before Jesus returns from the heavens. All of this world will worship the Anti-Christ except those whose names are written in the book of the Lamb slain from the foundation of the world (Rev. 13:8). Man was created to be in the image of God. Sadly, most will reject being what God created them to be, and settle for the extension of being formed of the dust of the ground.

Years ago an interesting test was given to help young children develop character and discipline. Each child was given candy at the start of the school day. They were then told that those who did not eat it would, at school closing, receive a double portion to take home. But those who ate their candy would not receive any more. It was amazing how many children ate their candy before school was out. And when these same children were given the same test years later, it produced almost identical results as it did when they were younger.

It is difficult for some to make wise choices at any age. The reason for this is that man's purpose often interferes with reason, or that which is right. "The Spirit of the Almighty gives man's spirit understanding during the night time. In a dream, a vision. Then he opens the ears of men and seals their instructions. - That he may withdraw man from *his purpose*, and hide pride from man. - To keep his soul from the pit." (Job 32:8, 33:15-18)

Two scriptures best explain what man has a difficult time conceiving while in this body of death. Luke 14:26-27 "If any man come to me, and hate not his father and mother, and wife and children, and brethren, and sisters, yea, and his own life also, he cannot be my disciple. - And whosoever does not bear his cross and come after me cannot be my disciple." Yes, he must hate his own life also. Romans 7:15 "For that what I do, I understand not, for that what I would, that do I not, but that what I hate, that do I." As we are to love our enemies, it is obvious this hating of father, mother etc. is revealing something else. The reality of the spirit is life that is eternal and flesh that is temporal.

These words of Paul in Romans are the result of knowing the Lord through Jesus. During the encounter Paul had on the road to

Damascus, the Lord took his sight for a season that he might see. Later, filled with the Holy Spirit and receiving his sight, Saul became a follower and prophet of God. He affirmed and then accepted these words his spirit had been receiving for years from the Spirit of the Almighty during deep sleep. There must be a complete acceptance, to the point of hating their own life without the Lord. Receiving the Lord with the hope and assurance of receiving, at the resurrection, a new body to be raised incorruptible.

Christians have a peace and joy that the world can never know. The hating of their life is in comparison of what they aspire to be. All because of their receiving just a partial glimpse of the Lord. And when just this partial glimpse is seen, there is a dramatic diminishing of concerns of this life and self. The contrast is in being part of this light that overcomes darkness. As the Spirit of the Almighty continually reveals this vast contrast between man and God, choices are then being made where the things of this world lose all of their importance to the point of hating this life. But also, while in this world, to have a joy unspeakable that this world can never grasp. To the world, this is foolishness.

This is then put in its entire perspective when Christians are told that they must love those who hate them. Luke 6:27-28,35 "But I say unto you that hear, love your enemies, do good to those who hate you. Bless them that curse you, and pray for them that despitefully use you. - Love your enemies, do good, hoping for nothing, and you shall be the children of the Highest; for he is kind to the unthankful, and to the evil."

Man was created in the image of God; who is spirit. John 4:24 "God is Spirit, and they that worship him must worship him in spirit and truth." God does not create robots, but individuals and free moral agents. This created eternal spirit of man enters into the newly born temporal body of flesh. Its origin is found in Gen. 2:7 "And God formed man of the dust of the ground and breathed into his nostrils the breath of life. And man became a living soul."

FEW WILL ENTER INTO LIFE

Education should always question unreasonable conclusions for the purpose of obtaining a preconceived conception. Unreasonable conclusions are arrived at when false or faulty information is inserted, and when no information is allowed that will contradict a predetermined assumption. No educator could disagree with this statement. And yet the most important and far reaching theory that has ever confronted by man has this stipulation: No supernatural intervention is allowed as to how the heavens, earth and life itself came into being. It is quite interesting that modern man, in their effort to deny a spirit world, is constantly filling the airwaves with TV concerning supernatural themes – along with movies and books.

The overriding questions asked by all of mankind regardless of their mindset is: What is my purpose in life? Why am I here? And is this all there is? These questions begin with children, and never cease throughout life. Eventually it extends to the most important and reasonable question of all. Where will they spend eternity?

CHAPTER 19

SETTING OF STANDARDS

The Lord reveals in Eph. 6:12 that our warfare is spiritual. This began with Lucifer as an angel of light, with his wisdom becoming corrupted because of his beauty and pride. Even he did not deny God. But he did claim equality to the Lord, and that kind of thinking soon extended to the thought of rising above God. Isaiah 14:13 "I will ascend into heaven, I will exalt my throne above the stars of God." As the god of this world, he sets a standard that those of this world follow. And that is why he is the god of this world.

This raises several questions and offers several more dilemmas as to why our evolutionists insist there must be no supernatural intervention in the creation. And specifically, no intelligence of any kind. What if that statement was made about a house, automobile or chair? That is silly, but think on this. It is always the greater that makes the lesser. Death does not create life, it creates nothing. All of life dies; and all of life comes from life. "Life comes only from life. And after its kind." (Law of Biogenesis.) All of life came from the life giver, God. Each kind of life has the seed of life, given of the creator God to produce life after their kind. This is observed by all of mankind.

There is something else concerning standards of understanding that a secular world in their pride cannot even address. In fact, they ignore. While establishing no supernatural intervention in the creation theory, where does the thought process or the awareness with the ability to think and reason come from? This writer is not aware of any specific law that addresses this. As the supernatural world must involve an ability to communicate with remembrance without a computer, brain, written word or recorded communication, how do spiritual beings communicate? There are a number of authenticated incidences in which people have died in hospitals. Later they were revived, and attested to their spirit leaving their body and accurately hearing conversations, in many cases several rooms away. Most of these events involved a person who was clinically defined as dead. These cases are so numerous they are not even contested as anything but factual.

The enormity of this spiritual world cannot even be conceived. Christians are told that in God's Kingdom, there will be no remembrances of unpleasant events in this life. We have recorded factual events, not knowing how this can be. Then the Lord erases what cannot be understood to be. The word of God assures us it has not even entered the heart of man what God has prepared for them that love him. This rather limits any speculations as to what will transpire in the Kingdom of God.

Do not limit the Lord, or presume perfect understanding of his words. When Jesus was on the cross, in Luke 23:39-43 "And one of the malefactors who were hanged railed at him, saying 'If you be the Christ, save yourself and us'. - But the other, answering, rebuked him, saying 'Do you not fear God, seeing you are in the same condemnation? - And indeed, justly, for we receive the full reward of our deeds. But this man has done nothing amiss.' - And then said to Jesus, 'Lord, remember me when you come into your Kingdom.' - The Lord replied 'I say onto you, today you will be with me in paradise.'"

The world, not knowing the Lord, nor having any regard for his words, then stand as judges saying: It cannot be that this man could be with Jesus in paradise that day. As Jesus will spend the next three days and nights in the tomb. No, it cannot be that this man could be with Jesus in paradise. (No one disputed the empty tomb after the third day.) This very conversation of the empty tomb rather overshadows whether this thief could be in paradise with Jesus that very day. Those that delight in pointing out this apparent impossibility of Jesus being in the grave and in paradise with this man on the cross at the same time then lose any sense of victory by their very attesting to the empty tomb. This is but one of countless examples of this world that loses every time it declares victory.

The word of God clearly states it is Jesus who created the heavens and earth. And that this same Jesus is sustaining and upholding every element of the universe. And this also while in the flesh, and also while in the tomb. Colossians chapter 1 and Hebrews chapter 1 declare Jesus is the creator of all there is, and the image and express image of God. And as by him all things were created, he also upholds and sustains all things. Also Acts 17:28 "For in him we live, move and have our being." This also while in the flesh for 33 years and in the tomb for three days and nights. Jesus was and is fully God and fully man.

As such, he is Omnipresent and beyond time. Yes, this man was that day in paradise with the Lord.

FALSE TEACHERS

Paul told the believers to work out their salvation with fear and trembling. (Phil.2:12) We are also told to be wary of false teachers who pervert the simplicity of the gospel. Then the Lord himself addressed the result of this grace beyond comprehension. And all that is necessary to receive this gift of life is to believe. Matt. 7:13-14,21-23 "Enter in at the narrow gate, for wide is the gate, and broad is the way, that leads to destruction, and many there be who go that way. - Because narrow is the gate and hard is the way, which leads to life. And few that be that find it. - Not everyone that says to me, Lord, Lord, shall enter into the kingdom of heaven, but he that does the will of my Father, who is in heaven. - Many will say to me in that day, Lord, Lord, have we not prophesied in your name? And in your name cast out demons? And in your name done many wonderful works? - And I will profess unto them, I never knew you. Depart from me, you that work iniquity."

THE SIMPLICITY OF THE GOSPEL

These are not words to the world and its false religions, but to professing Christian churches or off-shoots professing to be Christian. The simplicity of the way of salvation is revealed in Jesus' words. You must believe as a child. This childlike faith and simplicity is revealed in the story of the Philippian jailer.

Acts 16:25-31 "Paul and Silas prayed and sang praises unto God; and the prisoners heard them. - Then there was a great earthquake, and immediately all the doors of the prison were opened, and everyone's bands were loosed. - And the keeper of the prison, awaking out of his sleep and seeing the prison doors open, drew out his sword and would have killed himself, supposing the prisoners have been fled. - But Paul cried with a loud voice, saying, 'Do thyself no harm; for we are all here.' - And bringing them out, trembling, he asked, 'Sirs, what must I do to be saved?' - And they said, 'Believe on the Lord Jesus Christ, and you and all your house shall be saved.'"

And Jesus said "You must believe as a child." So why does the Lord say "Hard is the way and few find it"? What is hard about believing? The prophet Ezekiel was addressing this very subject: The thing that is hard is the heart of man. This can only be remedied by a new heart. Ezekiel 11:19 "I will take the stony heart out of their flesh and give them a heart of flesh." This is a prophetic pronouncement of those who believe. And when confronted with what has been done on the cross, they receive the Lord Jesus as Savior by simply believing. The term often used is "being born again". The gospel in its simplicity is: Man is a sinner and in need of a savior. This expands to a logical process of a savior that not only forgives, but takes or took their sins on the cross. Then all who believe, and receive the grace of God, are made pure.

But then reason rushes in, presenting a problem. As man is a sinner, and none are righteous, this leaves us with the picture of a hog being washed. Then the hog returns to the mire, with nothing being changed but for a short season. This awareness should increase as knowledge of the Lord increases, as with more knowledge, the greater the contrast that can be seen. But also the greater the peace, because of the light that overcomes our darkness. Believers know they are sinners. But what overwhelms them is that he has cleansed them.

True believers in the Lord abhor the things of the world, and overcome most. What is being addressed here is: Because of knowing the Lord, there is an increased awareness of how even the greatest of man's righteousness are truly as filthy rags. This brings a realization that there has to be a specific time when this hog returns no more to the wallowing in in the mud. And that specific time can only be when they see their Savior as he is. But that cannot be possible until believers are completely changed. They have to be completely cleansed in order to be fit to enter the kingdom of God and able to see the Lord as he is.

Jesus explains this to Nicodemus by two births. The first to *see* the kingdom of God, and the second to *enter* the Kingdom of God John 3:3. "Jesus answered, 'Except a man be born again, he cannot see the kingdom of God.'" This the first birth in which the way, truth, and life is seen and believed. What is seen is Jesus, and what is believed are his words. Then Jesus says to Nicodemus, "Except a man be born of water and of the Spirit, he cannot enter the Kingdom of God." 1st Cor. 15:50 "Flesh and blood cannot enter the kingdom of God: neither does corruption inherit incorruption." This second birth then occurs when entering the Kingdom of God, as this corruption becomes incorruption. (1st Cor. 15:51-53). This is when the Lord greets the believers, both dead and living, as they rise to meet him in the air. When they see him as he is, it is then that they will be changed to be as he is: Incorruption.

ETERNAL SEPARATION

These words are very plain and straightforward. All are born of the flesh. But those born of the Spirit, as a direct result of believing in Jesus, are special. And they are called the sons of God, or Christians. They are born again, eagerly awaiting the time they will see their Lord with new eyes and bodies. They are special because they are chosen. And they are chosen because they believe in, and want, what their heavenly Father wants for them. This is the great commandment of God. Matt. 22:37-38 "Jesus said, 'You shall love the Lord your God with all your heart, and with all your soul, and with all your mind. - This is the first and great commandment.'"

This commandment separates man for eternity: Loving God is wanting, more than *anything*, what God wants for you. "The Lord God formed man of the dust of the ground, and breathed into his nostrils the breath of life; and man became a living soul." This living soul is tried and tested for a season. But then returns to dust, with no life in it.

It is during this time, before returning to the dust, that standards and choices are being made. The most important is: Do you prefer your desires and wants to dictate to your creator how he is to finish his creation; do you wish to take over? This, in light of the knowledge that in the flesh your greatest righteousness are as filthy rags? This was authenticated 2,000 years ago when he who knew no sin, and was the express image of God, was crucified. The only one that protested his innocence gave in to the mob, and had him crucified; all the while professing him to be a just man, innocent, and their King.

CHAPTER 20

SEEING THE LORD AS HE IS

Man is faced with what should be the easiest decision of his life. That is, loving their creator who became man for a season. And this, becoming man for a season, was for the purpose of taking the sins of men who recognize there is this need and also understand and believe these words: "The Lord so loves the world and wants that none perish." This is quite humbling. The enormity of loving the Lord is consenting to and wanting, more than anything, for him to take your sin. Because that is the only way possible for man to become in his image and truly see and know the Lord as he is. How can it be that my Savior would die for me?

NON-CONTRADICTION

In the very first two chapters of the Bible there are statements that appear to contradict each other, or at least are confusing. This has been addressed here previously, for the sake of familiarity. This is not a contradiction, although the secular world still sees it as such. And this will cause anyone that is honestly searching for truth to recognize a clear and special teaching for those who know God is truth, and who hold the Bible as precious. Therefore, focusing greater attention on statements that appear to be errors. When reading a book, knowing there are no errors or contradictions, an obvious special truth is waiting to be revealed by the author to those who search his words with this understanding. Anyone desiring to know the truth of the Lord can find him in the word of God.

Because we are prisoners in the body of this flesh, we cannot have perfect knowledge. But Jesus is the Word of God. The more one searches out the word, the more clearly truth and deception can be seen. There is in this world both truth and error. And as none are all knowing, this is natural. However, because of the purpose of which man was created, imperfect man has this freedom to choose as he was created to be. Or, reject what he was created to be. Reason alone reveals that anyone that could reject the love of the servant of servants is completely sold out to deception and self.

First of all, the message of the gospel is quite pure and easy to understand. Not only because the Lord constantly reveals to the spirit of man the simplicity of the gospel to counteract the constant confusion and distractions while in the body of this flesh, but it is also given to mankind in a vision of the night, in a dream, by the Spirit of the Almighty. "That he may keep man from his purpose, to deliver him from the pit. Stating I have found a Deliverer, a ransom." (Job 32:8 and 33:1-30)

Job 33:14 "God speaks once, yea twice, yet man perceives it not." What is the full meaning of 'yet man perceives it not"? It needs to be understood that man is body, soul, and spirit; of which the spirit of man is the life and finality of man. When there is a rejection of this simple biblical truth, it is impossible to understand this biblical statement and its full implications. Eph. 6:12 "We wrestle not against flesh and blood, but against principalities, against powers, against the rulers of the darkness of this world, against spiritual wickedness in high places."

SPIRITUAL CHOICES

These words: "The Spirit of the Almighty that speaks to the spirit of man". This would have absolutely no meaning or comprehension, were it believed what is being presented in our secular education system; evolution, in that man has no spirit. That life came from non-life. This is a theory that contradicts all basic laws of science and reason. And it could not possibly have gained a foothold in any country unless there was complete control of children in the educational system. This, too, has spiritual roots.

This is why we have professing atheists also stating that man has no spirit. It is an absolute necessity for them to teach that man evolved, and was not created. Being created logically means there would be a *purpose* for creation. All of man's creations have a purpose, how much more so of the Creator of all there is? What is presented in Isaiah are these same people that have also rejected the Creator God who so loved the world that he sent his only begotten Son; that whosoever would believe in him would have everlasting life. This is the same Son who also created all there is, and spoke life into being. Isaiah 5:20-21 "They who call evil good, and good evil; who put darkness for light, and light for darkness; who put bitter for sweet, and sweet for bitter. - To them who are wise in their own eyes, and prudent in their own sight."

CHOICES MADE BY MAN AND ANGELS

There will be an abbreviated look at this world of angels, whom also were created for a purpose. Man was created to be in the image of God, who is spirit. "Angels were created to be ministering spirits, sent forth to be ministering spirits unto them who shall be heirs of salvation." (Hebrews 1:14) Then as these words are understood by Bible-believing Christians, it is often assumed there should also be close communications with these angels of God who are to minister to these special people who believe and receive the Lord through his Son. Instead, we are given warnings not to engage in any communication with these angels.

Jesus said our prayer and communication is to be with the Father. And anything to be asked for, is to be asked in His name. As we search out the word of God, we discover this world of the spirits is out of bounds. And for a reason. These words seem to come in conflict with what the resurrected Jesus spoke to the believers just before he was taken into heaven. Luke 24:49 "I send the promise of my Father upon you. But tarry in the city of Jerusalem, until you become endowed with power from on high." Acts 1:8 "But you shall receive power after the Holy Spirit is come upon you, and you shall be witnesses unto me."

This is not seeking spirits, but the Holy Spirit sent of God. The Spirit of God directs and guides, and the Lord gives instructions as to the proper and improper use of this power. There is improper use of this power, as man has not been given authority to control this power. There are three chapters that address this. As our battle is spiritual, you can be sure many will lose this spiritual battle because of pride, and forgetting who is to be lifted up. That, along with forgetting whom your prayers and conversation are to be with.

CHAPTER 21

ANGELS AND DEMONS

This writer has chosen not to go into depth and detail concerning Angels, as there would be much speculation concerning this spirit world. We are given basic information of a far different world than ours, and should trust completely the word of God. This has placed the world of spirits and angels out of bounds. Man is not to engage in any communication or contact with angels, nor with any spirits. These are not contradictory statements but common sense, with anyone willing to learn from God's word why man is not to attempt contact with this spirit world. This is clearly revealed in the third chapter of the Bible, with continual information until the very last book. Trust in and belief that the Bible is the word of God will give complete protection from deception. All deception is brought about by blatant rejection of the word of God, and then doing what is clearly told not to do. This will be touched on in greater detail later, as a few of the religions of man will be addressed.

Trust in the Word of God can only come about when it can be conceived and desired that there is a God who finds sin and evil such an abhorrence, that there would be zero tolerance. And that this same God would then send his only begotten Son to be the sin of all that believe in him. These are just words with no real meaning unless, if you yourself would have such a son. Your only son, whom you love. And then to give him to take the penalty of just one guilty person, that his evil would be made pure. Perhaps a man would pay for a man's debt. Or even die for another. But to send his only son to do so?

It is then that every word of God is searched out as never before, as what kind of God is this? As you now have a glimpse at the heart of God. This is then what separates man for eternity. Yes, to them that perish the preaching of the cross is foolishness.

VIOLENCE IN HEAVEN

Jesus was speaking of John the Baptist, and then gave some rare but important insight into the kingdom of heaven. Matt. 11:10-12 "For this is he of whom it is written, Behold, I send my messenger before my face, who shall prepare thy way before thee. - Among those born of women there has not risen greater than John the Baptist; notwithstanding, he that is least in the kingdom of heaven is greater than he. - And from the days of John the Baptist until now the kingdom of heaven suffers violence, and the violent take it by force." Two amazing Theological statements are made here. The greatest in the kingdom of heaven are servants, and the violent are in control of heaven and will continue to be so until Satan and his angels are cast out of heaven 2,000 years later.

This is the same time event revealed in the 12th chapter of Revelation, where the violent take the kingdom of heaven by force. Rev. 12:1-4 "And there appeared a great wonder in heaven. A woman clothed with the sun, and moon under her feet, and her head a crown of twelve stars. - And she being with child, cried, travailing in birth, and pained to be delivered. - And there appeared another wonder in heaven; and behold, a great red dragon, having seven heads and ten horns and seven crowns upon his heads. - And his tail drew the third part of the stars of heaven and cast them to the earth."

This prophesy in Rev. 12 is quite extensive and will only be addressed in part. Jesus was born of Judah, but is one with Jacob, of which are the twelve stars (sons). Receiving the same promise as Isaac and Abraham, the woman is identified as all of Israel. The child is clearly Jesus, born of the tribe of Judah, not to be separated from all of Israel. The time frame is the birth of Jesus. The red dragon is Satan, and the wording that his tail drew the third part of stars of heaven and cast them to earth, signifies the means these stars or angels were cast out of heaven; not drawn or led. The significance of this is reveals the heart, and the shrewdness of the dragon.

A third event concerning this time frame continues to a prophesy concerning these same angels 2,000 years later, in which many questions will be answered. As in all prophesy, with each understanding there is a realization of how much more there is to know. Jude 1:6 "And the angels who kept not their own habitation, he has reserved in everlasting chains under darkness unto the judgment of the great day." These angels are of those same angels that will be loosed for five months, and are part of the one third that Satan will cast out. Or perhaps they are individual angels, as when Satan wandered the earth. But unlike Satan, they would not obey the Lord. As recorded, Satan exhibited tremendous destructive power. When told he could not touch Job, but only what he had, he took the very lives of Job's children. The range of this power was quite extensive, to the influencing of man to do his will.

Had Satan attempted to harm Job by defying God he would have left his habitation, or bounds the Lord had set for him. The result would have the bounding of chains under darkness unto the judgement of the great day. Or these angels that left their own habitation could include both groups.

SATAN CAST OUT

Rev. 12:7-10 "And there was a war in heaven; Michael and his angels fought against the dragon, and the dragon fought and his angels, - And prevailed not, neither was their place found any more in heaven. - And the great dragon was cast out, that old serpent, called the Devil and Satan, who deceives the whole world, he was cast out into the earth, and his angels were cast out with him. - And I heard a loud voice saying in heaven, 'Now is come salvation, and strength, and the kingdom of our God, and the power of his Christ, for the accuser of our brethren is cast down, who accuses them before our God day and night.'"

Rev. 9:1-6 "And the fifth angel sounded, and I saw a star fall from heaven unto the earth, and unto him was given the key to the bottomless pit. - And he opened the bottomless pit, and there arose a smoke out of the pit, like the smoke of a great furnace, and the sun and the air were darkened by the reason of the smoke of the pit. - And there came out of the smoke locusts upon the earth, and unto them was given power, as the scorpions of the earth have power. - And it was commanded them that they should not hurt the grass of the earth, neither any green thing, neither any tree, but only those men who have not the seal of God in their foreheads. - And to them it was given that they should not kill them, but they should be tormented five months; and their torment is like the torment of a scorpion, when he strikes a man. - And in those days shall men seek death and shall not find it; and shall desire to die, and death shall flee from them."

COMBINING FIVE PROPHETIC MESSAGES

These prophetic messages start with a specific time. A time that God established before the very foundation of the world. Rev. 13:8 "All that dwell on the earth shall worship him, whose names are not written in the book of life of the Lamb slain from the foundation of the world."

God's angels know the word of God is true, and it cannot be broken or altered. And this includes those angels who rejected the purpose for which they were created, of whom Satan has been identified as their leader.

Starting with the angelic visitation to the priest Zacharias, the father of John the Baptist, proclaiming he shall have a son (John), who in the power and spirit of Elijah shall prepare a people for the Lord. (His birth took place 6 months before the birth of Jesus) (Luke 1:18 - Luke 2:11)

Matt. 11:12 "And from the days of John the Baptist till now the Kingdom of heaven suffers violence. And the violent take it by force." The "violent" are clearly referring to Satan and his angels. This reveals that most of the angels violently reacted to the announced appearance of God himself, as the ultimate ministering spirit through Jesus. Truly God, truly man. The timeframe of this violence continues from the beginning of John's ministry until the crucifixion of Jesus. The reason for this violence is obvious, as these angels know God's word cannot be broken. Therefore, Jesus must not be allowed to establish his everlasting kingdom, as the Bible clearly states will happen. Because they knew the next prophetic event would be Satan and his angels being cast into the pit.

These angels did not want to be demons. This explains the serpent casting them out, as there was no other way to stop the birth and purpose of the promised Messiah. The result of this violence is demonic activity on the earth. There was no such activity recorded in the Bible until this specific time. These angels have but one hope left. The word of God must be broken. That is the only hope they have. This was evidenced by the fact that demons were terrified when they came into contact with Jesus. "Jesus, Son of God. Have you come to torment us before the time?"

The time of this violence, and the why, is recorded in Rev. 12:1-4. This is when one third of the angels were cast out of heaven by the tail of the Serpent. Satan did not lead them. Being cast out, these angels became demons. It is then that they control man by various degrees. Satan is not yet a Devil, nor the rest of his angels whom he did not cast out. But soon the Kingdom of heaven will be cleansed for the bride of the Lord. Until then, Satan accuses the saints before God, day and night. (Rev. 12:12)

FIVE PROPHESIES

These five prophesies cannot be separated, as they concern these angels that have rejected the very purpose for their creation. There is a direct correlation between them and mankind that have also rejected what they have been created to be. Starting with the kingdom of heaven suffering violence from John the Baptist till Jesus' birth and ministry, this violence continues on the earth. This is evidenced with a madness of man beyond description with the culmination of the crucifixion of Jesus.

Pilate proclaimed Jesus as King of the Jews, and of doing nothing worthy of death, saying "I find no fault in this man, and the blood of this innocent man be upon you." And then he turned the man which he had just proclaimed innocent over to be crucified. This authenticated that Jesus was ordained to die as the Passover Lamb of God on that day. Most, if not all, of this mob knew of or were beneficiaries of the miracles of Jesus. Yet, while Pilate proclaimed Jesus innocent, asking "What he has done to deserve death?" the mob cried all the louder, "CRUCIFY HIM!" But he had to die that day, and that year. 1st Cor. 2:7-8 "But we speak the wisdom of God in a mystery, even the hidden wisdom, which God has ordained before the ages unto our glory. Which none of the princes of this age knew; for if they had known it, they would not have crucified the Lord of glory." Pilate, knowing and proclaiming Jesus innocent, had him crucified that day.

The disobedient angels of the Lord knew the word of God. Yet they crucified the Lord of Glory. An image of these disobedient angels can be seen in likeminded rebellious man. It is not that difficult to see an almost identical image of fallen man in these fallen angels. Jesus alone is called the image of God. And in Hebrews 1:3, the express image of God.

WHAT MUST I DO TO BE SAVED?

When the Philippian jailer asked "What must I do to be saved?" Paul answered: Believe. Just believe.

To reject Jesus and his words is to reject his standards and morality. And to do so reveals a moral flaw that defies all logic. Even if a person honestly believed Jesus never existed, wouldn't all but the sickest of minds choose to live in a nation or community that lived by Christian laws and standards? And if not for themselves, at least for their children? All of mankind are aware of the necessity of moral standards for any society to continue. This is the wisdom of God in a mystery. Mystery, because this perfect love is far too often rejected, and deeply offends the heart of man that is referred to as "the world".

And the wisdom of God because of those who hunger for this perfect love. They, desiring more than anything – even life itself – the eternal presence of He who died for him. The Lord desires such as these to worship him. These scriptures best explain this wisdom of the Lord. Luke 17:20-21 "The kingdom of God comes not with observation. - But the kingdom of God is within."

All the disobedient angels of God knew the Word of God. Yet they crucified the Lord of glory; on the *very day* it was prophesied, and by the *very means.* Thus, fulfilling the very scriptures they came to change. Take, for example, Psalm 22. The words that start the first verse of this chapter were spoken by the Lord 2,000 years later, just before he gave up the spirit. Thus authenticating them. Psalm 23:1 and Matt. 27:46 "My God, my God why have you forsaken me?"

Psalm 22:7-8 "All they that see me laugh me to scorn. And the shoot out the lip, they say. - He trusts on the Lord that he would deliver him. Let him deliver him, seeing he delights in him." 22:14-18 "I am poured out like water, and all my bones are out of joint. My heart is like wax, it is melted within me. - My strength is dried up like a potsherd, and my tongue cleaves to my jaws, and thou has brought me into the dust of death. - For dogs have compassed me. The assembly of the wicked have enclosed me, they pierced my hands and my feet. - I may count all my bones, they look up and stare at me. - They part my garments among them, and cast lots for my vesture." This is a clear eyewitness of a crucifixion. Then with the added information, it identified Jesus' *specific* crucifixion.

This prophetic event was fulfilled exactly as spoken. These events depict an undeniable picture of someone dying on the cross. This mode of torture and death was not even used until hundreds of years after it was prophesied! The most important thing gained from this is what separates for eternity: The simplicity and clarity that defines the heart of God. This is desired more than life itself by some. And they will receive it, beyond their wildest expectations.

THE HEART OF GOD

This world, and the god of this world, believes the preaching of the cross is foolishness. And they are unified in their effort to hinder any mention of this Savior... with a special emphasis and targeting of children. What separates them is the absolute assurance that there is a judgment, and that, only by degrees, is understood. All know that there is a creator God, and judgment. This is the wisdom of God that separates the servant heart from the serpent heart.

Isaiah 53 and other scriptures clearly define Jesus and his dying for the sins of man. So the question arises: Satan and his angels knew Jesus and the scriptures. Why, then, did they not protect him, and keep him from the cross? There is only one reasonable answer. It would appear that these angels – as well as fallen man – cannot, *will not* accept or comprehend the heart of the Lord, nor do they desire such for themselves. However, for those who do desire Him, more than anything they desire to be as they were created to be: in the image of God.

As we continue into the time of the wrath of God, this very wrath reveals, to a greater degree, the grace of God. And then in the last 1,000 prophetic years, the grace of God will completely dominate all of this world. No sin will be allowed, to the point that the lion will lay down with the lamb. Lies, deception and evil will not be seen at all in God's kingdom. Then after this 1,000 years and just before the New Heaven and New Earth, an event takes place that reveals the hunger for one of two hearts. The serpent heart, or servant heart. And this is answered in a dramatic way.

No one knows exactly when the date of the rapture or the cleansing of heaven will be. But Jesus upbraided the Pharisees for not knowing the time or season for his coming. This was revealed by the prophetic signs. The signs revealing these last days, which are fast arriving, are much more apparent.

THE LATTER TIMES

1st Tim. 4:1-2 "Now the Spirit speaks expressly, that in the latter times, some shall depart from the faith, giving heed to seducing spirits, and doctrines of demons, - Speaking lies in hypocrisy, having their conscience seared with an iron."

These five prophesies involve a specific change in this world that must be revealed in an attempt to make sense of a soon coming world that Jesus spoke of. Were he to delay his coming, there would be no flesh saved alive. This involves a violence beyond description.

FATAL (DEADLY) WOUND TO THE HEAD

The 13th chapter of Revelation uses much symbolism to identify nations, individuals, and timeframes. This writer has difficulty clearly identifying all these symbolisms in a clear fashion, and has refrained from doing so. As these later times arrive there will be greater recognition; for both those in the image of the beast, and those fast approaching to be in the image of God. Already there can be seen groundwork being laid for the doctrine of demons. This actually has been in place for centuries, but will expand to a blatant degree.

CHAPTER 22

FOUR BEASTS

There are four beasts that are identified in this 13th chapter of Revelation. Theologians have spent much time and effort seeking to identify them. The first three are a fallen angel and two fallen men. If the first three are living entities, would not reason dictate that it would also be so with the fourth? Logically it should be, and then factually it is the fourth beast that has the clearest biblical identification. And it is this fourth beast that the Lord has revealed with extraordinary regularity and clarity throughout the Bible, starting in the book of Daniel. And as this same book of Daniel reveals, it is the Lord himself who has sealed this revelation until the last days. Daniel 12:4 "O Daniel shut up the words, and seal the book, even to the time of the end; many shall run to and fro, and knowledge shall be increased." It is now the time of the end.

Actually, this fourth beast is the central character and concern in the Bible. This will become clearer as we address these last three and a half years before Jesus returns from the heavens. As we continue addressing the first three, it is hoped that the obvious will be brought to a greater light. The light being the complete contrast between light and darkness. The contrast is absolute. It is defined by Jesus, who is the express image of God; and Satan, of whom this world is the image of. Jesus addressed those who were of the beast in John 8:44. "You are of your father the devil, and the lusts of you father you will do. He was a murderer from the beginning, and abode not in truth, because there is no truth in him. When he speaks a lie, he speaks of his own, for he is a liar, and the father of it." Fallen man - the fourth Beast? Or image of the beast?

CHRIST'S INTERCESSORY PRAYER

Jesus' prayer is found in the 17th chapter of John. Two verses of his prayer are particularly revealing of the vast contrast that separates those who are of the image of the beast, and those in the image of God. John 17:14-15 "I have given them your word. And the world has hated them, because they are not of the world, even as I am not of the world. - I pray not that you should take them out of the world, but that you keep them from the evil."

The time is fast approaching when the Lord will take the believers out of the world. This is when the saints are given their new resurrected bodies as they greet their Lord in the air. As believed here, this is to be an event separated by 3 ½ years after Satan and his angels are cast out of heaven. And those left behind will be left in a world where, as in Matt.16:25, "Whosoever will save his life will lose it; and whosoever will lose his life for my sake shall find it."

The realization of knowing they were left behind should fill them with an overwhelming grief, and then terror. It would be impossible to describe their feeling of rejection. This would be followed by witnessing world changing events unfolding exactly as foretold in the Bible. And finally, they will understand that they were left behind not because God had rejected them, *but because they had rejected the Son of God.*

Gradually, they will come to understand the gravity of embracing absolute truth and purity. They will desire the foundation of morality, love, and peace... and suddenly long to be united with their Savior. They will want, more than life itself, to join and be part of the body of Christ. To be as they were created to be; in the image of God. They will know, as Satan also knows, that there is but little time left. It is then that this world will have an outpouring from these new Christian witnesses with an urgency as never before.

Then the full impact of Jesus' words from John 17:15 will hit them. "I pray not that you should take then out of the world, but that you would keep them from the evil." This, along with these prophetic life-giving words of the Lord in Luke 9:24 (which echoes Matt. 16:25) "Whosoever would save his life shall lose it, but whosoever shall lose his life for my sake, the same shall save it."

Rev. 13 clearly states only Christians will be killed during these last days, in which a world leader will reign for 42 months. These three and a half years of Satan's reign will see continual turmoil and disasters; called by many 'the time of the Lord's wrath'. This writer has placed a five month hindering of Satan that will affect his reign. During this five months no one will die. A plague will affect most people, and those affected will desire to die. But God will not allow death. This is the beginning of Satan's three and a half year reign. After this time of terrible wrath, in which God reveals his unbelievable grace, death will be of such that were Jesus to delay his coming there would be no flesh saved alive.

OBSTACLE

The United States of America has been recognized as an obstacle to the plans already in place to establish a one world government. This because of its constitution and the Judeo-Christian Bible, its standards, and its love of Israel. This nation is moving perilously close to embracing this soon coming government.

This rejecting of the Lord is accelerating at a breath-taking pace in this nation. First, there was the rejection of the Bible. And then the rejecting of God's people Israel. Two 4-year cycles of electing a president (Obama) that agreed with Iran that Israel's existence is not negotiable. A clear declaration that there is no objection to Israel's destruction by Iran. Then with the same negotiations, assuring the means by which Iran can accomplish this: by removing any obstacle of Iran developing the atomic bomb.

This is an evil beyond description. And then there is the further rejection of God's morality by rejecting marriage which God has established between a man and woman. It is the opinion of this writer that this next election will define if this nation will have a short reprieve, before embracing this coming one world government.

THE HEART OF MAN

Communism most perfectly fulfills this coming one world government. Except this will be a New World Order or a One World Government in which religious acceptance will be a key element. The Bible defines the main player bringing this about as a harlot committing fornication. And because she is called a harlot, this identifies her as a false Christianity being responsible for this unity of confusion (Babel). Then the Bible makes it abundantly clear she has gone beyond harlotry, calling her a great whore. Rev. 17:1 "I will show you the judgment of the great whore that sits on many waters (nations)."

Religions are not defined as committing adultery or fornication. This applies only to Judeo-Christianity that has become perverted. In verse 2: "With whom the kings of the earth have committed fornication, and the inhabitants of the earth have been made drunk with the wine of her fornication" And then Rev. 17:5-6 "And upon her forehead was a name written, Mystery Babylon the Great, the Mother of Harlots and Abominations of the Earth. - And I saw the woman drunk with the blood of the saints, and with the blood of the martyrs of Jesus." This reveals a history of murdering true Christians.

IDENTIFYING THE HARLOT

This world government will be a religion that is violently anti-Bible. Not because they do not know its contents, but because they *do*, and have rejected its words. "And I saw the woman drunk with the blood of the saints, and with the blood of the martyrs of Jesus. And I wondered with great admiration." Rev. 17:7,9 "Why do you marvel? I will tell you the mystery of the woman, and of the beast that carries her, which has seven heads and ten horns. - And here is the mind which has wisdom. The seven heads are seven mountains, on which the woman sits." Because Rome is called the city of seven hills, and has killed countless Christians and Jews through the centuries, most religious scholars have named her as this harlot. (The identifying of The Roman Catholic church as this woman has decreased in number, as man has become more ecumenical)

Dave Hunt, in his book The Woman Rides the Beast, wrote

extensively and quite convincingly concerning identifying the Roman Catholic Church as this woman. There is no argument here on his logic, reasoning, and scriptural references. This harlot is called Mystery Babylon. Probably because the extent of this harlotry also involves Christian principles, leading to the final solution to eliminate any and all presence of biblical Christianity.

To understand and identify this woman are helpful, but not critical. Every individual who receives Jesus as Lord and Savior does so only because of this: His words are true, and their need of a Savior is absolute. It has nothing to do with having been forewarned as to whom to believe or not believe by some writer or orator. The world is deceived simply because they do not believe.

BABYLON IS FALLEN

Shortly after the flood, when all of the earth had one language, the people joined together. Their purpose and agenda was to stay as one people, with the intent to build a tower to heaven (the tower of Babel, in Gen.11:1-9). Having one religion in which man reaches heaven by their own effort is an absolute impossibility, and this was realized by these builders. It left an obvious spiritual effort of their own to reach or contact spiritual powers in high places. As the Lord has strictly forbidden this practice, this type of effort to communicate with any spirits will not end well.

At this time, shortly after the flood, man's effort to reach the heavens on his own was completely stopped by the Lord. This was accomplished by the Lord confounding their language. It is in the very last days that man will finally accomplish what back then he had set out to imagine, or be, or do. But man was created to be so much more than what we imagine; man was created to be in the very Image of God. The special attribute that mankind has been given by their creator is something no one can take away; the freedom to choose what to believe, which is then followed by receiving our desires.

Fallen man is pretty much the same as fallen angels. The words of Satan are similar to fallen man's desires. Those are also the desires of this people of Babel, that by their power they would reach the heavens. Isaiah reveals this world of unity that fallen man will soon achieve. A world that used their freedom to reject what their creator prepared for them. The following scripture is a prophetic picture of Lucifer, from his fall to his final effort to destroy all there is.

Isaiah 14:12-17 "How you have fallen from heaven, O Lucifer, son of the morning! How you are cut down to the ground, who did weaken the nations! - For you have said in your heart, 'I will ascend into heaven, I will exalt my throne above the stars of God; I will sit also upon the mount of the congregation, in the sides of the north, - I will ascend above the heights of the clouds, I will be like the Most High.' - Yet thou shall be brought down to sheol, to the sides of the pit. - They that see you shall narrowly look upon you, and consider you, saying, 'Is this the man that made the world to tremble, who did shake the kingdoms, - Who made the world like a wilderness, and destroyed its cities, who opened not the house of his prisoners?'"

MAN'S FIRST ATTEMPT TO BUILD BABEL

Gen. 11:6-9 "And the Lord said, 'Behold, the people are one, and they have one language, and this they imagine to do. And now nothing will be restrained from them, which they have imagined to do. - Go to, let us go down, and there confound their language, that they may not understand one another's speech.' - So the Lord scattered them abroad upon the face of all the earth and they left off building the city. - Therefore, the name of it is called Babel."

This effort for all of man to be one, in which all of his imaginations may be achieved; yes, God created man as a free moral agent to choose. But along with this freedom there is given to all of mankind a clear awareness of what the Lord would have for man to be. And the purpose for it, along with the benefit. Job 32:8 "There is a spirit in man, and the inspiration of the Almighty gives them understanding." The next chapter reveals that this Spirit is the Holy Spirit. Job 33:4 "The Spirit of God hath made me, and the breath of the Almighty hath given me life."

This same Spirit, without which man would not even exist, does not abandon his creation and leave man to their own devices. Instead, he continually seals instructions in all of mankind. Continuing in Job, Elihu asks how it is possible to strive against the words of God. The Lord then reveals how and when the inspiration and instructions are given. Job 33:13-18 "Why do you strive against him? For he gives not account of any of his matters. - God speaks once, yea twice, yet man perceives it not. - In a dream, in a vision of the night, when deep sleep falls upon men, in slumbering on a bed; - Then he opens the ears of men and seals their instruction, - That he may withdraw man from his purpose, and hide pride from man. - He keeps back his soul from the pit, and his life from perishing by the sword."

CHAPTER 23

CHRISTIANITY

There will be at this time an effort to define with greater clarity this harlot that perverts the word of God (although his effort could not be accomplished in its entirety in several volumes of books). A short while ago this writer, a veteran of the Korean war, along with a few WWII veterans, were honored by many special people who showed their appreciation for our wartime service to this nation. This letter to a special teacher will hopefully explain what Christianity is.

Dear Bob;

I was told were I to go on this honor flight to Washington D. C. that it would be an experience that I would never forget.

This was correct beyond my wildest expectations, but not for the reason I had expected. The memorials of which I was familiar with, meant much more when visiting them in person. It was this realization of the amount of time, and labor of love, with complete commitment to these memorials to these veterans of our armed forces. It was then my attention began to focus more on these faceless volunteers and workers then on the veterans being honored. This alone makes this trip one which I can never forget. While in Washington D.C. we were greeted with crowds who shook our hands, thanking us for our service. This is special beyond description, as it was so personal.

Then there was this short return to Madison. Instead of being exhausted my mind could not forget this kindness and thankfulness from so many people. As we embarked from the plane in Madison we heard music, then as we turned a corner we were greeted with something I can never forget. A multitude of people greeting us, as though we were the most important celebrities imaginable. Everyone wanted to shake our hands. And thank us for our service.

And then there were a group of young boys and girls who also reached out their hands to touch and shake ours, as though we were very special. (They were from your class and a few others.) And then I finally recognized some people I knew. Most of my family. There is no way I can express this emotion of love and kindness that comes from all these strangers, along with my family that was exhibited toward me and these old veterans. To me it was very personal and special beyond my wildest dreams.

But as I realized before, the truly special ones were those who were so overwhelmingly thankful, and about what was done 64 and 74 years ago. And then show this overwhelming thankfulness to these old veterans, as though they had just returned from the battle.

My daughter Jenny later asked if I would go to the Middle School to have my picture taken with some of these children in your class. And it was then it became authenticated in my mind as to whom were the special ones. And this has far reaching consequences.

The truly special ones are those filled with appreciation and overwhelming thankfulness for what was done for them. But this was years ago, and these people made it continual as though it was yesterday. Afterwards having met with your class I read those letters from these children to me in which many wrote of my protecting them with my life in the Korea war. They were so thankful, that someone would give their life for them. (Even though I spent most of my time in Hawaii.)

I believe you are very well aware that it is those who appreciate the sacrifice of others, whether they be policemen, veterans, fathers, mothers or teachers, that are really the special ones. And it is those who recognize this; it is they who will reap the benefits of their conduct of thankfulness. You are laying a foundation that will define a moral direction for your students. And were this the norm for teachers, this nation would benefit to a degree beyond description. Thank you for your service.

As I do not know you, may I expand on my thanking you for your service? When this is spoken to the veterans, it is referring to their combined service to keep us safe. The service you continually offer is far more reaching, having eternal consequences.

What I am wishing to convey to you is not in line with religious correctness. But neither does truth. As two contrary religious beliefs cannot be correct. One must be in error and both could be. But two diverse views cannot be true.

Few people realize this, but Christianity is completely different than the religions of the world. Unfortunately, the lack of this understanding includes most professing Christians. The world's religions have nothing at all in common with Christianity, which is a deep and personal relationship with their creator. This could be referred to as a strange relationship. This is founded on accepting with great thankfulness what God has done for man. Or putting it another way, it could be phrased that those who appreciate with overwhelming thankfulness this ultimate kindness of the ultimate sacrifice reveals a character trait well pleasing to God.

The words of John 3:16 completely eliminate any suggestion that we all worship the same God. As an example, here are words that Islam's Holy books clearly state. This to affirm their belief that the Bible is in error. They state Allah has no son, and then that Jesus did not die on the cross. But had an imposter take his place. The Quran accepts the truth of the cross, then denies its authority. It is interesting that the religiously correct crowd is not then offended when Islam states emphatically that what defines Christianity, is a lie.

This is given as but one example of the absurdity of comparing all religions as the same. I suspect you understand the simplicity and purity of Christianity. The Judeo-Christian gospel is completely different from all of man's religions. As it is really a relationship. Christianity's foundations are defined and fulfilled in these words. John 3:16 "God so loved the world that he gave his only begotten Son, that whosoever believed in him would not perish, but have everlasting life."

All that is necessary for man to receive the benefits of this love, is to believe. This is evidenced by an overwhelming thankfulness. Yes the truly special are those who are building this foundation of thankfulness. Not just in the young, but in many old veterans whose foundations needed repairing.

I was going to mail this letter to you a few days ago, and when putting on my trousers a small quarter sized emblem fell out of my pocket. When this was given to me I paid little attention to it. It has a white cross on a black background with these small writings on it. John 3:16 God gave his only Son, that he who believes on him, will not perish but have ever lasting life.

May I ask, is this the motivation for what you are doing? As they are inseparable.

Thanks again for your service.

CONTINUAL SACRIFICE

It is hoped that by having a basic understanding of the gospel (which is far from simplistic) that there would be a hunger as no other to want to know all that is possible concerning our creator, who created us to be in his image. It seems this gospel must touch the heart of man with an understanding that there is such a God that could love with such overwhelming love.

All of this sacrifice and unconditional love is meaningless unless there is an overwhelming thankfulness and appreciation for what has been done for them, with full knowledge that this is a free undeserved gift.

This is why the letter written to this grade school teacher was inserted here. There are many such teachers in this nation. Sadly, cowardly and liberal administrators do all they can to silence these moral and thoughtful teachers that are building a foundation that will make this nation a far greater nation. With the greater benefit of eternal life.

Think on these things, as too often Christians have a tendency to lose track of the enormity of God's sacrifice. Right now, Jesus sits at the right hand of the Father. At the same time he is continually taking the sins of believers, to make them pure. And this will continue until there is a new heaven and new earth.

SUMMIT MINISTRIES

What will now be now given is an abbreviated lecture given by Dr. David Noebel at the 2014 Summit Adult Conference.

"William Bradford (History of Plymouth Plantation) When the Pilgrims came, they originally planned to establish the colony at Plymouth as a socialistic colony, following after Plato and the Republic. After three disastrous years, William Bradford came to a conclusion. God is smarter than Plato. So he then divided the land and each family got a portion of their own to take care of and be responsible for, establishing private property over socialism. (At the tower of Babel people also wanted to be one. And as one, reach to heaven. However the Lord, through Jesus Christ, establishes a personal intimate relationship with man individually, defined as a marriage. Man never gives up his individuality, only enhances it.) So where is the wisdom of the individual responsibility over the oneness of man?"

Dr. Noebel continues one hundred years later, with the question: "What can one individual do? There was a Scottish preacher named John Witherspoon. In his life, he had approximately 450 students. He founded Princeton University. And out of his 450 students, 114 became ministers, 49 became U.S. Representatives, 28 became U.S. Senators, 26 became state judges, 17 became members of their State constitutional conventions, 40 became delegates to the State Conventions that ratified the constitution, 12 became members of the constitutional congress, 8 became U.S. District Judges, five became delegates to the constitutional Convention, 3 became U.S. Supreme Court Justices, 3 became Attorney Generals, two became foreign ministers, 1 became Vice President, and one, James Madison, became president.

"And then there was Reverend George Whitefield. He preached to thousands, and befriended one man who some say did not believe all his words. That person was Benjamin Franklin, on whom he had a positive effect and influence. On the campus of the University of Pennsylvania that Franklin founded, there are two statues, as Franklin insisted there be one of George Whitefield alongside his. With these words "The Reverend George Whitefield Bachelor of Arts

1736, Pembroke College, Humble Disciple of Jesus Christ, Eloquent Preacher of the Gospel."

Others are mentioned. And then Dr. Noebel addressed the fact that Americans are the most generous people on the earth, because of this sound Christian foundation:

"Americans give billions to charity every year. They give more of their wealth away to help others than any nation or combination of nations or groups in the whole world. There are some nations that have no charity. Their whole attitude is the government takes care of it. "Let the government take care of it and do the charitable work." That's not true in this country. In fact in this country, the people themselves give more in charity than the government. There is no nation like it. In fact, it takes three Frenchmen, seven Germans, and fourteen Italians to equal the charitable contributions of one American.

"Those who come under the influence of Evangelical Christianity form the backbone of philanthropic, social interest, social reform, and popular education. They embody and express the spirit of kindly goodwill. John Dewey, a professed atheist, said 'Evangelicals Christians are the essence of charity.'

"When famine, natural disasters, Civil wars, and ethnic cleansing ravage foreign nations it is invariably the first and often the only nation to bring help. When the big tsunami hit Indonesia, we turned a whole navy group around.

"America with its system of government has done more to alleviate poverty than the rest of the world combined. And has provided more freedom to more people than any people in the history of mankind.

"America's hospitals, schools, universities, technologies, inventions, churches, courts, businesses, highways, airlines, cities, farms, water systems, food chains, super markets, military, and government structure are the envy of the world.

"America and its democratic capital system have done more to alleviate poverty than the rest of the world combined. America's work ethic, capital inventions, copyright and private property concepts, and production are copied throughout the world. America is the richest, most literate, most free, most productive country in the world. Whatever America's many faults, we have provided more freedom to more people than any nation in the history of mankind. And by the way, we're not even 300 years old.

"America did more to put down the 20th century's three most evil empires – Fascism, Nazism, and Communism – than the rest of the world combined. And then after World War II, America was the most powerful nation on the earth. We had 13 million men at arms and the A bomb. We could have conquered the world. You know what we did? We disarmed 13 million men and paid to help restore Germany and Japan.

"What's right with America? How about Tocqueville's answer. About 1831 de Tocqueville's looked at America and said there is no country in the whole world in which the Christian religion retains a greater influence over the souls of men than in America. We're mighty messed up at the moment, but we started well, and I pray to God, we will finish that way."

David Noebel ends up this lecture with 'we're mighty messed up. But we started out well.' Our prisons are full; all to protect our populace from a large violent element. And the use of illegal drugs, including alcohol, surpasses by far any nation in the world. Then there is this moral degradation and pornography.

This brings about an important question and quandary. To credit the exceptionalism of this nation because of Christianity, should not this debauchery, drug abuse and immorality also be the fruits of Christianity?

CHAPTER 24

TWO WORLDS

Most people are aware that having too much free time and no purpose for your life is not a good combination. When there is added to this having no incentive to work because a welfare system often results in a pay cut by working, it results in far too many who will reject work. When anyone accepts Jesus as Lord and Savior, by that very definition they desire and take on a new nature. They die to self. This means there is a greater concern for others and taking on a servant or giving, nonjudgmental attitude. This is as it should be.

A SERVANT

As a servant of God, Christians do not subject themselves to a world they are no longer a part of. Christ's prayer to the Father reveals this. John 17:14-16 "I have given them your word; and the world has hated them, because they are not of the world, even as I am not of the world. - I pray not that you should take them out of the world, but that you should keep them from the evil. - They are not of the world, even as I am not of the world."

Christians, as the salt of the world, are commanded not to compromise God's moral laws or standards. This nation was built on the firm foundation of the Bible. All of mankind are created with the free will to accept or reject the Lord. This right is given to all. Otherwise the Lord would not be a just God, but a tyrant. As a husband does not demand his wife to love him, neither does the Lord, but gives a reason for this love. Therefore, our founding fathers forbid the state to establish a state religion, and offered the right for all citizens the freedom to worship as they chose.

That is why our constitution does not infringe on the rights of religious freedom. Regardless of what choice the people would or would not make, our founding fathers followed the Lord's pattern. Actually, the Lord put in a system or government of laws, but the people wanted a king. The end result was that the Lord did indeed allow them to have a king. This also verifies that God does not demand or control as a despot. Only those who come to know the Lord, want more than anything to be as he wants for them.

Christians are not to be "taken out of the world," but to remain to be a light unto darkness. As Jesus prayed to the Father, "But keep them from the evil". What is the purpose or benefit of this? There are churches that teach that whenever anyone accepts Jesus as Lord that their sins are forgiven and they are saved. And a few actually believe they no longer sin. Both are true; but not yet. It is not what man proclaims. But whom the Lord has established who believed on him. Those who are truly born again, and remain in this world, are tried, tested and brought through the fire to be refined.

Our initial birth is physical and of this world. Our second birth is spiritual, but we remain in this world to be tried and tested. This was covered by Jesus in John 3:3-7 in which you cannot see the kingdom of God, except through Jesus. And then you cannot enter the kingdom until the Holy Spirit quickens our spirit; born of the Spirit. "That what is born of the flesh is flesh. And that what is born of the Spirit is spirit. Marvel not that I said unto you, you must be born again."

While in the flesh there are events and trials to prepare and make one's self strong by what the Bible calls a cleansing. It is always helpful to have direction or guidance. A two-way conversation is helpful. Discussing the Lord's words to you, presented in the Bible. There will never be an end of asking the Lord for clarity. And as this conversation increases, there is a greater clarity and intimacy, with the continued realization there is no end.

The very first process of asking the Lord why this is results in prayer. Many testify the Lord told them this or that. This is not disputed here. However it would seem to be more of a lasting and a personal relationship if there were dialog or conversation, along with listening to what the Lord has to say.

Our founding fathers set out to establish a lasting, godly government, also knowing the heart of man. Therefore, they were aware it was not to be. Having no illusions concerning the minds of men, they drew up checks and balances to protect this more perfect and special government of man. And we know this government was based on the Bible, as at the very founding of this nation chaplains were appointed and prayers offered at the beginning of each day. This was especially needful, as the government the Lord had established for Israel was a government of God's laws and commandments. A government in which the priests played a vital role.

After years of conflict with her neighbors, Israel eventually rejected the Lord God and at the same time embraced their neighbor's pagan gods. Therefore separating themselves from Him who had separated them from the world. Soon they became subject to and submissive to these peoples. And when it became unbearable, because their enemies became their rulers, they would then repent and cry unto the Lord for deliverance. The Lord would always send a deliverer. This went on for years until Israel wanted a king to rule over them, just as the nations around them had a king. The Lord, through his prophets, objected, and then eventually gave in because Israel insisted. So the Lord gave them a king, as they desired.

Now, our founding fathers did not want a king. Nor did they want priests interpreting God's laws and subjecting them to the Church's dictates. They were well aware of the Roman Catholic Church's Inquisition, in which Jews were forced to convert and submit to the Roman church or be killed. And an even larger number of Christians were punished, tortured and killed for the crime of heresy. That is, if they would not also submit to the doctrine and dictates of the Roman Church. As Christians, our founding fathers wanted a Godly government with true priests who understood that believers have an individual personal relationship, in which the Lord Jesus took each individual's sins. You are not to submit to a man-established church system. The *believers* are the church and the priests.

It is no wonder that there is such confusion when men appoint priests. At the tower of Babel, which means "gate of God", this effort to reach Godhood resulted in confusion. This is where the term "babbler" comes from. In the last days, this confusion or Babylon will be destroyed. Not directly by God, as God will put it in the hearts of lost men to destroy what they have built. Only to submit to and be in complete control of, worshiping a spirit of darkness. The Lord has clearly defined who are his priests are, as the Lord addresses his church. 1st Peter 2:9 "You are a chosen generation, a royal priesthood, a holy nation (not of this world), a peculiar people; that you should show forth the praises of him who has called you out of darkness into his marvelous light." It is important to remember, and not forget from where you were called.

CHAPTER 25

PURPOSE

The world cannot name even one of the 10 commandants that is not beneficial for any society. However, because they come from the Bible, they or their source must not be revealed in our educational system. This is the same with the pure and simple gospel. Has this happened because the Christians have capitulated, or are their numbers much smaller than realized? Our liberal or progressive element have managed to follow the Socialists and Communists, by the banning of the Bible that reveals the origin of life and matter. This has been replaced by what they call science, involving two inseparable theories: The Big Bang and Theory of Evolution. The Big Bang Theory contradicts the Law of Thermodynamics. Matter can be neither created nor destroyed, and the Theory of Evolution is based on mutations of existing life. However, it is known and proven that all mutations are harmful, with a loss of information (DNA). As has been mentioned previously, there has never been found a beneficial mutation. This quite pointedly reveals that at a certain time in the not too distant past, someone of inconceivable intelligence, ability and power created almost perfect life forms that can only deteriorate. And then this someone revealed this to his created mankind, who in turn is given the freedom to choose or reject his creator.

God has revealed to his creation exactly what his purpose was for each and every man, woman and child. Job 33:14-18 "For God speaks once, yea twice, yet man perceives it not. - In a dream, in a vision of the night, when deep sleep falls upon men, in slumbering upon the bed, - Then he opens the ears of men, and seals their instructions, - That he may withdraw man from his own purpose, and hide pride from man. - He keeps back his soul from the pit, and his life from perishing from the sword." And in Titus 2:11, "For the grace of God that brings salvation has appeared to all men." In John 6:45 Jesus said, "It is written in the prophets, 'And they all shall be taught of God.' Every man that therefore heard, and hath learned of the Father, comes to me."

These are very clear pronouncements that everyone has been told of the Lord, with no exceptions. However, it is stated that man perceives it not. There are two scriptures that make clarity on this, and both are addressing the same thing. One is in Job, for all of mankind. And this following one is specifically for Christians. 1st Cor. 2:9-11 "But it is written, Eye has not seen, nor ear heard, neither has entered into the heart of man, the things that God has prepared for them that love him. - But God has revealed them to us by his Spirit; for the spirit searches all things, yea, the deep things of God. - For what man knows the things of man, save the spirit of man that is in him? Even so the things of God knows no man, but the spirit of God."

Every Christian has a unique personal relationship with God through Jesus. This is defined as a marriage. This marriage is with Jesus as the groom, and believers as the bride. Each believer is individually, separately espoused to Jesus. And as individuals, it is difficult to explain this unique understanding that the Holy Spirit has in revealing to our spirit the deep things of God. Or exactly how it is conveyed. The only thing that can be given here that it is absolute, as there must be a complete acceptance of the Groom.

REVEALED TO ALL

Not only are the Father and Son revealed personally by the Spirit of the Almighty to the spirit of man, but God sent prophets and his written word. There is not one that can protest "I have never heard". You either continue doing what your purpose is, or embrace what the Lord has proposed for you. With this, there will be given a review to explain our purpose of being, and a clearer understanding of what is the essence of man.

CHAPTER 26

CREATION OF MAN

Two interesting written events are given in the Bible to give understanding and light. To one it is clear and beautiful. But to those who see darkness for light, it is darkness indeed. God made man in his image. The complete Godhead was involved in this endeavor. Gen. 1:26-27 "And God said, 'Let *us* make man in *our* image after *our* likeness.' - So God created man in his own image, in the image of God created he him, male and female created he them." And then in the next chapter God reveals man was formed. First created, and then formed. In the first chapter God, who is Spirit, created man in his image, a spirit. In the second chapter "The Lord God formed man out of the dust of the ground, and breathed into his nostrils the breath of life. And man became a living soul." (Gen.2:7)

Man is body, soul and spirit. The body is flesh, the soul is life, and the spirit is consciousness or awareness. The spirit is the essence of man. The body is nothing more than a living shell that returns to the dust. (1st Thes. 5:23) - Animals have a spirit, as does man. However the Bible reveals a very big difference between man and animals. Ecclesiastes 3:20-21 "All go to one place; all are dust, and all turn to dust again. - Who knows the spirit of man that goes upward, and the spirit of the beast that goes downward to the earth?" Animals and man have awareness or spirit, but the spirit of the animal goes downward. This spirit dies when its body dies. This is not so with the spirit of man.

The human brain can be best described as a computer. The design, sophistication and functions are such that man can scarcely comprehend. It is a computer that will return to dust along with the rest of this body of flesh. This body, without the spirit, would have no consciousness or awareness. Much as one in a coma or someone that is clinically dead. This is evidenced by flat lining. The spirit of man defines each individual, being unique one from another. The Bible reveals the Father, Son and Holy Spirit are involved in this creation to become in the image of God.

The Bible clearly states, "So God created man in his own image, in the image of God created he him; male and female created he them." Christians know the word of God cannot deceive, and they also know that no man is in the image of God. As there is none righteous, no not one. There is none that does good, no not one.

There are many answers to this apparent dilemma. The clearest answer reveals the enormity of God. Revelation 13:8 "All those that dwell on the earth shall worship him (the beast), whose names are not written in the book of life of the Lamb slain from the foundation of the world." This scripture was written for the very last days, just before Jesus returns to establish his everlasting Kingdom. The wording here states the very names of those not yet born. In fact the earth itself has not yet been created. But God already knows those that will receive Christ, and will be in his image, after his likeness. This is not predestination, but knowledge with no time restraints.

KNOWING GOD

The most important involvement is love. John 3:16 "God so loved the world." Love not embraced and returned is an incomplete love. Its fullness has not been accomplished. In love, the Lord went to the cross for all of man. However it is a meaningless event, unless there is complete awareness of the absolute necessity of their need to be washed from their sin. Also there must be a complete awareness that the Lord Jesus has the authority and ability to do this. And most importantly, those who receive Jesus must believe He himself is absolute purity, and want more than life itself to be with him, and be as he is.

ANGELS

Father, Son and Holy Spirit will not bring about this creative miracle without the complete and overwhelming desire for this to be so. For those who lack this absolute desire, it is a rejection. Rev. 3:15-16 "I know your works, that you are neither cold nor hot. I would you were cold or hot. - Because you are neither, I will spew you out of my mouth."

The Bible never discusses even the possibility of atheists. Only the worshiping of other gods or entities. There is but one God. With this in mind, Daniel defines this world prophetically, just before Jesus returns from the heavens to establish his everlasting kingdom. And when he returns, he will bring with him his saints. This world Daniel describes is a world that has taken on the image of the beast. Daniel 2:41-43 "And whereas you saw the feet and toes, part of potter's clay, and part of iron, the kingdom shall be divided. There shall be in it of the strength of iron, forasmuch as you saw the iron mixed with miry clay. - And as the toes of the feet were part of iron, and part of clay, so the kingdom shall be partly strong, and partly broken. - And whereas you saw iron mixed with miry clay, they shall mingle themselves with the seed of men. But they will not cleave one to another, even as iron is not mixed with clay."

Who or what is this that will mingle with the seed of men, but will not cleave one to another? This is answered in the 13th chapter of Revelation, revealing a terrifying chain of events.

NEAR SIMULTANEOUS EVENT

Christians have been waiting for centuries for the promised return of Jesus for his church; in which he will gather his church, the bride of Christ, meeting them in the air. It is true that no one knows the time or hour. But we can discern the signs; and there are a few. John 14:2-3 "In my Father's house are many mansions; if it were not so I would have told you. I go to prepare a place for you. - And if I go and prepare a place for you, I will come again and receive you unto myself, that where I am you may be also."

The preparing of his place would be the cleansing of the heavens to receive a cleansed and purified body of believers. As long as Satan accuses the Saints in heaven, the believers still bear the image of the earthly. But when they are changed to bear the image of the heavenly, Satan can no more accuse them. This would be the gathering of the saints to meet the Lord in the air. The believers will all be changed to be in the image of God. They will be made pure, as this heaven's mansions are being prepared for the saints. Meaning they also are made pure. And for this to happen, Satan and his angels must be cast out.

This event when heaven's mansions are being prepared is recorded in Rev. 12:10,13. "And I heard a loud voice saying in heaven, 'Now is come salvation, and strength, and the Kingdom of our God, and the power of his Christ. For the accuser of our brethren is cast down, which accused them before our God day and night.' - And when the dragon saw that he was cast unto the earth, he persecuted the woman which brought forth the man child."

His angels were also cast out. Rev. 12:7-8 "And there was war in heaven. Michael and his angels fought against the dragon, and the dragon fought and his angels. - And prevailed not; neither was their place found any more in heaven." We do not know the exact date this rapture will take place. Except logically this will be a near event with Satan and his angels being cast out.

TWO WONDERS IN HEAVEN

The 12th chapter in Revelation reveals a wonder in heaven. 12:1-5 "And there appeared a great wonder in heaven, a woman clothed with the sun, and the moon under her feet, and upon her head a crown of twelve stars. (Identifying her as from Israel) - And she, being with child, cried, travailing in birth, and pained to be delivered. - And there appeared another wonder in heaven; and behold, a great red dragon having seven heads and ten horns, and seven crowns upon his heads. (Identifying specific time frames) - And his tail drew the third part of the stars of heaven, and did cast them to the earth. And the dragon stood before the woman which was ready to be delivered, for to devour her child as soon as it was born. - And she brought forth a man child, who was to rule all the nations with a rod of iron. And her child was caught up unto God and his throne."

Rev. 12:6-10 "And the woman fled into the wilderness, where

she has a place prepared of God, that they should feed her there a thousand two hundred and threescore days." (Three and a half years) - And there was a war in heaven. Michael and his angels fought against the dragon; and the dragon fought and his angels, - And prevailed not, neither was their place found any more in heaven. - And that great dragon was cast out, that old serpent called the Devil and Satan, which deceives the whole world; he was cast out into the earth, and his angels were cast out with him. - And I heard a loud voice saying in heaven, 'Now has come salvation, and strength, and the kingdom of our God, and the power of his Christ, for the accuser of our brethren is cast down, who accused them before our God day and night.'"

There is a gap of 2,000 years between that red dragon casting a third of the stars (angels) of heaven to the earth, to devour the child (Jesus) as soon as the child was born. Jesus later was caught up to heaven, and he will return to rule the nations with a rod of iron. The gap of 2,000 years is between the unsuccessful effort to destroy this child as soon as it was born and "the woman fled into the wilderness to a place prepared of God that they should feed her there for (three and a half years)". This along with Satan being cast out of heaven and his angels.

We will address this in part: "The woman fled into the wilderness to a place prepared of God that they should feed her there a thousand two hundred and threescore days." This miraculous event we will explore later, along with a series of events that do not seem possible unless the Bible is accepted as literal (other than obvious allegory). They will also affirm other hard to accept scriptures. Scriptures that are presumed to be allegory, but actually mean what they say, are subject to a wide range of interpretation.

During the time of Jesus' ministry there were those who did not believe in the resurrection as factual but allegory, because this appeared to be an impossible task. Even more of an impossible task than creation. This religious group were called Sadducees. Just one of many endless interpretations that result in another gospel.

The god of this world is completely blinded to this wonder in heaven. The extent of this is revealed as he himself was instrumental in his deadly (fatal) wound to his own head. This wound was inflicted when Jesus cried out "It is finished" while on the cross; and then Jesus gave up the spirit. The fatality of this wound will come about when Satan is cast into the lake of fire. (Rev. 20:10)

Of course, when Jesus rose from the dead that old serpent realized his mistake, but still cannot comprehend how this could be. How can it be that man would worship a servant God? Nor can those of the world comprehend this. They are unable to understand that this is the power of God that cannot be separated from his love and absolute truth, revealed in his Son. James 2:19 "Thou believe there is one God; you do well. The demons also believe, and tremble." Satan and the world knows there is but one God, and tremble. Both find him unacceptable, but yet an absolute reality.

What is inconceivable to Lucifer and this world is the express image of God who is both truth and a servant. (Why does mankind not curse using the name of Allah, Buddha, or any man's gods names in vain?) It is inconceivable to the world that such a God would actually take these sins, as though *he* is the guilty one. All this because the Lord wants that none should perish, and that all receive eternal life. And most importantly that all would receive such a heart.

This is completely opposite of any of man's religions. The New Testament clearly speaks of what the Old Testament reveals. There is a complete dependence and trust in the Lord. So why would the creator do such a thing? What is the motive? Man has motive, but God has purpose. This purpose is defined as love. Man's self-love has but one beneficiary, self, and is quite limited in its scope.

We are told that while in the presence of the Lord, all of eternity is not enough time to know him to our complete understanding and satisfaction. Psalm 27:4 "One thing have I desired of the Lord, that will I seek after; that I may dwell in the house of the Lord all the days of my life, to behold the beauty of the Lord, and to inquire in his temple."

But to answer that question now – as to why God would take all of man's sin? What is his purpose? This can only be completely understood and comprehended by those completely cleansed. So this cannot be fully grasped until this mortal takes on immortality, and this corruption takes on incorruption. John 3:3,7 "Except a man be born again he cannot see the kingdom of God. - Except a man be born of the water and the Spirit he cannot enter the Kingdom of God." 1st John 3:1 "Behold what manner of love the Father has bestowed upon us, that we should be called the children of God. Therefore, the world knows us not, because it knew not him."

CHAPTER 27

SATAN AND HIS ANGELS CAST OUT

But now continuing with the casting out of Satan and all his angels from heaven. It is assumed this dividing of the world into ten sections has been mostly accomplished, but not finalized. Israel is not of this ten-part world, but will be involved in this new covenant that the world is trying to negotiate with her. Or more likely, certain forces in Israel are trying to bring about this new covenant with the world. But what logically must be addressed is this reality: Israel not being of this world. This is part of Jesus' prayer to the Father. John 17:14-17 "I have given them thy word, and the world has hated them, because they are not of the world, even as I am not of the world. - I pray not that you should take them out of the world, but that you should keep them from the evil. - They are not of the world, even as I am not of the world. - Sanctify them through your truth. Your word is truth."

Christian Jews in Israel are not of the world, the same as all Christians. All Christians will be raised to meet the Lord in the air at the same time. This includes those of Israel. The nation of Israel, which also is not of this world, is separate from the world in an unusual and special way; involving supernatural protection and purpose. This we will examine later. But because of this obvious hand of God on Israel, she will play an intricate part in these end time events. But first we will take a brief look at this world becoming more terrifying each day, with no direction or Christian influence.

CLEANSING, RAPTURE, AND ANTICHRIST

It is before and during the time of the rapture, or taking away of the Church, that the world has established their ten-toed world government. The kingdom of heaven has been cleansed before the resurrected saints are brought home. This world will, at the same time, be overwhelmed with demons that know that they have but a little time. Rev. 12:12 "Rejoice you heavens, and you that dwell in them. Woe to the inhabitants of the earth, and the sea. For the devil is come down to you having great wrath, because he knows he has but a short time."

FALLEN ANGELS

These fallen angels are referred to as Satan's angels. When that old dragon cast them out to the earth to accomplish his desire, they became demons with their power limited to control only those who are foolish enough to allow them access. Those so foolish are also subject to illusions and physical anomalies. Some would refer to this as power; but they are lying wonders. This is possible for these spirits, having access to this computer of unbelievable powers of misdirection (the mind of foolish man). 2nd Thes. 2:9 "Even him whose coming is after the working of Satan with all power, signs and lying wonders."

In the book of Job, Satan would not go beyond what the Lord allowed. It is assumed he would lose any access to return to heaven, along with this loss of power, which is significant. So he did not go beyond what the Lord dictated. He did not touch Job at the first encounter. But he destroyed all that he had; including his children. Then in the second encounter, the Lord forbid Satan to kill Job. So he tormented him with boils, but dared not kill him.

Satan's angels lost access to heaven and whatever status or power they had before becoming demons. All to prevent the birth of the Son of God. Satan, as their leader, did not lead, but cast them out. Yes, he cast his followers to earth knowing what their fate would be. This contrasts what Jesus does for those who follow him. He sets them free from the bonds of this earth and their temporal body. The Lord is revealing, and then presenting, two completely different images to choose from. And this contrast is not hidden.

This mystery of God is something the world can neither

understand nor grasp. We will continue with this fascinating story of man as prophetically foretold. Mankind themselves are given the right to choose or reject what they were created to be. Now we will continue with this soon to come madness as the result of not only rejecting Jesus the Son of God. But also a mad vindictiveness and hatred that grows with each rejection of his words, morals and standards. And at the same time, with others there also becomes a greater awareness, because of this obvious blatant rejection of truth.

Satan and his angels have now lost their considerable angelic power, except for manipulating weak, prideful, and disobedient mankind that God had formed out of the dust of the ground. The same people that angels were created to be ministering spirits to. And now Satan has no power other than what he has been given by manipulating this same prideful man. Satan is filled with wrath when he is cast down. And when confronted with this realization, his wrath becomes rage. He is the God of this world only because this world has made him so.

A NEW WORLD

Christians are not of this world. And now this becomes a reality, as the church has been raptured. 2nd Thes. 2:6-7 "And now you know what restrains, that he may be revealed in his time. - For the mystery of iniquity does already work; only he who hinders will continue to hinder, until he is taken out of the way."

Now will that wicked one be revealed, or present himself as God sitting in the temple of God? 2nd Thes. 2:4,6 "Who opposes and exalts himself above all that is called God, or that is worshiped, so that he, as God, sits in the temple of God, showing himself that he is God. - Now you know what restrains, that he might be revealed in his time." The length of time involved between the taking away of the Church and the revealing, or antichrist revealing himself, most likely will not be that long.

REVELATION 13

An effort will be made to make sense of this chapter and identify antichrist and all these beasts. The prophetic book of Daniel helps to understand Rev. 13 and in turn, the book of Revelation helps us to understand Daniel.

PURE JUSTICE

There will be a falling away, which involves the accelerated rejection of truth and Christian standards. Having pleasure in unrighteousness clearly involves moral and sexual standards. This world has continually rejected the Creator Lord and his words. Then the Lord, in the fullness of time, revealed absolute truth and love in the express image of himself.

At this time 2,000 years ago the Lord revealed himself, truly man and truly God; born in Bethlehem. This was Jesus, whom the world then crucified. This was the final act of rebellion against God; the murder of His only begotten Son. Then incredibly, He used this final rebellion of man to achieve the very reason for which man was created. To be in His image, after His likeness.

And all that is necessary for man to receive this incredible free gift is to believe that there is such a God, and then in true thankfulness receive this gift of life. A God that would take man's sins, that man may achieve a purity of which he is incapable of achieving by himself? What kind of God is this? Hebrews 12:2 "Looking to Jesus, the author and finisher of our faith, who for the joy that was set before him endured the cross, despising the shame, and is set down at the right hand of the throne of God." This defines those who not only believe this, but have an overwhelming desire to worship and be eternally in the presence of this, their Lord and Savior.

Jesus then rose from the dead after three days and nights in the tomb, as attested to by the prophets, both before and after this event. And for forty days after his resurrection he showed himself alive. After that, he was seen rising to heaven. Luke 24:51-52 "And it came to pass, while he blessed them, he was parted from them, and carried up into heaven. - And they worshiped him, and returned to Jerusalem with great joy." Acts 1:9-11 "And when he had spoken these things, while they beheld, he was taken up, and a cloud received him out of their sight. - And while they looked steadfastly toward heaven as he went up, behold two men stood by them in white apparel; - Who said, 'You men of Galilee, why stand you gazing up into heaven? This same Jesus, who is taken up from you into heaven, shall so come in like manner as you have seen him go into heaven.'" Angels themselves were testifying the manner in which he will return; and that will be from the heavens.

Chapter 28

Image of the Beast

The 13th chapter of Revelation introduces the dragon, beast, and false prophet. This could be a very confusing project in identifying or separating these three. Especially because all three are identified as beasts. By combining this chapter with the book of Daniel a lot of confusion is cleared up, along with insight received. Daniel identifies beasts as nations, along with time frames. Then Revelation 13 reveals the entrance of the beasts along with the specific mention of Satan, being what would be the first, or father of beasts. Having been revealed as the god of this world, and affirming this world to be identified as beasts, followed by these two specific beasts identified in Rev. 13, who both receive their prospective positions of authority and power in this world from this dragon.

Rev. 13:3 "And I saw one of his heads, as it were wounded unto death." As beasts also define times, this identifies one of his heads. A timetable. Not a nation, but an event that brings identity to this father of beasts. The understanding of what this deathly wound is has the utmost importance as to, is it a nation? Who or what is it that receives this wound? As we shall see, it is Satan who receives this fatal wound. Then, as Satan is also revealed as the father of beasts, reason and logic help to clear this up by revealing what this wound to death is, and how he obtained it. And most importantly, we shall see that this mortal wound extends to all images of this beast as death. In contrast, all images of God extend to life. John 3:5,15-16 "Except a man be born of water and of the Spirit, he cannot enter the Kingdom of God. - Whosoever believes in him shall not perish. - For God so loved the world that he gave his only begotten Son, that whosoever believes in him should not perish, but have everlasting life."

Continuing to the 13th chapter of Revelation concerning this beast that rises out of the sea (of man); Rev. 13:4-8 "And they worshiped the dragon who gave power unto the beast and they worshiped the beast… - And power was given unto him to continue forty-two months (three and a half years.) - And he blasphemies against God and his tabernacle, and them that dwell in heaven. - And it was given unto him to make war with the saints, and to overcome them, and power was given them over all kindreds, and tongues, and nations. - And all that dwell on the earth shall worship him, whose names are not written in the book of life of the Lamb slain from the foundation of the world." It is the belief here that this worship of this beast from the sea of man is not the taking of his name and number. Rather, it is a spiritual misdirection. As the world moves to a ten world anti-Christian government, there will be an actual worship as God to the beast from the land.

Rev. 13:9-10 "If any man has an ear, let him hear. - He that leads into captivity shall go into captivity. He that kills with the sword, must be killed with the sword. Here is the patience and faith of the saints." This unusual wording is confusing unless combined with the 11th chapter of Revelation that involves the same time and events.

During this time, the Lord sends two witnesses. And they will prophesy forty and two months at the temple of God. Rev. 11:5 "And if any man will hurt them, fire proceeds from their mouth, and devours their enemies. And if any man will hurt them, he must in this manner be killed." These two men of God will hinder the dragon, and the beast from the sea, and the beast from the earth. Their ministry lasts for three and a half years. This is from Israel and makes clarity of what doesn't make sense, unless you believe in a literal interpretation of the Bible. Whenever a scripture starts with this type of reference: "If any man has an ear to hear, let him hear" or any scripture that is pointed to, special attention reveals special insight and wonders.

Rev. 13:11-12 "And I beheld another beast coming out of the earth (Israel) and he had two horns like a lamb, and he spoke as a dragon. - And he exercises all the power of the first beast before him." The political beast from the sea appears first. Then very shortly afterwards the beast from Israel. This is the one from Israel that sits in the temple of God, as God. And he causes the earth and them who dwell in it to worship the first beast whose deadly wound is healed. This is not the beast from the sea of man, but Satan.

Rev. 13:13-14 "And he does great wonders, so that he makes fire come down from heaven to the earth in the sight of men. - And he deceives them that dwell on the earth by the means of these miracles which he had power to do in the sight of the beast, saying to them that dwell on the earth, that they should make an image to the beast, that had the wound by a sword, and did live." So now we must identify this sword and wound that is mortal.

THE SWORD

John 19:30 "And when Jesus had received the vinegar, he said 'It is finished.' And he bowed his head and gave up the spirit." What was finished? It was the Lord's purpose for which he was born. Jesus came to die for the sins of mankind; the innocent taking the sins of the guilty. Jesus' purpose of dying for the sins of fallen mankind has now been fulfilled. "It is finished." But what does speaking *that* have to do with a *sword*? The answer is that these are the words of God, and they cannot fail. They accomplish all that they purpose to do. The word of God is the sword of God.

John 1:1 "In the beginning was the word, and the word was with God, and the word was God." - And then Revelation itself defines this sword that inflicts this mortal wound to the god of this world, along with the book of Hebrews that gives more understanding of this sword. Hebrews 4:12 "For the word of God is quick, and powerful, and sharper than any two-edged sword, piercing even to the dividing asunder of soul and spirit, and the joints and marrow, and a discerner of the thoughts and intents of the heart." Rev. 1:16 "And he had in his hands seven stars; and out of his mouth went a two-edged sword. And his countenance was as the sun shines in its strength." Rev. 19:15 "And out of his mouth goes a sharp sword, that with it he should smite the nations, and he shall rule them with a rod of iron; and he treads the winepress of the fierceness and wrath of Almighty God." - Rev. 2:12 "... These things says he who has the sharp sword with two edges." - Rev.

2:16 "Repent, or else I will come unto you quickly, and will fight them with the sword of my mouth."

We now return to this beast from the earth (an Orthodox Jew that rejected Jesus and was waiting for the promised Messiah), deceiving them that dwell on the earth by the miracles which he has power to do in the sight of the beast. This wording "in sight of the beast" reveals not only the source of this power and lying wonders, but Satan's actual presence in this man. 2nd Thes. 2:9 "Even him who whose coming is after the working of Satan with all power and signs and lying wonders of falsehood." Foolishly ignoring God's warnings results in allowing spiritual control. These at this time are probably not real miracles, except in the minds of those who are controlled and blinded.

THREE BEASTS

Rev. 13:12 "And he exercised all the power of the first beast before him, and causes the earth to worship the first beast, whose deadly wound was healed." It is clearly stated that he exercises all the power of the first beast before him. And the one to be worshiped is the first beast, whose deadly wound was healed. The first beast before him received the deadly wound, and is the political world leader from the sea of Man. The first beast is Satan.

Rev. 13:13-15 "And he does great wonders, so that he makes fire come down from heaven on the earth in the sight of men. - And deceives them that dwell on the earth by the means of these miracles which he had power to do in the sight of the beast, saying to them that dwell on the earth to make an image to the beast, that had the wound by the sword, and did live." It is believed here that initially there were actual miracles done. (The same as when Satan had permission from God to touch all that was of Job, but not Job himself.) This was the cause of Satan and his angels being cast out of heaven. The time being seven years before Jesus returns from the heavens with his angels and resurrected saints. And he had power to give life unto the image to the beast, that the image of the beast should both speak, and cause those that would not worship the image of the beast to be killed.

This man is now the image of the beast. Rev. 13:15 "And causes that as many as would not worship the image of the beast should be killed." As Satan occupies this particular man and has complete control, this man is now more than an image of the beast that the world must worship, completely losing his identity. He now is completely controlled by Satan indwelling his flesh. And as for Satan, he now is the Devil and no longer has the power or beauty beyond description as God created him. If he did, men would have a reverence for him befitting his grandeur and excellence. What a degrading experience for this would-be God to be seen as a man!

CHAPTER 29

MAKING AN IMAGE TO THE BEAST

Continuing with these words from Rev. 13:14b-15, "Saying to them that dwell on the earth, that they shall make an image to the beast, which had the wound by the sword, and did live. - And he had power to give life unto the image of the beast." Only God gives life, so this cannot be correct. In checking the proper Greek translation of this word life (Pneuma), we see that it means "breath" or "current of air", not life. This completely changes the meaning. It now makes sense, and does not contradict the Bible. But even without knowing the proper translation of this one word, reason and other scriptures would reveal the Bible is not referring to a robot, statue, android or even a man. The only reasonable conclusion is fallen man.

The early translators were very thorough, dedicated and efficient. But it is always the responsibility of the believers to examine any scripture that seemingly contradicts God's word. It is always beneficial to have a personal searching of the word of God, as our relationship with the Lord is personal.

Satan cannot give life. If "breath" or "speech" is used instead of "life", we have an understanding that does not confuse, but clarifies. "He has power to give speech to the image of the beast." This means he has power or control over this image of himself. The words following in Rev. 13:15, "He has power to give life (breath) that the image of the beast should both speak and cause as many as would not worship the image of the beast should be killed", are obviously referring to an absolute control of their words and their life. Rev. 13:8 - "And all that dwell on the earth shall worship him, whose names are not written in the book of life, of the Lamb slain from the foundation of the world." This image that would follow such an edict is flesh and blood man. Those of the world are now the image of the beast. All that have taken his name or mark now worship the dragon and this image he now possesses. Rev.13:17 "And that no man might buy or sell, save he who has the mark or name of the beast." The next verse verifies the image is man. "Here is wisdom. Let him that has understanding count the number of the beast, for it is the number of man; and his number is 666."

This writer does not know Greek, so has inserted the Zondervan interlinear Greek, English translation, without the Greek words. Rev. 13:15 "And it was given to it to give breath to the image of the beast, that also should speak. And the image of the beast would cause as many not would do homage to the image of the beast that they should be killed." This is quite difficult to follow as written, but it does confirm that the original Greek states it is breath, and not life that the beast gives to the image of the beast. Then states after giving breath that also is speaking the image of the beast; or complete obedience. This seems quite clear, (but poor English) this breath is speaking the image of the beast. The first priority is that all who do not do homage to the image of the beast (whom he occupies) should be killed. As this is immediately implemented, it verifies there is a single purpose and direction involving a worldwide flesh and blood beast.

UNDIVIDED KINGDOM

Jesus spoke these words to his apostles. Luke 11:18 "If Satan be divided against himself, how shall his kingdom stand?" Satan's angels are called his angels because they are his. And this has an undivided agenda. This is affirmed by the fact that that both Satan and his angels are cast out of heaven. Satan is the devil (singular), and these - his angels as demons (plural) - occupy and control these people. But they can only control those who allow or invite them in. As Satan's angels, they will control whoever they indwell. Just as Satan will control this one particular man.

Rev. 12:9,12 "And that great dragon was cast out... into the earth, and his angels were cast out with him. - Therefore rejoice, ye heavens and you who dwell in them. Woe to the inhabitants of the earth and of the sea! For the devil is come down to you, having great wrath, because he knows he has but a short time."

Jesus spoke of this time to come. Matt. 24:21-22 "For then shall there be great tribulation, as was not since the beginning of the world to this time, nor shall ever be. - And except those days should be shortened, there should be no flesh saved. But for the elect's sake those days shall be shortened." It is the last three and a half years that this scripture is referring to. Satan oversteps his bounds at the start of the last seven years before Jesus returns. As antichrist demands worship as God, he is hindered for three and a half years by God's two witnesses. And this author adds another five months of hindering. The Bible speaks of this time, not telling when it will take place. This writer added this event in the middle of the seven years. Otherwise I could not see any possibility of anyone living to populate the world in the last 1,000 years.

It is the book of Daniel that probably gives the clearest explanation as to how it is possible for the world will be in the image of the beast in a manner that reveals absolute submission and control. But first, clarity on what all Christians must understand. That is, the eternal spirit of man is the essence of man. The flesh is temporary.

IMAGE OF GOD AND IMAGE OF THE BEAST

The first chapter of the Bible reveals God created man in his image, after his likeness. Male and female created he them. But a just God has given mankind the right to reject what they were created to be. Then, in the fullness of time, the Lord revealed his express image in his only begotten Son. Man then desired to make him king as they witnessed his creative powers, miracles and healings. As the time of our Savior's purpose approached, the Lord revealed to the world his Son's heart as the Lamb of God. It was now the Lord's time to try the hearts of man. This is when things took a nasty turn, and the heart of man was exposed. Jesus submitted himself to this world. They took him captive, beating him and having apparent power over him. And then when Pontius Pilate desired to release him, the mob preferred another. Pilate then asked the people, what should then be done with their King (Jesus)? They cried out to crucify him. And Pilate asked why, what has he done? They cried all the louder... CRUCIFY HIM!

The cross separates mankind. 1 Cor. 1:18 "For the preaching of the cross is to them that perish foolishness; but unto us who are saved it is the power of God." The world does not comprehend this power that is the heart of God. And it is this heart that created life and gives life anew. This power of God is often revealed in a glorious and unusual way. Just as in the entrance of Satan and his angels, being cast out of heaven. And at the cross, there is a clear contrast of choices to be made. Then the iron and the clay shall be exposed. There will be no compromise, nor political or religious correctness.

BABYLON

At this present time, this world is identified as the Babylon of Revelation. A Babylon that has reached their objective as a one world government, having not quite completely implemented it (Israel will not be of this this unified world). This one world government will be established for world unity and peace. There will also be a religious unity with acceptance of all religions, with one exception. The exception will be biblical Christianity; those who hold to the absolute authority of the Judeo-Christian Bible. This writer does not wish to hazard an opinion as to the extent of outlawing or restrictions imposed on biblical Christians at this time in history. But at this present time, converting to Christianity can cause your death in many nations. The United States is considered the most Christian at this time, with each year witnessing a steady decline of any influence. Same-sex marriage is the latest mocking of the word of God. And at the last days there will be a falling away. The falling away will increase, exposing the iron along with this clay.

The Bible itself addresses this. This Babylon is the same Babylon as from the beginning. Rev. 18:20-21 "Rejoice over her, thou heaven, and you holy apostles and prophets; for God has avenged you on her. - And a mighty angel took up a stone like a great millstone, and cast it into the sea, saying, 'Thus with great violence shall that great city Babylon be thrown down, and never be found anymore.'

This stone cast into the sea reveals it is the sea of man that will destroy her. There are several scriptures that identify Jesus as a great stone, and waters as mankind. And the word "sorceries" involves spiritual involvement or knowledge that is not of the Lord. This warning to not inquire of this spiritual knowledge and influence is commanded by the Lord. And Rev. 18:23-24 reveals the consequences of this deception. "For by your sorceries were all the nations deceived, - And in her were found the blood of the prophets and the saints." This is also authenticated by a violence that extends to "all that were slain upon the earth."

CHAPTER 30

TRIED AND TESTED

Man, by his efforts, has tried to solve this problem of violence and wars since being cast out of the garden. But he cannot; because of the very reason they were cast out of the garden. They rejected the word of truth. This is authenticated, and not only because they were deceived by the words of he who is a liar with no truth in him. And then, regardless of man's stubbornness, in the fullness of time God sent the word of truth in the form of a man. Man once again rejected the Word of Truth, and then crucified him. And by this very act the Lord showed the only way for man to obtain eternal peace and joy unspeakable; just believe that this was indeed the Son, the Lamb of God. He who had no sin shed his blood, so that he who was sin would be washed by the blood of He who cannot sin.

MAN TO DESTROY HIS DREAM

Fallen man does not need a spiritual element to do evil, since man's greatest righteousness is as filthy rags. But because of this spiritual element, a bondage of unimaginable terror will occur as fallen man will destroy what he has built. All in an attempt to be free, in exchange for a world devoid of any freedom. A world that the Lord warned man not to become involved with. This spiritual element is defined by these words: "For by thy sorceries were all nations deceived." Man was created as a living spirit, inhabiting a body of flesh. The eternal essence of man is spirit. It is the *spirit* of man that must be made in the image of God. Not the flesh, which is a body of death.

Romans 7:21-25 "I find a law that, when I would do good, evil is present with me. - For I delight in the law of God after the inward man (our spirit) - But I see another law in my members, warring against the law of my mind, and bringing me into captivity to the law of sin which is in my members - Oh wretched man that I am! Who will deliver me from the body of this death? - I thank God through Jesus Christ, our Lord. So then, with the mind I myself serve the law of God, but with the flesh, the law of sin."

Paul is explaining the state of all of mankind since being cast out of the garden, caused by believing the liar who has no truth in him and rejecting the words of his creator. This authenticates that each of mankind is free to choose his destiny. The grace of God is revealed in Paul's words. "Who will deliver me from the body of this death? I thank God through Jesus Christ." And this is what separates Christianity from all religions. Just believe that he who is without sin died, and that he who has no righteousness will be made pure. Just believe there is such a God.

BABEL AND BABYLON

From the beginning of time man has strived to obtain peace and order without God, and yet at the same time to please God. This involved various ways to please him. And most often in this process, man has rejected the only way this is possible. God did not create man for the purpose of blindly worshiping him, but to *know* him. And when man comes to know the Lord, worshiping of the Lord is what he will do. But this worshiping takes on a whole new meaning. It is not blind submission, but a thankfulness beyond description. Knowing, in part, a love beyond comprehension that is freely bestowed upon all of man.

KNOWING GOD

Through Moses the Lord revealed that through the shedding of blood, the children of Israel were set free from Egypt. But not their own blood. Rather, the blood of the lamb. This is called the Passover lamb. In Exodus 12:1-11, each household was to take a lamb without blemish and examine it for four days to have complete assurance this lamb indeed was without blemish. Then the whole assembly of the congregation was to kill their lamb in the evening and put the blood on the top of the doorpost and the two side doorposts. "And I will pass this night to smite all the first born in the land of Egypt. - And when I see the blood I will pass over you."

So as we search out these words concerning this lamb that is to be examined for imperfections; first, each household was to have their own lamb to examine. If this lamb had any imperfections it would not be acceptable to the Lord. A lamb is very trusting, and easy to become attached to. Especially as they had this specific lamb in their home with their family for four days to observe. This went beyond simply physical imperfections; this lamb's gentle and trusting nature also came into play. They were then to kill and eat what had come to be a family pet to many.

Christians are now aware this Passover lamb is a picture of Jesus the Son of God. This is prophetically revealed as "slain from the foundation of the world" (Rev. 13:8). The children of Israel did not understand this. And, at first, neither did Jesus' disciples. In fact, what Jesus had revealed to them was apparently taken as a parable. Until he rose from the dead and revealed himself to them and many more for forty days before he was taken up to the heavens before their eyes.

This scripture is one of many that reveal God's ways are not man's ways. And man's ways often coincide with the god of this world's ways. Matt. 16:21-23 "Jesus began to show his disciples how he then must go to Jerusalem, and suffer many things from the elders, and chief priests, and scribes, and be killed, and be risen the third day. - Then Peter took him, and began to rebuke him, saying. 'Be it far from thee, Lord. This shall not be unto you.' - And the Lord said to Peter, 'Get thee behind me, Satan. Thou are an offence unto me, for you savor not the things that are of God, but those things of men.'"

It is interesting that neither Peter, nor apparently any of the rest of the disciples, regarded or asked concerning these very next words of the Lord: He would then rise the third day. In fact, later they asked Jesus: Was he now going to establish his kingdom? What he was saying simply did not register to them.

LOVE

Earlier, it was addressed here that certain truths have been revealed to every man, woman, and child by the inspiration of the Almighty.

These truths are that God had *created* man in his image, after his likeness; and then placed this image of God in a body of flesh for a season. This body of flesh was *formed* of the dust of the ground and will return to dust again. But the *creation* of male and female is spirit, and eternal. As God is Spirit, so must his image be spirit. It is this spirit that must then be tried, tested and sent through the fire to be purified or burned.

There is a problem involved in explaining with any kind of clarity how man can be created in the image of God, as the Bible makes it very clear this does not define man. God is the Alpha and Omega, the beginning and the end. He is beyond time, and when he proclaims or speaks anything to be done, it is then done. Perhaps not in *our* time frame, but it is done. No one can undo what God has done. However, a just God allows man to reject what will be completed at the gathering of the Saints. That is, man's spirit being born again to enter the Kingdom of God. When this corrupt takes on incorruption. And then we will receive the fullness of God's greatest gift… love. It is not possible to force anyone to love. Love is a gift. We are told to love that what is good and hate that what is evil. But we are not forced to love. Nor can we - it is given as a gift.

God is Spirit and God is love. In Chapters 12-14 of 1st Corinthians, the Bible explains spiritual gifts the Lord gives to man, along with the purpose and proper administration of them. But then in the thirteenth chapter we are told that the greatest gift is Love.

Love is defined in part. And we are told man cannot obtain the fullness of this love at this time, but will in the future. 1st Cor. 13:9-12 "For we know in part, and we prophesy in part. - But when that what is perfect is come, then that which is in part shall be done away. - When I was a child, I spoke as a child, I understood as a child, I thought as a child; but when I became a man, I put away childish things. - For now we see in a mirror darkly; but then face to face; now I know in part, but then I shall know even as I am known."

We all are created with the free will to reject as we were created to be. Then when that which is perfect is come (Jesus at the rapture, who is perfect), that what is done in part shall be done away with. (Believers being born again. When this mortal takes on immortality, and this corrupt take on incorruption.) "Then shall I know even as I am known." There is only one truth involved. That is simply accepting the only way man can be made pure. This necessity is only presented in the Judeo-Christian Bible, along with the only way it is possible.

If man believes he can, by himself, make himself pure, he has judged himself as God. No, if the criteria begins with the fact that man must be without sin to enter a paradise, then man must be completely washed of all sin. Then there must be an advocate or mediator. Not to only forgive our sins, but a sinless mediator must *take our sins as if they were his.* For to simply forgive the sins of man would neither be justice or truth. These truths are evident to some, and to others foolishness. John 15:15b-16 "All things I have heard of my Father I have made known unto you. - You have not chosen me, but I have chosen you."

There is pure reason why the Lord chooses whom he does. The Lord put David in place of Saul as King of Israel. The reason being, David was a man after God's heart. David wanted the heart of the Lord. 1st Samuel 14:14 "But now your kingdom shall not continue. The Lord has sought him a man after his own heart." Saul's heart is a picture of Babylon, and of the same mind of those at the tower of Babel. His heart was not after the heart of God, but of a different spirit, that he may then decide whom to follow. As Babel he, by his own ways, was going to build his tower to heaven and make a name for himself.

This spiritual Babylon is well aware of the Lord, as all are receiving inspiration from the Lord. The Almighty speaks to the spirit of man during the night time when man is not involved in the things of this world. Many are as Eve, who was convinced that she had to have the only fruit she was told not to eat. Even when told if she did eat of this fruit she would die. This comes from a heart that was not thankful to her creator, who talked directly to Adam and Eve in the cool of the day. This is not just making a decision as to whom to believe. Eve was well aware of whom she was not willing to believe, and thought that God was withholding knowledge from her and Adam. Gen. 3:4-5 "And the serpent said to the woman, 'You shall not surely die. - For

God knows that in the day you eat thereof, then your eyes will be opened, and you shall be as God, knowing good and evil.'" He was reinforcing her thoughts.

This was the first step of man being of Babylon. Rejecting God's words expanded to rebelling against his words. This leads to these final days when mankind will destroy what he himself has been building on and striving for. Replacing and denying God in exchange for being in the image of the beast. In man's desire to become free, he will put himself in bondage. The Lord created man to be in his image. But a second birth is involved with an absolute necessity; seeking, more than life itself, the heart of the Lord. All that is necessary is to believe, and desire such a God. As man proceeds to the end of times, when Satan and his angels are cast out of heaven, this world will have established their long-awaited one world city of Babel (Babylon). A world of selective political and religious correctness.

Man will have achieved their tower of Babel of ten toes or horns of unity. Rev.17:12-13, 16-18. "And the ten horns which thou saw are ten kings, who have received no kingdom as yet, but will receive power as kings one hour with the beast. - These have one mind, and shall give their power and strength unto the beast. - And the ten horns you saw upon the beast, they shall hate the harlot, and shall make her desolate and naked, and eat her flesh, and burn her with fire, - For God has put in their hearts to fulfill his will, and to agree, and give their kingdom unto the beast, until the words of God shall be fulfilled. - And the woman whom you saw is that great city, which reigns over the kings of the earth."

CHAPTER 31

THE IMAGE OF THE BEAST

Throughout the years, theologians have speculated on who this scarlet colored beast, Babylon, and the woman who rides the beast are. We do know the name of the woman. Rev. 17:5 "And upon her forehead was a name written. MYSTERY, BABYLON THE GREAT, THE MOTHER OF HARLOTS AND ABOMINATIONS OF THE EARTH." She and Babylon are one and the same, they are intricately entwined. She is the people who have created Babylon. We are given more information that the woman and the beast are one in Rev. 17:1b "Come here. I will show you then the judgment of the great harlot that sits on many waters (peoples)." As she rides the beast and sits on many waters, we have a oneness of this people and the dragon who is Satan, the god of this world. This woman has been riding or building a one world system for herself.

The Lord has strictly forbidden to inquire from the source of this system (spiritual wickedness in high places). This world has rejected what the Lord has created man to be, along with the Kingdom of God. The Lord has put in their hearts to hate what they have achieved and give this kingdom unto the beast. The subjects of this kingdom become the subjects of whom they give this kingdom to. They then become the image of the beast.

Rev. 17:12 "The ten horns upon the beast are ten kings, who have received no kingdom as yet, but receive power as kings one hour with the beast." It would seem the world has just established a one world government. The finalization of appointing these kings, or rulers, is not to be completed until the time that they receive this power one hour (a short time) with the beast. They have now given their kingdom to the beast. What is involved? And what are the consequences of becoming this image?

Rev. 17:16 "And the ten horns shall hate the harlot and make her desolate and naked and eat her flesh and burn her with fire." This is quite a graphic description of the revulsion they would have for what they, lost man, have been building without God. Why will this be so? Rev. 17:17 "For God has put it in their hearts to fulfill his will, and to agree, and to give their kingdom unto the beast." Man has been building this one word government for themselves. All the time it has been for the god of this world. The book of Daniel reveals much of this time of great sorrow and depravity of man. But at the same time, the greatest victories and rejoicing. The victories and rejoicing as a direct benefit from God from some of those hating of the harlot, of which they became. But for others, the finalization of becoming of the image of the beast.

IRON AND CLAY

Daniel 2:41-43 "And whereas you saw the feet and toes, part of potter's clay and part of iron, the kingdom shall be divided; but there shall be in it of the strength of the iron, forasmuch as you saw the iron mixed with miry clay. - And as the toes of the feet were part of iron and part of clay, so the kingdom shall be partly strong and partly broken. - And whereas you saw iron mixed with miry clay, they shall mingle themselves with the seed of men; but they shall not adhere one to another, even as iron is not mixed with clay."

There are two separate revelations. One, the kingdom will be divided since it is of iron and clay. And two, this kingdom shall be partly strong and partly broken. Just what does this imply? And then who or what is this "they" that shall mingle themselves with the seed of men, but not adhere to one another, even as iron will not adhere with clay? The "they" referred to are fallen angels, or demons, and the clay, or the broken, is mankind. Men have seed; angels do not. The demons will mix with, or possess, men; the strong indwelling the weak. As these are now the latter days, when Satan and his angels have been cast to the earth. They are no longer angels, but the Devil and his demons. As such, the only way their presence can be exhibited is through a human host.

It may appear at first glance that the strong indwelling the weak would be the mix of iron and clay. However, there is a greater strength in this kingdom.

This writer believes the *real* iron in this prophesy will be those who had neither denied nor professed the Gospel message. The rapture will happen soon after this, which will be explained later in this book. At that time, they will be left behind – and soon after will clearly see the contrast between the Christian message and the evil of this new world of madness. They will then be filled with the realization of the huge mistake they made by being lukewarm with their faith, and understand that the only way to save their life is to lose it. This will be a small price to pay, as the reality of the Word of God becomes their only reality. This is their new-found strength. They become the iron.

Thus, it would appear that what would make this kingdom partly strong and partly broken would be a world of demon-possessed people whose first agenda is to kill only those whose names are written in the book of life of the Lamb slain from the foundation of the world - the Christians. The brokenness and clay of this world would be those who are not Christians, and are possessed by demons. By trying to save their earthly lives, they lost them. At this time, the strong, or iron, are clearly identified in the paragraph above.

Rev. 13:7-8 "And it was given unto him to make war with the saints and overcome them; and power was given him over all kindreds and tongues and nations. - And all that dwell on the earth shall worship him, whose names are not written in the book of life of the Lamb slain from the foundation of the world."

The last chapter of Daniel speaks of this very time. Daniel 12:8-10 "I heard but understood not. Then I said, 'O my Lord, what shall be the end of these things?' - And he said, 'Go thy way, Daniel, for the words are closed up and sealed till the time of the end. - Many shall be purified, and made white, and tested. But the wicked shall do wickedly, and none of the wicked shall understand, but the wise shall understand.'" This last three and a half years will have a revival as none other, as those that lose their lives will save them.

LEFT BEHIND

The Bible is very clear that only the Father knows the time of the rapture or taking away of the church to meet the Lord in the air. But what will happen at the time of this event is clearly defined. Several things concerning this event will happen. The mortal believers will become immortal, and their corruption will become incorruption. The Lord will bring a cleansed bride to a cleansed kingdom, as Jesus told the believers in John 14:2-3. "In my father's house are many mansions, and I go to prepare a place for you. And if I prepare a place for you I will return for you, and receive you unto myself, and where I am you shall be." Heaven must be cleansed to receive the cleansed believers. Then the Lord will return to receive the believers unto himself at the rapture, and "where I am they shall be also".

This future event was recorded in Rev. 12:9 "And that great dragon was cast out, that old serpent called the Devil and Satan." This is the cleansing of the heavens to receive the saints. (There are arguments against this. One widely held one is that the rapture will be long before Satan and his angels are cast out of heaven.) Jesus said he would prepare a place for the believers and then receive them unto himself.

The believers have now become of the kingdom of heaven. It is this evil spiritual presence that has tried, tested and refined the saints in the fire of this world; a world that has made Satan the god of it. But the dragon and his angels are stripped of their power when cast to the earth, which is impressive. Paul spoke of this spirit of man. "Who will deliver me from the body of this body of death?" He then stated that only Jesus can do this. The spirit of man programs this body of flesh through a sophisticated computer beyond comprehension, which is man's brain. This is the reason for the strict warning not to have any contact with spiritual forces in this world, or high places. If we do, we then have the combination of the spirits of fallen man and fallen spirits both having access to this computer. This extensive spiritual warfare will be briefly addressed.

Most people are aware of voodoo witch doctors that gain power to control of man through evil spirits, as depicted by movies and T.V. As our secular humanists and our educational system assures us there are no spirits, nor God, it would appear educated people reject this as fake and great fun. But the Lord God has revealed himself to all. In truth, there are no atheists. All of mankind knows there is a creator God and a redeemer. Not only does man know this, but the Lord reveals, with absolute clarity, exactly how this is possible for man to know. The Spirit of God speaks continually to the spirit of man when the essence of man is not distracted by the things of this world.

Job 32:8 "The Spirit of the Almighty gives them understanding." And the next chapter reveals what this information is, and when it is given. Job 33:4 "The Spirit of God has made me and the breath of the Almighty has given me life." Job 33;14-18 "God speaks once, yea twice, yet man perceives it not. - In a dream, in a vision of the night, when deep sleep falls upon men, in slumbering on the bed. - Then he opens the ears of men and seals their instructions - That he may withdraw man from his purpose and hide pride from man. - And he keeps back his soul from the pit, and his life from perishing by the sword." (Science has revealed the brain of man is most active during deep sleep. These words from Job give a reasonable explanation.)

Then Jesus is identified. Job 33:19-22 "He is also chastened with pain upon his bed, and the multitude of his bones with strong pain. - So that his life abhors bread and his soul dainty food. - His flesh is consumed away, that it cannot be seen, and his bones that were not seen stick out. (The visible effects of hanging on the cross) – Yea, his soul draws near to the pit, and his life to the destroyers." (The innocent's life for the guilty.)

This demands repeating. Christianity is completely contrary to all religions, in that there is nothing that anyone can do to achieve their salvation. Absolutely nothing. And anything that is done for the purpose of attaining or the helping of obtaining eternal life, actually hinders what Jesus has done. When what Jesus has done on the cross is believed and accepted, a new heart desires a new life and conduct, which is then evident to the world. But to the believer, there comes an even greater understanding and knowledge of the Lord. There then comes the awareness that their "greatest righteousness is as filthy rags." (Isaiah 64:6) And nothing they do can further their salvation. How can this be? This can only be grasped by those who ask, "What kind of God is this, that my savior would die for me?" And then to want, more than life itself, to spend eternity with such a God. It is profitable and wise to take our minds off ourselves. Job 33:16-17

"Then he opens the ears of men and seals their instructions. - That he may withdraw man from his purpose and hide pride from man."

GOD'S TWO WITNESSES

God will send his two witnesses three and a half years before this world submits to and become of the image of the beast. The Lord's grace and love will be exhibited worldwide in miraculous signs, wonders, and truths in prophesies and testimonies from Jerusalem to all the world. This, along with the world receiving bold witness in all nations from the soon to be raptured saints, to be gathered to meet the Lord in the air. Affirming these things are what God's two witnesses will proclaim.

The Lord, whom the world has rejected, is still stretching out his arm to receive them. Rev. 11:3 "And I will give power to my two witnesses, and they shall prophesy for one thousand two hundred and sixty days, clothed in sackcloth." And to assure that this truth may not be interrupted, so that all may hear, the Lord then does several things. Rev. 11:5 "If any man will hurt them, fire proceeds from their mouth and devours their enemies; and if any man will hurt them, he must in this manner be killed."

But how will they be able to understand their speech worldwide? And why will this world continue to televise these words that infuriate them? They will broadcast these words because God is God. And for the same reason, all people will understand these words spoken in a tongue they should not understand. To affirm the complete authenticity and the foreknowledge of God, this understanding in their own language has been prophesied by the prophet Joel and affirmed by Peter.

PENTECOST

The special day of Pentecost was a day that Jesus told his believers to wait for, in which they would receive power from on high. These were the last words that he spoke to his disciples. This was after appearing to them four various times in his resurrected body, during the forty days just before he was taken up to heaven. Luke 24:44-52 "And he said unto them, 'These are the words I spoke unto you, while I was yet with you, that all things must be fulfilled, which were written in the law of Moses, and in the prophets, and in the psalms, concerning me.' - Then he opened their understanding, that they might understand the scriptures. - And he said unto them, 'Thus it is written, and thus it behooved Christ to suffer, and to rise from the dead the third day. - And that repentance and remission of sins should be preached in his name among all the nations, beginning in Jerusalem. - And you are witness of all these things. - And behold, I send the promise of my Father upon you. But tarry in the city of Jerusalem, until you become endowed with power from on high.' - And he led them out as far as to Bethany, lifting up his hands, and blessed them. - And it came to pass, while he blessed them, he was parted from them, and carried up into heaven. - And they worshiped him and returned to Jerusalem with great joy."

And when the day of Pentecost was come, Acts 2:2-7,12-13 "Suddenly there came a sound from heaven like a rushing mighty wind, filling the house where they were sitting. - And there appeared unto to them cloven tongues as of fire, and it sat upon each of them. - And they were all filled with the Holy Spirit, and began to speak with other tongues, as the spirit gave them utterance. - And there were dwelling at Jerusalem Jews, devout men, out of every nation under heaven. - As this became known the multitude came together, and they were confounded, because every man heard them speak in his own language. - And they were all amazed and marveled (as they heard them speak in their own language) - The wonderful works of God. And they were all amazed and perplexed, saying one to another, 'What does this mean?' – Others, mocking, said 'They are filled with new wine.'"

This what the Lord has revealed, where some heard language they knew they could not possibly know, but did. And what they clearly heard were words speaking of the wonderful works of God. Others said they were filled with new wine. This writer is assuming all heard with clarity these words. This was a special day - Pentecost. Elijah was in a mountain and a great wind came. But the Lord was not in the wind. Then there was an earthquake. But the Lord was not in the earthquake. Then a great fire. And the Lord was not in the fire. And then a still small voice; of the Lord.

Some can never seem to hear the Lord no matter how loudly he speaks to them. But to others, they listen intently and this still small voice gets easier to hear the more often they listen.

Acts 2:14-21 "But Peter, standing up with the eleven, lifted up his voice and said unto them, 'You men of Judea, and all that dwell at Jerusalem, be it known unto you, and hearken unto my words. - These men are not drunk as you suppose, seeing it is but the third hour of the day. - But this is that which was spoken through the prophet Joel, - 'And it will come to pass in the last days that I will pour out my Spirit upon all flesh; and your sons and daughters shall prophesy, and your young men shall see visions, and your old men shall dream dreams. - And on my servants and on my handmaids, I will pour out in those days of my Spirit, and they shall prophesy. - And I will show wonders in heaven above, and signs in the earth beneath: Blood, and fire, and vapor of smoke - The sun shall be turned into darkness, and the moon into blood, before that great and notable day of the Lord comes; - And it will come to pass that whosoever shall call on the name of the Lord shall be saved.'"

This obviously is two different prophesies, or an extension of the day of Pentecost. Jesus himself answers this, while telling his believers to tarry at Jerusalem until they receive power from on high. Luke 24:47 "And that repentance and remission of sins should be preached in his name among all nations, beginning at Jerusalem." Pentecost started at Jerusalem. Joel takes us to the end times, also beginning at Jerusalem, At Pentecost all men heard them speak, in their own language, the wonderful works of God. This the same as when God's two prophets speak of the wonderful works of God. Now the whole world hears them in their own language. This lasts for three and a half years.

With the two witnesses, there are also signs and wonders involved in the whole world as Joel stated, thus revealing this expanded prophesy. That these are one and the same prophesy is affirmed by the Lord's supernatural intervention that all heard, in their own language, the wonderful works of God.

Acts 2:6 "The multitude came together and were confounded, because every man heard them speak in their own language." Acts 2:8 "And how hear we every man in our own tongue, wherein we were born?" And they were amazed and perplexed, saying to one another, "What does this mean?" But others said, "These men are full of new wine." Not because they did not know what was being said, but because they did. 2nd Cor. 4:3-4 "If our gospel be hidden, it is hidden to them who are lost. - In whom the god of this world has blinded the minds of them who believe not, lest the light of the glorious gospel of Christ, who is the image of God, should shine unto them."

At the time of the prophesies of God's two witnesses, the world has been successful in establishing this Babylon (which the Lord had delayed long before, by confusing their language). And now the Lord allows all of Jerusalem, and then the world, to hear of the wonderful works of God. These amazing conclusions are affirmed by Peter. Standing up with the eleven, he quoted the prophet Joel concerning multiple signs, along with events as dreams, visions and signs that reveal this rebellion against the word of the Lord. A separation revealing time does not lessen man's rebellion to reach their own godhood.

Reason confirms this time of combining these two events. As Peter stated, these are the words of the prophet Joel. In Luke 24, Jesus revealed the things that were to happen to him on the cross and his sufferings revealed in the scriptures by Moses, the prophets and psalms. And that he must die, and then raise again the third day. Then, he told them to wait for the Holy Spirit. But before revealing these things, he opened their understanding that they might understand the scriptures (Luke 24:45.)

CHAPTER 32

FATHER, SON AND HOLY SPIRIT

We Christians have an incompleteness that involves the Father, Holy Spirit and Jesus, who is the Word of God. This incompleteness is that we are not yet as we shall be, in the image of God. We have previously addressed this as Jesus spoke to Nicodemus. (John 3:3,6. This concerns being born again, to see the kingdom of God. And then being born again of the Spirit and the water (word) to enter the kingdom of God. This is the single reason for the creation of man, which separates us from a mindless existence void of logic, reason and purpose. Our purpose, without direction from the Lord, is more than flawed... it is meaningless. Man is completely self-centered without inspiration. This inspiration, which is from the Lord, has goals and standards that cannot be comprehended in our present state. Job 33:16-17 "Then he opens the ears of men and seals their instructions. - That he may withdraw man from his own purpose, and hide pride from man."

PRIDE OF MAN

The Lord has created man to have purpose and meaning, along with all of creation. Our secular world defines and theorizes what it does not understand. An example of this is the DNA of Man. Just one part of this DNA involves the immune system, of which books are written on. And they are no sooner published when more discoveries and knowledge reveal the vastness and intricacies of new discoveries that can't be explained, other that they are miraculous in their scope. And yet evolutionary scientists state that 95 to 98% of DNA is junk DNA left over from man evolving. This is akin to a man stating the blueprints to the most sophisticated designs of men would function far greater with only 2 or 5% of this information. DNA is a living blueprint. The madness that causes man to believe this nonsense can only be explained by someone or something messing with the thinking processes of man. What is being taught is that ignoring 95% of the designer's blueprint will result in a much-improved product. What this reveals is the ignorance and arrogance of man without direction.

The creative designs of man have been unbelievable in their scope and brilliance. Does not reason reveal that something is going on? Those with the ability to comprehend and appreciate creative design know that this demands a creator. This gets the attention of those who believe as a child. The word of God is quite clear that those who are blinded are willingly ignorant. (2nd Peter 3:5) This in itself is an even greater blindness, a self-imposed blindness that reveals pride and arrogance. This is verified by the Lord's words. Luke 18:16-17 "Permit little children to come unto me, and forbid them not; for such is the kingdom of heaven. - Whosoever shall not receive the kingdom of God like a child shall in no way enter in." This is not mindless gullibility, but accepting simple truths.

WHY?

The Lord has revealed that he indeed is love. This is seen in the express image of himself in his Son. Jesus, the Word, defines God; who has then, with full knowledge, created an angel who is an adversary to both God and man. This particular created angel, Lucifer, was made indescribably beautiful and full of wisdom. And then? He apparently contradicts the word of God by revealing he is all but full of wisdom. Or... is the Lord revealing that wisdom and beauty are anything but that without love? 1st Corinthians chapter 13 expresses it this way: "Though I speak with the tongues of men and angels, and have all gifts, understanding, faith, and could move mountains; yet if I do not have love, I am nothing."

The Lord has revealed his love for man by exposing this deception of beauty and wisdom void of purpose and love, and full of pride. And he speaks of John the Baptist. Luke 7:25-26 "What went you out to see? A man clothed in soft raiment? Behold, they who are gorgeously appareled, and live delicately, are in king's courts. - But what went you to see? A prophet? Yes I say unto you, much more than a prophet." And then came he who is much more than a prophet, proclaimed the servant of servants, who takes the sins of the world. The Lamb of God.

The Spirit of the Almighty gives understanding and inspiration to the heart of man. But the preaching of the cross is foolishness to them that perish. For those who have eyes to see, and a heart to feel, no explanation is necessary. The word of God was given to man, to examine this fallen angel Lucifer, or Satan. And these examples are quite detailed throughout the Bible. First, his rejection of the purpose for his creation. Then, his effort to kill the Son of God at his birth. His tempting of Jesus in the wilderness. Then finally succeeding in his purpose – so he thought – only to fulfill the Lord's purpose instead, resulting in this mortal wound to his head. Thus, fulfilling the word of God. And then from the prophetic revealing of Lucifer making the world a wilderness, to him being cast into the lake of fire. And much, much more. All of these things are recorded in the Judeo-Christian Bible. And yet, man has made him the god of their world.

Writers and some theologians go into great detail explaining this battle for man's souls, the great conflict between God and his adversary Satan. In many minds there are two Gods in combat, and Satan is ruling from hell, which is his domain. Hell is not only not his domain, but a place of torment prepared for him. Matt. 8:28-29 "There met him two (men) possessed with demons - And they cried out, 'What have we to do with thee, Jesus, thou Son of God? Are you come to torment us before the time?'"

Satan is not now on this earth, but will soon be cast out of heaven. Man's misconceptions of the Bible are the results of not accepting *all* of its words as true, but picking and choosing what to accept and reject. Why would men take on the name of Christians, not believing what it clearly states? Of all religious writings, only the Judeo-Christian Bible demands that you prove it to be as it claims to be; the word of God.

This is more than a narrative of this battle or conflict, but a historical account of what will be. With man actually having a part in the writings of the most important part of the final chapter... their names.

Satan is not God's adversary, but man's. But is this entirely so? Yes, he is man's adversary. However, he is also serving a purpose. Man is to observe his conduct. We are told to love that what is good, and hate that what is evil. This includes lies, which defines that old dragon. There is a statistical study that is quite troubling, but not surprising. It is stated that up to 16% of young men in Iran are converting to Christianity. It is because of the Bible's message of love and forgiveness, which is completely contrary to Islam. This is wonderful, but here is the troubling part. In the United States of America, new converts to Christianity in the same age group is only about one half of 1%.

The people of Iran are well aware that the religious rulers of their nation are continually calling for the complete annihilation of all Jews, along with their cries of death to America. The economy in this nation controlled by Islam is in shambles. Although this seemingly endless war with Iraq has finally ended, it resulted in something that cannot be forgotten by anyone with any moral decency, nor should it be. This an evil that in the annals of history has not been equaled: the religious leaders of Islam, sacrificing their citizen's children in the name of Allah in this long war against Iraq. This should stand out in the minds of every Iranian with absolute disgust. During this war they sent their young children out to clear the mine fields. They were not trained to defuse the mines, but to detonate them.

This is an evil that has been surpassed by the silence from the world, and then Iran itself. How is it possible that our country's secular and political leaders define this religion as a religion of peace? And yet they have managed this, from our last two Presidents down to our press and academia. This is mindless evil.

A GREATER EVIL

But what is an even greater evil is being perpetuated on all the children of this nation. This is the constant all-out siege to eradicate from their minds any factuality of the creator God of the Christian

Bible. This nation is not sending our children out to detonate these mines, which would result in their physical deaths. But a different minefield, having far deadlier eternal consequences. An all-out assault not to destroy their bodies before their time, but an all-out effort to deny them eternal life. This evil cannot be surpassed in its magnitude.

All sciences are strictly followed and taught in our schools, in order to prepare students for this life. However, there is an unscientific process involved in all our schools – which are federally funded – which is strictly adhered to. Any theories are allowed as to how life, the planets and all matter came into being. All possibilities are allowed to be pondered… except for divine intervention. This is not even allowed as an option. The logic presented is that this would then force a scientific solution by eliminating any outside influence from the Judeo-Christian Bible. But in so doing this did not eliminate outside influence. Rather, it embraced it.

Science itself reveals there must be a creator God for life and matter to even be present. This short sightedness was immediately recognized (or was well thought out) and then ignored, because this truth is unacceptable. Thus revealing this outside source of a far greater evil than Iran's Mullahs. This is a well thought out evil because academicians are well aware that both the Big Bang and Evolution theories are an absolute impossibility, by the very first Law of science.

This is not mindless evil, but a well thought out evil. Purposely setting out to train children about Science, then inferring that science has revealed there is no God, when you know the opposite is true… this is, with open arms, embracing the ultimate evil. Does this not explain the small percent of this nation's youth becoming believers? When, by the heart alone, young men and women of Iran recognize the significance of the Christian God, who sent his Son to die for mankind, compared to Islam's god, who calls man's children to die for him.

THERMODYNAMICS

Here is an interesting verification that academia is well aware of their deception, but not aware of their being deceived; they themselves warn against publicly debating any creationist who knows science. They state: Do not debate a creation scientist, as you will lose. And as true science progresses, the greater this assurance is. They are willingly ignorant, then in this process gain access to spiritual wickedness in high places.

This evil knows that if you can control the children, in a few years you will control the nation. If, as they say, it took billions of years for the universe and life to appear, then how is it possible for the Lord Jesus to have spoken the worlds and life into being in six days? And then this same creator God will recreate everything in a moment of time. (Actually, the Bible states in the blinking of an eye.) 1st Cor. 15:52 "In a moment, in the twinkling of an eye, at the last trump; for the trumpet shall sound, and the dead shall be raised incorruptible, and we shall be changed." They receive a new incorruptible eternal body. We are also assured of more than a new eternal body, but a new heaven and earth. As this old heaven and earth, in a moment, will be done away with. Rev. 21:1 "And I saw a new heaven and a new earth, for the first heaven and the first earth were passed away, and there was no more sea."

2nd Peter 3:10-14 "But the day of the Lord will come as a thief in the night, in which the heavens shall pass away with a great noise, and the elements shall melt with fervent heat; the earth also, and the works that are in it, shall be burned up. - Seeing, then, that all these things shall be dissolved, what manner of persons ought you to be in all holy living and godliness, - Looking for and hasting unto the coming day of God, in which the heavens, being on fire, shall be dissolved, and the elements shall burn with a fervent heat? - Nevertheless we, according to his promise, look for new heavens and a new earth, in which dwells righteousness. – Wherefore, beloved, seeing that you look for such things, be diligent that you may be found of him in peace, without spot, and blameless."

GOD REVEALED

As science increases in knowledge and understanding, some particle scientists state there is a mysterious particle called the Higgs Boson particle. And by this particle, all matter consists and exists. This is more than a glue that holds everything together. The Bible says the very same thing, only stating that it is the Lord that has created this world and all life, and sustains it, and not this Higgs particle. Otherwise there seems to be agreement that without Higgs, or the Lord, there would be nothing; absolutely nothing. This is the pride and arrogance of man.

The world's scientists are so convinced of this that they built a massive multinational Hadron Collider in Switzerland in the search of this particle. Have the world's scientists gotten religion? This seems an unlikely answer, because the religions of the world that have searched out spiritual forces in high places (Buddhism, Hinduism, American Indians, the Jewish Kabbalah, or Cabbala) have received a creation very similar to the big bang and evolutionary theories.

In August of 2014, Pope Francis stated that evolution and the Big Bang theory did not conflict with Catholic teaching. He stated that God is not a magician, with a magic wand able to do everything. Then why does he call the Lord God?

It appears that there continues to be not several beliefs, but one. Are the words of the Judeo-Christian Bible and the historical accounts of Jesus and his apostles accurate? And if God is not a magician, then what is he? This writer is not denigrating Pope Francis, as he is only speaking honestly what others hypocritically state. The Lord is still reaching out, by revealing to these scientists his presence, that they would then receive his overwhelming love. Why is it only offensive to tell the truth? It has been stated here several times that there are no atheists. Only "professing" atheists. And the more knowledge acquired by man, the greater the assurance that there is a creator God.

Paul addressed the men of Mars' Hill two thousand years ago, with an announcement almost identical to these scientists, in their search for this elusive unknown particle of which they profess is responsible for life and all there is. Paul calls them very religious. (Atheism is a religion. This has been affirmed to be so by the Supreme Court.) But these scientists profess atheism, while at the same time saying there would be nothing, absolutely nothing, were there not for this mysterious unknown particle. This is the definition of a Creator God. And yet more than that; a *loving* God that has just revealed himself to all of mankind. With the world doing the testifying. These men and women, with full knowledge, know who they are rejecting; that is with one clarification. They, being suborned, will never have this true knowledge of who they are rejecting… other than it is a truth beyond their comprehension.

Acts 17:22-28, 30. (Paul said) "You men of Athens, I perceive you are very religious. - For as I passed by, and beheld your devotions, I found an altar with this inscription: TO THE UNKNOWN GOD. Whom you ignorantly worship, him I declare unto you. - God who made the world and all things in it, seeing he is the Lord of heaven and earth and dwells not in temples made with hands, - Neither is he worshiped with men's hands, as though he needed anything, seeing he gives to all life, and breath, and all things; - And has made of one blood all nations of men to dwell on the face of the earth, and has determined the times before appointed, and the bounds of their habitation, - That they should seek the Lord, if perhaps they might feel after him, and find him, though he is not very far from every one of us; - For in him we live, and move, and have our being; as certain of your own poets have said, for we are also his offspring. - And the times of this ignorance God overlooked, but now commands all men everywhere to repent."

Before continuing, what should be addressed is this statement that God commands all men everywhere to repent. And by whose standards? Not too long ago a young couple told me there is no such thing as sin. I then asked them, what would they call an act where someone severely beat, and then robbed them? This question did not have any effect on them at all, because it is the Lord's righteousness that offends, not the sins of man. Before dismissing this thought, think out the gospel message. Who was offended, and why?

FORGIVENESS

It is not that difficult to understand forgiveness and love. But can anyone really comprehend complete forgiveness, or complete love? The Bible reveals man cannot comprehend this love that defines God. As we are told, there is none good, no, not one. And our greatest righteousness is as filthy rags. This is not very flattering. Religious men have set standards for man to follow to be accepted by God. But isn't it God who wants to be accepted of man? And then he sets impossible standards that only those who know they cannot meet, do meet. They meet these standards by believing, and more importantly wanting, to worship a God of such love. How can it be that the creator and sustainer of all life desires to be accepted by creatures of which, as was stated above, "there is none good, no, not one"? The enormity and scope of this love has been put in place by the Father from the foundation of earth. With their names already written in the Lamb's book of life, this reveals a love and power surpassing time itself. Mankind cannot even begin to understand who God truly is, and yet will state God is not a magician. Matt. 19:13-14 "Then there were brought unto to him little children, that he would put his hands on them, and pray; and the disciples rebuked them. - But Jesus said, 'Permit the little children, and forbid them not to come unto me. For of such are the Kingdom of heaven.'" The wording "For of *such* are the Kingdom of heaven" reveals childlike trust.

2 Cor. 12:1-7 "It is not expedient for me to glory. I will come to visions and revelations of the Lord. - I knew a man in Christ above fourteen years ago (whether in the body or out of the body I cannot tell: God knows), such a one caught up to the third heaven. - And I knew such a man (whether in the body, or out of the body, I cannot tell; God knows) - How he was caught up into paradise, and heard unspeakable words, which are not lawful for a man to utter. - Of such a man, I will glory; yet of myself I will not glory, but in my infirmities. - For though I would desire to glory, I shall not be a fool, for I will say the truth. But now I forbear, lest any man should think of me above that which he sees me to be, or that he hears of me. - And lest I should be exalted above measure through the abundance of the revelations, there was given unto me a thorn in the flesh, the messenger of Satan to buffet me, lest I should be exalted above measure."

Paul was taken into the third heaven and heard things that are unlawful to speak. The word gives absolute awareness that all of eternity will not contain time to fully comprehend the magnitude and completeness of what we define as God. And as we continue with a few more events leading up to the New Heavens, Earth and Jerusalem, hopefully this contrast of images will become more and more evident.

TRUTH AND ITS REJECTION

The statement "Christianity is not about man, but about God" should be clarified. Exactly what is this implying? Is it that everything is centered on God, and his wants and desires? Yes, that is true. However, what *are* his wants and desires? And as we analyze the complete scriptures it seems it is not about God, but what God wants for man. Man's general concept of an all-powerful God is that all of his creation will eventually submit to him in absolute obedience. This also is true, but not for the reason of his absolute power. No, the reason is his love. This love cannot be separated from truth. This defines God's power.

The dictionary definition of truth means "lack of any falsehoods". Because of the nature of man, it seems there is a necessity of emphasizing *absolute* truth. But truth is absolute. This is the same for lies. Jesus emphasizes this when stating "Satan is a liar, with no truth in him." Any rejection or perversion of truth is a lie. By accepting of the words of the Judeo-Christian Bible, there must be a rejection of all the religions of man as being false.

An element has emerged in this nation that is specifically hostile to the Judeo-Christian Bible. There is a pretense of an equal acceptance of all religions; except for Christianity, which is offensive to them. This is nothing new, as fallen man has forever done this. The difference is that our universities and government have now become involved in this divisiveness that has a spiritual agenda. But to successfully carry out their agenda they incorporate non-spiritual elements, such as race, financial and etc.

Christianity pleads for open discussions with the religions of this world. And specifically, with Christian denominations that reject the Bible as literally the Word of God. No religions outside of Christianity incorporate factual historical evidences that become part of its teachings. The Bible also demands for us to "Prove all things that even they proclaim and hold fast that what is good." The Bible itself establishes historical documentation along with prophetic proofs. Prophesy amounts to up to 20% of its writings. Man's religions do not contain documentation or prophetic pronouncements to verify or disprove its writings.

It begins with the very first family – Adam and then Eve, along with the creation of the worlds and all life. And then the lineage from Adam and Eve, from birth to their ages at death. From there it is recorded up to the flood with Noah, his wife, and their three sons and their wives that entered the Ark. This documentation continues to the birth of Jesus, born of a virgin as prophesied. Fully man, fully

God. It leads up to his dying on the cross, as he gave up the spirit, and then raising from the dead three days later. This was also prophesied.

There are continual documentations and proofs to examine. This is not true of even one of man's religions. And yet, it is only the Judeo-Christian Bible that comes under attack in our Universities. Not honest scrutiny, but mindless attacks that demand proof. These mindless attacks are yet another proof of the reliability of the Bible, as it not only reveals this will happen, but tells the source of this. Then, it extends to revealing the final chapter of the history of man.

The Bible has accurately foretold man's history up to the coming of the Messiah (Jesus), continuing to the re-gathering of the twelve tribes of Israel into a single nation (on May 14, 1948). This comes after thousands of years of the Jews being separated. The Bible also accurately names the Muslim nations who will immediately attempt to wipe them of the face of the earth. And yet it is only the Judeo Christians that come under attack as being bigoted.

A bigot is defined in the dictionary as being against someone, or a view without cause or reason. This is not defining Christian belief based on factual evidence, but rather a mindset completely contrary to or unconcerned with truth. Like placing one's head in the sand and accusing ignorantly, except there is no ignorance involved. Would not any religion, if it were true, desire to be openly examined? This is the single most important subject that man could possibly examine. Both cartoons and thoughtful mankind have asked these questions: Why am I here? What is my purpose? What is the purpose of life? Even evil men cannot keep these thoughts from their minds. Can the thought police that poison children's minds not be aware of what they are doing?

This, which appears to be mindless lack of reason and common sense, reveals just the opposite. There is clearly a self-centered, evil agenda at play. And the Bible is quite clear in continually identifying this source. The very presence of these actions – which could be best described as less than adult behavior – further authenticates the truth of the Bible. The understanding of this truth was played out recently. A homecoming celebration revealed, in dramatic fashion, how the purpose for man's existence is hidden in plain sight.

CHAPTER 33

HOMECOMING CELEBRATION

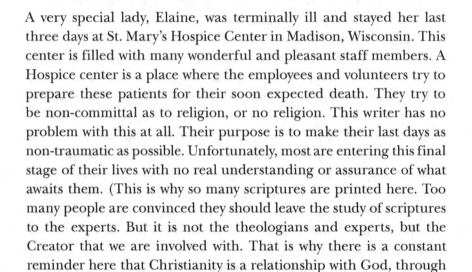

A very special lady, Elaine, was terminally ill and stayed her last three days at St. Mary's Hospice Center in Madison, Wisconsin. This center is filled with many wonderful and pleasant staff members. A Hospice center is a place where the employees and volunteers try to prepare these patients for their soon expected death. They try to be non-committal as to religion, or no religion. This writer has no problem with this at all. Their purpose is to make their last days as non-traumatic as possible. Unfortunately, most are entering this final stage of their lives with no real understanding or assurance of what awaits them. (This is why so many scriptures are printed here. Too many people are convinced they should leave the study of scriptures to the experts. But it is not the theologians and experts, but the Creator that we are involved with. That is why there is a constant reminder here that Christianity is a relationship with God, through Jesus his Son. And it is the Bible that is the word of God. And not your church, pastor or priest. It is encouraged here to engage in conversations with them.)

So now these patients have whatever time is allotted to them to ponder, and, not really understanding, they can choose to be part of what their heart has longed for. It is never too late. Even for a wasted life fighting against the thought that he that is pure. But all of us are guilty of this to varying degrees. It is the Spirit of the Almighty that has been directly giving inspiration to their spirit from their very beginning. The end of the existence of the body of this flesh comes very quickly. For some of those fortunate enough to enter Hospice having not yet made a decision, they will finally understand the lifelong inspiration from the Almighty to their spirit during these last days. (Job 32:8) To others, the preaching of the cross is still foolishness. And to yet others who already know and love the Lord, the inspiration from the Almighty will flow in unbridled abundance during this time when their spirits come closer and closer to seeing their beloved Savior.

UNDERSTANDING

This special lady Elaine received this overflowing of understanding with great joy. Unfortunately for the Hospice center, she was not there that long. Only three days. And the last two days were very special for her family and the Hospital. The day before she died, a beautiful Christian family came up to her quite large room. Bob and Cindi Carlson and their three children Karissa, Julia and Isaiah, along with a huge harp. They stayed for two hours, with the children singing Christian songs and playing beautiful harp music. The harp was so fitting and special in this setting. There were many positive remarks from many people, even those passing by in the hall, saying they had never witnessed such a beautiful and moving event.

The next night Elaine's family and friends sang Christian songs. And then as they were singing Amazing Grace, suddenly the family became so excited, you would have thought they had all just won the lottery, as they cried out: Mother's gone! This was not a time of mourning, but a homecoming celebration. There was real joy and excitement that would not be considered normal behavior unless you believed what the Judeo-Christian Bible clearly states. However, there was one girl there that proclaimed she was an atheist.

Later she sent a message out on the Internet concerning what she witnessed when Elaine departed. That she wished she could have been part of this feeling of joy and assurance. She said she felt so left out, and isolated. What she did not mention was what happened the day before, in which her spirit was convicted by the Spirit of the Almighty. The spirit of truth touched her heart as no words can.

Elaine would awaken for just a moment to acknowledge someone's presence. As she came in to visit and woke her, Elaine opened her eyes and said, "My dear, do you have Jesus in your heart?" And then she closed her eyes again. This young lady sobbed uncontrollably for a very long, long time. She did not cry - she sobbed. The Holy Spirit is the most convicting force for revealing the presence and reality of the Lord. There are no atheists. Only "professing" atheists, who are engaged in a losing spiritual wrestling match while in this body of flesh. (Eph.6:11-17) How is it possible to deny such a presence? Actually, no one can. You cannot deny truth, only reject it.

Shortly before this event I had about a one-hour conversation with this young lady and her boyfriend, who also professed to be an atheist. That is, believing there is no God or spirits. Both are a nice and intelligent couple. But there was no progress, as they would not budge. So finally I asked them, how about these thousands of authenticated documentations of people in hospitals that apparently die and are later brought back, claiming they saw their own body and then floated to another room, accurately revealing who was there and their conversation? Both repeated the same thing, which is that the human brain is amazing in its capabilities to stir up false illusions. I then repeated that these people accurately saw and heard. This was immaterial to them. Accuracy and truth are the same, just as falsehood and lies. There is but one reasonable possibility: the denying of truth, or the blinding of the minds, being replaced with a lie. This authenticates Eph. 6:12 "Spiritual wickedness in high places."

GEORGIAN

Not being able to deny the special truth of the Gospel, but only reject it was revealed through a very lovely lady named Georgian. This Catholic Nun has called me about three times since my wife's passing, asking how I am doing. And then the conversation eventually gets to the Carlson family, and our celebration of my wife's departure; because of the lasting effect this had at the Hospice center at St. Mary's. This dear lady is such a delight, and her love of the Lord is so evident as she speaks with such joy about him. During one conversation, the subject got to professing atheists. I then asked her if it was true, that it is a terrible thing to witness a professing atheist die? She then told me an amazing story. A story that authenticates that you cannot deny truth, only reject it. This is that special truth, the Son of God.

Georgian had engaged this man, whom I assume was at Hospice as a patient, in conversation where he revealed he was an atheist. And, I presumed, he was quite proud of this fact. This is how Georgian's narrative began as she addressed this man: "Now as you are a college professor at the University of Wisconsin, rather than debate with you whether there is a God or not, I will be as one of your students and bring my pad and pencil and take notes as you state why you know there is no God." The professor agreed to this. So then begin this arrangement of professor and student as she would visit him. He would state all the reasons why there can be no God, and Georgian would quietly write in her pad and say nothing. And as they progressed this professor's wife told Georgian there was a steady and dramatic change in her husband, for the better. There was increasing notability with each teaching seminar he spent with Georgian. And then his wife said he became a new man. She could not believe this transformation; this wonderful transformation which brought great joy to her.

What happened to her husband that brought about this change as he became closer to death? And at the same time, would cause his wife to become so overjoyed? Her husband was a professing atheist, who no doubt for years had pridefully told her how many Christians he had freed from the ignorance and bondage of Christianity. And now there is this Christian nun writing on her pad, as he is actually making an argument for atheism to himself; as he knows he cannot convert or convince this lovely Nun. And as a professor, he has access to information that he knowingly withholds from his students. Pride would not allow him to so much as address the possibility that even one of his students could possibly be correct, that there must be a creator God. And by extension this would make him wrong, which, of course, would be totally unacceptable.

But now he is not only teacher, but also student. Georgian is a student just taking notes. But this student has committed herself to such an extent of acknowledging and knowing this creator God. She has taken vows of marriage to Jesus to the extent that she will marry none other. Of this he is aware. He does not know what she is writing, except she is a believer and is knowledgeable about what he says does not exist. How does anyone get knowledgeable about anything that is not? And to the extent that the one who has this knowledge, quietly takes notes while the other does all the speaking.

This professor became silent for a while. He then asked Georgian to quit writing, stating "I know there is a God." His improved demeanor revealed a new heart long before he professed this to Georgian.

He had entered a realm where pride and arrogance are supreme. And all that was necessary to be freed from this bondage was to embrace truth. This is really quite simple to accomplish: Reject that which is false. Now he is not upholding what he had been taught, as the stakes have eternal consequences. Truth now has special meaning, as there is no one to impress. He, as all of mankind, must honestly look for contradictions and truths. And for this reason (as a teacher) he must carefully choose his words and give great thought to them as never before. As now, he is addressing himself. And it is the most important matter he can address. All else has no real meaning. It is the reason he was created – to be in the image of God. There is another element involved: the Spirit of truth. Man is well aware of this. The word used for this truth is often the conscience of man. (Their conscience bothered them, which restrained them from evil. Or, they are evil because they have no conscience.) This is the spirit of truth given to all of mankind.

It is not just enough to know there is a creator God. The demons and all of mankind know as much. James 2:19 "Thou believes there is one God; you do well. The demons also believe, and tremble." This is not just an intellectual conclusion that decides the outcome. The outcome is based on the overwhelming desire to, more than life itself, spend eternity with this God who sent his only begotten Son to pay the ransom for us. What kind of a God is this, who would die for me? Job 33:24 "Then he is gracious unto him and says, 'Deliver him from going down to the pit. I have found a ransom.'"

This desire to become as one with this special truth overrides pride itself. Very shortly this truth that cannot be denied confronts all of mankind. Along with the understanding that he has been rejecting what his heart has always known. But for him to then have this dramatic change, there must be more than just knowing there is a God. There must be a verbal confession of this ultimate truth. Matt. 10:32-34 "Whosoever therefore shall confess me before men, him will

I confess before my Father, who is in heaven. - But whosoever shall deny me before men, him will I also deny before my father, who is in heaven. - Think not that I am come to send peace on earth. I came not to send peace, but a sword."

This last verse was not left out, because this is what defines Christians. They are taken through the fire to purify them as gold and harden them as steel. This writer finds a similar event concerning the Lord Jesus. An event where the teachers also needed teaching. This was when the religious leaders brought before Jesus a woman taken in adultery. Instead of writing on a pad, he wrote on the ground.

John 8:4-11 "They said to him, 'Master, this woman was taken in adultery, in the very act. - Now Moses, in the law, commanded us that such should be stoned; what say you?' - This they said, testing him, that they might accuse him. But Jesus stooped down, and with his finger wrote on the ground. – When they continued asking him, he stood up, and said to them, 'Whosoever is without sin cast the first stone at her.' - And he again stooped down, and wrote on the ground. - And they that heard it, being convicted by their own conscience, went out one by one; and Jesus was left alone with the woman. - Then said Jesus, 'Where are your accusers? Has no man condemned you?' - She said 'No man, Lord.' And Jesus said, 'Neither do I condemn you. Go, and sin no more.'"

These final words to this woman; "Go, and sin no more". These words would be devastating to the professor. As how could he make right this evil he had done? As shortly he must meet his maker whom he has not only denied, but because of his position, bullied these students to reject and deny him. This is the sin in which he has not only denied the Lord before men, but has incorporated this in his position, in his life's work. This we know, as he confronted Georgian proudly. Was it to boast of his lifelong accomplishments to this lady as perhaps his last chance to offend the Lord? This revealed the grace and love of the Lord and Georgian in never giving up on this man.

There must have been such sorrow for these wasted years specifically targeting Christian students. He must have wept bitterly at the realization of the evil he had done. This writer is convinced that he did just that. Had he not, his demeanor would not have changed in such a dramatic fashion. As much as this must have bothered him, he also realized the magnitude of this love that revealed what the

Lord has done. This what defines God. This light far outshines any darkness. And all have sinned.

Just as Peter did, after he had denied Jesus the third time; exactly as Jesus said he would. Matt. 26:69-75 "A maid came to Peter, saying 'Thou also was with Jesus of Galilee.' - But he denied it before them all, saying, 'I know not what you are saying.' - Then another maid saw him, and said to them that were there, 'This fellow was also with Jesus of Nazareth.' - And again, he denied with an oath, 'I do not know the man.' - After a while others said to Peter, 'Surely you are one of them, for your speech betrays you.' - Then he began to curse and swear, saying, 'I know not this man.' And immediately the cock crowed. - And Peter remembered the words of Jesus, who had said to him, 'Before the cock crows, you shall deny me three times'. And he went out and wept bitterly."

It is interesting to note that with each denial of the Lord, this brought a greater and more emphatic denial, which finished with his cursing and swearing. Does not reason suggest the Lord is revealing that each compromise or denial of him widens this breach to the point of becoming an enemy? This clearly reveals spiritual warfare that is gaining control. And to break this control requires a complete and dramatic awareness of what they have done.

Most all that come to know the Lord go through a cleansing of joy. A part of this is uncontrollable sobbing, which is better defined as tears of joy. Words cannot define this joy of unspeakable kindness that has been received from their Lord.

Because of the change in this professor, it is obvious he received Jesus as Lord and Savior. He is completely forgiven of all sins. The joy of receiving and knowing the Lord completely overshadowed his own failings. How can one dwell on one's own self after coming to know the Lord? Were this professor's life to be prolonged, he would no doubt with joy proceed to try to rectify this evil he had done. But few of us can do this.

CHAPTER 34

SPIRITUAL WARFARE

Eph. 6:11-17 "Put on the whole armor of God, that you may be able to withstand the wiles of the devil. - For we wrestle not against flesh and blood, but against principalities, against powers, against the rulers of darkness of this world, against spiritual wickedness in high places. - Wherefore, take unto you the whole armor of God, that you may be able to withstand in the evil day, and having done all, to stand. - Stand, therefore, having your loins girdled about with truth, and having the breastplate of righteousness, - And your feet shod with the preparation of the gospel of peace; - Above all, taking the shield of faith, with which you will be able to quench all the fiery darts of the wicked. - And take the helmet of salvation, and the sword of the Spirit, which is the word of God."

As we see, the Lord is revealing that this wrestling match is spiritual. This should not come as a surprise, as the essence of man is spirit; spending but a short season in this body of flesh, a body that will return to the earth. This is difficult to put in its proper perspective as there are so many that envision and proclaim spiritual warfare as where they test their spiritual strength against Satan. Commanding and demanding him in the name of Jesus. Special insight is recorded in the book of Jude. Jude 1:9 "Yet Michael, the archangel, when contending for the body of Moses, dared not bring against him a railing accusation, but said, 'The Lord rebuke you.'"

Satan, the chief of fallen angels, and Michael, one of the chief angels, were contending for the *living* body of Moses, not his dead body. Satan, in order to misdirect him, and Michael, as a ministering spirit sent to minister to one of God's special heirs of salvation. It also is seen that Michael's actions are in line with following the Lord's directions. Why did Michael dare not bring against Satan a railing accusation? Because it is not ours or Michael's will that we want to impose on the world. It is the Lord's purpose that we desire.

This is why our spiritual battles are defined as wrestling, and not warfare. The only offensive weapon at our disposal is the word of God, along with the admonition to take on the whole armor of God. For that reason, Christians dare not accuse the world. It is the Lord that takes our greatest righteousness, which are as filthy rags, and cleanses them. Yes, we are to rebuke, but as sinners we dare not make railing accusations.

In the same way, it is the word of God proclaiming there is but one way to life, which is believing on the Son of God. This includes all religions. So a question comes up: Where in the world did this political and religious correctness come from? And does the Bible identify this source? Yes, the Bible does so, and constantly. In the 6th chapter of Ephesians it names one source that occupies two places: Against the rulers of the darkness of this world, and spiritual wickedness in high places.

ONE TRUTH

There is only one religion or truth, and the rejection or acceptance of this truth. The Lord has given us enough information that this can be understood. But there are literally thousands of religions. What will be offered in as short a time as possible, using the Bible and the Law of non-contradiction, is an explanation of Christianity. We will start with the creation of the heavens, earth, and man, in which the angels rejoiced. This was recorded in the book of Job, believed to be the oldest book in the Bible. Job 38:4,7 "Where were you when I laid the foundations of the earth? - When the morning stars (angels) sang together, and all the sons of God shouted for joy."

All angels in heaven know with absolute awareness of who Jesus is. They know he is the prophesied Messiah who was crucified, rose from the dead, ascended to heaven, and will return to the earth and judge man and angels. We know this because the demons themselves affirmed this. Demons are cast out, fallen angels. Matt. 8:28-29 "The demons cried out, – 'What have we to do with you Jesus, the Son of God? Are you come to torment us before the time?'"

SPIRITUAL POWER

This writer has little understanding of this spiritual world, and the Lord has made it clear man is not to search out this kingdom directly. That is inquiring directly from this world to reach the spirit world. The term often used from those who ignore the Lord is that they are 'obtaining extra spiritual knowledge'. Jewish scholars have for years done this very thing, to their own detriment. This special, extra school of thought or learning comes from what is called "spiritual wickedness in high places". "The rulers of the darkness of this world" is referring this same element, but through men of this world. (Eph. 6:12) This is the source of what is defined as extra spiritual knowledge. Satan is the god of this world, and Christians are not of this world.

KABBALAH - (CABBALAH)

Webster's dictionary defines this Jewish school of learning as the Kabbalah. This an actual teaching and learning, which Webster's Dictionary defines as such. If possible, it is suggested that you look up these words as given in Webster's Dictionary: "A medieval and modern system of theosophy, mysticism, and thaumaturgy marked by belief in creation through emanation and a cipher method of interpreting scripture." The knowledge from these teachings comes from entering an altered state of consciousness. New converts are not discouraged from entering into these altered states of consciousness. When praying or inquiring of the Lord, your mind and thoughts should be very clear. (It is difficult to obtain an actual time frame of this spiritual inquiring.) The 5th And 6th Century is given.

When it actually started was much earlier, as recorded in the book of Judges. This was shortly after Joshua led the Israelites out of the wilderness as they began to occupy the land Abraham was promised. They were not to mix with the occupants of the land, as their worship involved this spiritual wickedness in high places. Judges 2:11-13 "And the children of Israel did evil in the sight of the Lord, and served Balaam. - And they forsook the Lord God of their fathers, who brought them out of the land of Egypt, and followed other gods of the people who were round about them and provoked the Lord to anger. - And they forsook the Lord and served Baal and Ashtaroth."

SOURCE OF EVOLUTION AND BIG BANG

Look up the meaning of these confusing words to establish a discipline of verifying the accuracy of this very important revelation: there is only one truth. And a single entity against this truth. What these words reveal is a wide range of confusion, even to mixing miracles and magic together, involving evolution that must start with a Big Bang of disorder to evolve. It does not address if God caused the Big Bang, or simply used it. The teachings of the Kabbalah are evolution (Theosophy). This is also the teaching of Buddhist and Brahman theories of evolution. These are used to advance pantheistic evolution, or reincarnation. These eastern religions, voodooist, etc. and the Kabbalah all get their information from the same source.

THE LIE

Western society has for years prided themselves, using both Charles Darwin and science, in freeing man from the ignorance of the Judeo-Christian Bible and the myth of creation. Both statements are in error. The laws of science prove there must be a creator God. Not only to create, but to sustain creation. And centuries before Darwin, the Kabbalah and Eastern mysticism were well entrenched with this deception received from the father of lies.

Does not reason reveal that all of this knowledge comes from the same forbidden source? This is the same source that the Lord strictly warns against inquiring of. And as Jesus states that Satan is a liar with no truth in him, would not this also affirm this to be a lie? The more one searches for truth using the law of non-contradiction, the greater the affirmation there is but one truth, and but one lie to distract from this truth. It would seem man is being tested and tried. And this test is not that difficult to pass.

With a very unusual twist, those who fail the test seem to have an awareness of those who pass the test, even before they are graded. And this in itself reveals there is one truth… a *rejection* of, not ignorance, of this special truth. This includes a wide range of rejection, from rage and anger to indifference. This extends to those who wish they could have the special joy and peace of those who believe. Christianity cannot be ignored. A just God will not let man ignore his Son; just as the spiritual forces in this world cannot. This is increasingly becoming evident.

OCCULT PRESENCE INCREASING

There isn't much need to explain witchcraft, voodooist and other occultist practices, as TV and movies are awash with this. And those that engage in such practices are open in their purpose. And that purpose is to contact these spirits. Why does this change into a religion when reaching to these spirits for guidance? The Lord calls this evil. So what is the difference? Or is there any?

HOLY SPIRIT

This is a completely opposite spirit from the Holy Spirit of the Bible. He is called the Comforter and the Spirit of truth, whom the world cannot receive. The Lord sends the Spirit of truth, and he testifies of Jesus. And he comforts, not controls. John 15:26 "When the Comforter is come, whom I will send unto you from the Father, even the Spirit of truth, who proceeds from the Father, he will testify of me."

Christianity is an extension of the Old Testament's promises and the fulfillment of them through the promises of the coming Messiah. This is given through the prophets of God. Any contact with this spirit world will deny or diminish Jesus. But the word of God more than affirms that Jesus is the Son and Word of God. Rev. 19:10 "Worship God; for the testimony of Jesus is the spirit of prophesy." The prophetic book Isaiah defines fallen man. Isaiah 64:6 "We are all as an unclean thing, and all our righteousness are as filthy rags."

What effect will that understanding have upon man? This all depends on their hearts. The more people are convinced or convicted of the reality of the cross and its necessity, the more it will affect them. This truth can only be revealed to them if the reality and truth of Jesus is absolute to them. Then, and only then, can the enormity of this sacrifice be understood. Then a question arises: How is it possible that those who believe these things are correct? That is, as it is revealed that their greatest righteousness are as filthy rags? As it would be devastating.

But this is not a reality, and is meaningless until the Holy Spirit reveals the righteousness, beauty, and love of Jesus, the Son of God. So, with the awareness and belief that this is the heart of the God who created the whole world and all that is, how can man be devastated when confronted with this presence and sacrifice? Our heart is overtaken and consumed, no longer with self, but with the Lord. It is then that our minds become engaged in this spiritual wrestling match.

CHAPTER 35

ONE GOD - ONE TRUTH

What defines a Christian is they have no doubt that the Bible is the word of God, with no error, no deception, and absolute truth. We have the word of prophesy announced in writing, hundreds and thousands of years before it happens. This defines the creator God as the Alpha and Omega. Rev. 22:13 "I am Alpha and Omega, the beginning and the end, the first and the last." The fullness and enormity of this is incomprehensible to man. Along with this is what this writer calls the law of non-contradiction; just as sure as irrefutable prophesy. Oftentimes well-meaning men have agreed with men who reject part of God's words. Often because theologians before them were in error. We are to inquire of hard to understand scripture with the help of the Spirit of the Almighty, whom Jesus calls the Comforter, the Spirit of Truth. This is really quite simple to understand. If it doesn't make sense, the Lord is revealing something special to special people. Ask the Lord.

Daniel himself said in Dan. 12:8-10 "I heard, but understood not. Then said I, 'O my Lord, what shall be the end of these things?' - And he said, 'Go thy way, Daniel. For the words are closed and sealed till the time of the end. - Many shall be purified and made white, and tested, but the wicked shall do wickedly, and none of the wicked shall understand, but the wise shall understand.'"

As there is but one God, there is but one truth. Therefore, the rejection of truth is the rejection of the God of truth. All of man's religions must therefore be false. And as "we but know in part" this would include, to various degrees, all Christian churches. There is only one thing that man can do. And that is to believe there is such a God that so loved the world that he gave his only begotten Son, that whosoever believes in him will have everlasting life. There is nothing man can do to receive salvation but believe.

The very definition of God demands absolute perfection. If these things are true, God's eternal kingdom must also be pure. Only He who is pure can purify. For there to be such a kingdom, it must be also defined. This has been done though the prophets of God. No other religions use prophets, as very quickly they will be exposed as false. The gospel of salvation is written for the solitary purpose of revealing the coming Messiah of God. This is written with over 120 clear and distinct prophesies; including that Jesus Christ must die, and then rise from the dead. This also authenticates that he himself will raise the dead, and has the authority to do so. This Messiah is revealed as the express image of God, in the person of his only begotten Son who went to the cross as the only possibility to affirm this truth. The innocent dying for the guilty... the just for the unjust.

This is incorporated with prophetic and scientific proofs, which have barely been touched on here. The greatest proof is that which touches the heart of man. And it is this which ultimately reveals the spirit of man. This choice, which our heart alone makes, defines what we desire to be.

We will continue with this orderly chain of events which confirm one another. This is with the full knowledge that volumes more could be written. The Bible confirms this Law of non-contradiction, starting with the first two chapters of the word of God. And by believing that these are indeed the words of God, this special law of non-contradiction becomes more evident. There is only one way the truths that will be presented here can be understood, or made sense of. It is only if those that are pursuing hard-to-understand scriptures pertaining to these two births, or creations, believe that they are true. These scriptures span 6,000 years.

THE PROMISE AND ASSURANCE

God created man to be in his own image. The created have the freedom to reject or accept what God has created them to be. Gen.1:26-27 "And God said, 'Let *us* make man in *our* image, after *our* likeness.' - God created man in his *own* image, in the image of God created he him, male and female created he them." But if man was created in the image of God, it would be impossible for man to sin. And the Bible is clear that there is none righteous. No, not one. This understanding does not cause a problem, but is the start of solving and revealing a special Lord beyond comprehension. And only because of our assurance in the word.

During this combining of scriptures, be mindful of one of God's attributes. Rev. 1:8 "'I am Alpha and Omega, the beginning and the ending', says the Lord, who is, and who was, and who is to come, the Almighty." God is beyond time. It is stated in Genesis chapter 1 that God created them male and female and in his own image. John 4:24 "God is Spirit; and they that worship him must worship him in spirit and in truth." So as man is flesh, and a sinner, therefore man cannot fully worship God in truth... and is not in his image.

Then in the next chapter we have God (singular) forming man of the dust of the earth. Also note that it is God alone that formed man. There is no "us" or "our" involved in this creation. Nor is there female created or formed. Gen. 2:7 "And the Lord God formed man of the dust of the ground, and breathed into his nostrils the breath of life, and man became a living soul." This living soul is life, along with consciousness or awareness. This is what the Lord has given to all flesh. Ecclesiastes 3:21 "Who knows the spirit of man that goes upward, and the spirit of the beast that goes downward to the earth?" No creatures were made in God's image, and all need the breath of life to become living souls.

God is Spirit, whereas man is spirit and flesh, the same as all of created life. But the spirit of man goes upward (continues after death). In 1st Thessalonians 5:23, Paul wrote concerning Christians keeping moral standards, "And the very God of peace sanctify you wholly; and I pray God your whole spirit and soul and body be preserved blameless unto the coming of our Lord Jesus Christ."

We have clarified here that Jesus, as the God of peace, sanctified the believers completely. He purified this body of flesh from all sin from the beginning of our life, to be preserved blameless onto a specific time. That time will be the coming of our Lord. This will be verified with other scriptures shortly. But first Jesus will make clarity concerning the two different births, or creations.

John 3:1-5 "There was a man of the Pharisees, named Nicodemus, a ruler of the Jews. - The same came to Jesus by night, and said unto him, 'Rabbi, we know you are a teacher come from God. For no man can do the miracles that you do except God be with him.' - Jesus said unto him, 'Unless a man be born again, he cannot see the kingdom of God.' - Nicodemus said, 'How can a man be born when he is old? Can he enter a second time into his mother's womb?' - Jesus answered, 'Verily, verily I say to you, Except a man be born of water and of the Spirit, he cannot enter the kingdom of God.'"

First, Jesus said to Nicodemus that he could not *see* the Kingdom of God until he is born again. Then he said he could not *enter* the Kingdom of God unless he was born of water and of the Spirit. Christians use this term. They are born again when they accept Jesus as Lord and Savior. It is at this time they are aware of, or see, the Kingdom of God. But they do not *enter* the Kingdom of God until they are born of water and of the Spirit. Which will happen at a clearly defined time.

This birth of the Spirit is the completeness of what was done in the very first chapter of the Bible. Let us make man in our image - After our likeness - Male and female. All of the Godhead is involved in this specific time or event of Jesus' coming. This writer believes being born of the water involves more than the water birth, as the word of God is often referred to as the water of life and the word of life. But you must be completely cleansed to enter the kingdom of God.

There are a few more scriptures that will be used here that will make clarity of this' the most momentous change in the life of mankind. A time expressed in 1st Cor. 2:9 "Eye has not seen, nor ear heard, nor has entered the heart of man, the things God has prepared for those that love him."

When God created man, it was stated in his word "Let <u>us</u> make man after <u>our</u> image, after <u>our</u> likeness." This reveals an extension of much more than just Jesus creating. There is an extra involvement that includes man being spirit. Also, he made them male and female. Thus, "created he *them*" in Chapter 1. As we carefully examine Chapter 2, God (singular) formed man out of the dust of the ground. There is no mention of female, who was later taken from the rib of Adam. Had the Bible stated male *and* female were formed, as it was so stated male and female were created in Chapter 1, there would be a contradiction. What we have is not a contradiction, but an attention getter. To those who know the Bible is truth, this will get their attention because of these little truths or clues that can be so easily missed.

Chapter 36

Believers Changed

This specific moment in God's timetable which Jesus spoke to Nicodemus about – when man will enter the Kingdom of God – is also the moment that mankind will be changed. Not to the express image of God, but after his likeness, in his image. This specific time is referred to as the rapture, or taking away, or gathering of the Church to meet the Lord in the air, as Jesus comes from the heavens for them. 1st Cor. 15:51-54 "Behold, I show you a mystery: We shall not all sleep, but we all will be changed, - In a moment, in the twinkling of an eye, at the last trump; for the trumpet shall sound, and the dead in Christ shall be raised incorruptible, and we shall be changed. - For this corruptible must put on incorruption, and this mortal must put on immortality. - So, when this corruptible shall have put on incorruption, and this mortal shall have put on immortality, then shall be brought to pass the saying that is written, 'Death is swallowed up in victory.'"

1st Thes. 4:13-17 "I would not have you to be ignorant, brethren, concerning them who are asleep, that you sorrow not, even as those who have no hope. - For if we believe that Jesus died and rose again, even so them who also sleep in Jesus will God bring with him. - For this we say unto you by the word of the Lord, that we who are alive and remain unto the coming of the Lord shall not precede them who are asleep. - For the Lord himself shall descend from heaven with a shout, with the voice of the archangel, and the trump of God; and the dead in Christ shall rise first; - Then we who are alive and remain shall be caught up together with them in the clouds, to meet to Lord in the air; and so shall we ever be with the Lord."

The exact moment in which the believers will be changed will be when they see the Lord. We are told the dead in Christ shall see him in the blinking of an eye before the living do, and will be changed to be as he is. Since hundreds and thousands of years can separate the sleeping, or dead, saints from those who are raptured while living, this brings a question. Where were these deceased saints, and what kind of body do they have before being changed? They could not have been changed to *be* as he is, as that will not happen until they *see* him as he is.

1st John 3:2 "Beloved, now we are the children of God, and it does not appear what we shall be. But we know that when he shall appear, we shall be like him; for we shall see him as he is." Exactly what does this mean? We cannot now see the Lord as he is, because this ability to see Jesus in his fullness cannot be accomplished until we are given new eyes and understanding. We must be changed for this to happen. And because we will be changed when we see him, it is then that we will see him as he is. This will occur when born again Christians are changed when they meet the Lord in the air at his coming for them.

GULLIBILITY

So many reject the Bible as the word of God because of not questioning biblical events that appear to contradict others. When you have complete belief, there is a real assurance. This is faith. Christians are to search out all of God's words with absolute assurance that they *are* God's words. 1st Thes.5:21 "Prove all things and hold fast that what is good." Unfortunately, there is this odd belief that it is a lack of faith to question those few scriptures that appear unreasonable or contradict other scriptures. However, the Lord has especially inserted them for those who have a strong faith in the word of God. Because of the assurance that the Bible is the word of God, by searching out these scriptures the Lord can enter into what evolves into conversation as insight and faith are increased.

To blindly accept as truth that which you believe in your mind is contradiction. This is not faith, but gullibility. And it diminishes your ability to understand or properly proclaim the gospel. But the closer you examine scripture that appears to contradict, just the opposite happens. The Lord reveals truth to special people who have a loyalty to God's words. And not the whims of unfaithful man, to gain their favor for a season. These truths which are eternal cannot be revealed unless there is assurance. "All scripture is given by inspiration of God, and is profitable for doctrine, for reproof, for correction, for instruction in righteousness." (2nd Tim. 3:16) This can never be realized unless there is absolute confidence the Bible is the word of God.

Few to none have access, time nor the education to search out every accusation against the Bible. And why would you waste your time? The Bible can be proven correct in investigating, say, 100 events. But then a false accusation is made. And then it is found out, after much digging, the Bible was correct after all. There is never an apology, only a new accusation of error. This accusing continues from the same element or group constantly. Soon we have a total of 110 false accusations, all of which have been proven false. What is never mentioned is that the false accusers will be 100% wrong. Reason reveals a rather bankrupt logic in even considering the words of anyone who is never right. This writer encourages the questioning and proving of all the Bible, all the time. This should be done by believers and non-believers.

What have been given as examples here are these two creations spanning six thousand years in the first book, Genesis, Chapters 1 and 2. And in the last book, Revelation 12, there are two events of angels being cast out, spanning two thousand years. Both are usually stated as single events, or ignored, or considered as contradictions. There are many more. And then we have the rejection, and ridicule of creation.

This, even as the advancements of science affirm there must be a creator God. But these evolutionists are not embarrassed by their insistence that all there is was created by a speck that exploded. Contradicting all laws of science concerning Matter and Life, this also includes logic, reason and common sense. And because science has proven evolution to be such a bankrupt theory, there is now a new or expanded theory which attributes creation to ancient aliens or astronauts. Completely ignoring the question: Where did they originate? The gullibility of man is amazing. Just as the demons know there is one God, and tremble, so all of mankind knows there is a creator God. And they are all without excuse.

It is really an embarrassment to deem it necessary to even address both the Big Bang and Evolutionary theories. But both are being taught in our schools, and not by ignorant people. This both presents and answers a lot of questions. How can it be that all of these intelligent people are wrong? This really plays on the mind of a lot of people. As after all, would not all want to believe there is eternal life? But then another strange worldwide phenomenon is evident. The so-called uneducated people of the world completely accept this spirit world with a God or gods.

PURPOSE

Does it not seem that there is a testing and trying of mankind? And then there is the Judeo-Christian Bible that gives historical and prophetic statements to prove its reliability. But most of all, why did this world find it necessary to kill the prophets of God? And then, to kill the Son of God who healed the sick, opened the ears of the deaf, and eyes of the blind; and did harm to no one? And then we have constant attempts to wipe tiny Israel off the face of the earth, and to make sure that no Israelites exist. And it seems that the only people who object to this are Bible believing Christians. And of course, Israelites. It should not be necessary to point out there is confusion and blindness, with an evil that is growing in this world. And it is evident that it is very specific. These events reveal intelligence to determine, with positive testing, where the heart lies. There is something else concerning this word of God. It is quite clear that the greatest enemy is self, and the greatest friend is God.

The answer to combating this evil is first being able to recognize it. Again, the Bible reveals this evil and gives the only way to defend oneself against it. It *can* be defeated, and it is revealed that it is an absolute necessity to begin with self. Ephesians 6:12 "We wrestle not against flesh and blood, but spiritual wickedness."

There are some victories, and it is called upon us to stand and fight for that which is pure. This is really quite simple. There is only one thing that is pure in this world: the word of God. Just because the world is offended at these words, must we be fearful of offending this world? Of course, the world is offended. And this will increase with greater frequency, until there are only two images that will define man. And what's more, none will be able to say "I didn't know."

What is amazing is that even with our children being targeted specifically, it is still impossible to convince anyone, including children, that there is no God. So what must be done is to denigrate the Bible as being reliable. Theories of science must be made up that conflict with the laws of science, as all laws of science reveal that matter and life require a creator God. This in itself reveals the justice and grace of God, as it takes very little effort to recognize nonsense.

Does not reason, to the point of being obvious, reveal someone or something is involved in this rejection of their creator? And since it is impossible to convince anyone there is no God, the obvious ploy is to remove credibility of the Judeo-Christian Bible. Christians are constantly being tried and tested, and this is as the Lord promised. In school, students are tested to ascertain what they know and are able to apply. There is a much greater test applied by our Lord. And you do not need to be an A student to pass with flying colors. How much longer will it be before this nation will be tried and tested as in North Korea and other Communists nations, or especially Muslim nations, where to affirm Jesus the Creator as Lord and Savior often requires the ultimate sacrifice? But always requires the loss of worldly comforts, to beatings and imprisonment.

All of mankind is tested and tried. Let us therefore continue with this taking away of the saints, fit to enter God's Kingdom. There a specific time in the not too distant future when the Lord will show unbelievable grace and love toward a world that continues to reject God's word, and at an accelerated rate. One of the reasons the rapture is rejected is because of this question: what kind of body do these deceased Old Testament and New Testament saints have now?

SOUL SLEEP

What happens to the souls of those who died hundreds and thousands of years before this? After they died, do they enter into a soul sleep until the Lord comes to give them a new body? Many hold this view. The Bible does not answer the kind of body that

Christians occupy immediately after death. As we are told, it has not even entered into the heart of man what we will be. This would include before the rapture. It appears there is a recognition ability in place beyond our present capabilities. At the transfiguration on the mount, when Moses and Elijah appeared to Jesus in the presence of Peter, James and John, they recognized both of them. (Matt.17:1-4) Then Jesus appeared for 40 days after his resurrection. In Luke 24:31, the term used when they then recognized Jesus was "and their eyes were opened".

Jesus spoke of Lazarus and the rich man, in which Lazarus was taken to a place called Abraham's bosom. And then Revelation 6:9-11 "And when he had opened the fifth seal, I saw under the altar the souls of them slain for the word of God, and for the testimony which they held. - And they cried with a loud voice, saying, 'How long, O Lord, holy and true, do you not judge and avenge our blood on them who dwell on the earth?' - And white robes were given unto every one of them, and it was said to them that they should rest for a little season, until their fellow servants also and their brethren, that should be killed as they were, should be fulfilled."

It is clear there is no such thing as soul sleep, but a rest, and in a much better place; with an apparent awareness of what is going on. As they will also be changed. This writer does not know what believers will be changed to. Except that it will no doubt be an improvement on our present bodies. But it will not be this body, which is not fit to enter the Kingdom of Heaven. This will happen only after the gathering of the saints to meet the Lord in the air.

CHAPTER 37

THREE AND A HALF YEARS OF GRACE

Does the Bible reveal when this mystery of the ages, and the very purpose for the creation of man will take place? Are there any specific clues or a string of events leading up to this, the most glorious climatic event in human history? (Following the resurrection of Jesus the Christ, which makes all this possible.) The answer to that would have to be a resounding yes. And it would be logically proceeded with a worldwide preaching of Jesus as Lord and Savior; with a nonstop testimony of Jesus, happening from the same Jerusalem where our Lord was crucified. Then the mystery of God will be revealed with an uninterrupted and unbelievable clarity, as the grace of God is clearly seen and heard. And yet, it will be vehemently rejected by many. This will continue for the three and a half years in which the Lord's two witnesses will prophesy. There will be none who can dispute their words, because of the special miracles and plagues by his two servants. All of this will happen from Israel, as all the world will hear them speak in their own language. This will be in the same manner as the day of Pentecost, when all heard, in their own language, words spoken in a language foreign to them.

THE TEMPLE OF GOD

Rev. 10:10-11 "And I took the little scroll out of the angel's hand and ate it up. And it was in my mouth sweet as honey, and as soon as

I had eaten it, my belly was bitter. - And he said unto me, 'You must prophesy again about many peoples, and nations, and tongues, and kings.'" Rev. 11:1-2 "And there was given unto him a reed like a rod; and the angel stood, saying, 'Rise, and measure the temple of God, and the altar, and them that worship in it. - But the court, which is outside the temple, leave out, and measure it not; for it is given unto the nations, and the holy city shall they tread under foot for forty and two months (three and a half years).'"

The angel told John to measure the temple of God. This was to confirm or authenticate this special time; the very purpose for man's creation. The temple of God being measured are the saints measured or being made white, to become of the image of God. 1st Cor. 3:16 "Know you not that you are the temple of God, and the Spirit of God dwells in you?" And of course, those who are outside the temple are the world that has rejected the word of God. Now as for the bitterness in his belly that follows the sweetness: The sweetness is the washing of those soon made white, to the gathering of the saints to meet the Lord in the air. Their corruption becomes incorruption and mortality becomes immortality as they are born again, to be in the image of God. And the bitterness is what then follows. Three and one half years of unimaginable terror, as a far more different image fills this world.

GOD'S TWO WITNESSES

Rev. 11:3-12 "And I will give power to my two witnesses. And they will prophesy for a thousand two hundred and threescore days (three and a half years), clothed in sackcloth. - These are the two olive trees, and two lampstands (Zechariah 4:2-3) standing before the God of the earth. (The translators put a large G in God where perhaps a small g would be more proper.) - And if any man should hurt them, fire proceeds from their mouths and devours their enemies; and if any man will hurt them, he must in this manner be killed. - These have power to shut heaven, that it rain not in the days of their prophesy; and have power over waters to turn them to blood, and to smite the earth with all plagues, as often as they will. - And when they have finished their testimony, the beast that ascends out of the bottomless pit shall make war with them, and overcome them, and kill them. - And their dead bodies shall lie in the street of the great city, which spiritually is called Sodom and Egypt, where also our Lord was crucified. - And they of the peoples and kindreds and tongues and nations shall see their dead bodies three days and a half, and shall not permit their dead bodies to be put in graves. - And they that dwell on the earth shall rejoice over them, and make merry, and shall send gifts one to another, because these two prophets tormented them that dwell on the earth. - And after three days and a half the spirit of life from God entered into them, and they stood upon their feet, and great fear fell upon them who saw them. - And they heard a great voice from heaven saying unto them, 'Come up here.' And they ascended up to heaven in a cloud, and their enemies beheld them."

THE WICKED ONE REVEALED

Now that he is no longer hindered, this man of sin shall be revealed. The two witnesses of the Lord are visibly taken to the heavens after lying dead in the streets of Jerusalem. Those dwelling on the earth shall rejoice for three and a half days after their deaths. They will make merry, sending gifts one to another, because these two prophets tormented them. The people's minds were, no doubt, also on the Christians worldwide who aligned themselves with the two witnesses, and who had also testified these things were so. Then those very Christians who had been testifying of the Lord were taken at that same moment. But perhaps not visibly seen rising. And all the nations of this world will be well aware of their sudden disappearance at that same moment of time. And because of the gospel that had been given during the last three and a half years, they will know exactly where the Christians went, and why.

And great fear fell upon this world as they stood upon their feet, and then after a voice from heaven called them. Rev. 11:13 "And the same hour was there a great earthquake, and the tenth part of the city fell, and in the earthquake, were slain seven thousand men. And the remaining were terrified and gave glory to the God of heaven." The events which take place, beginning with the two prophets of God standing on their feet, taken visually to the heavens, and then the earthquake... all of these caused fear, then terror, and then giving glory to the God of heaven. All of mankind knows what is going on, in which one of two choices are to be made. Give glory to the God of heaven, or rejoice for a season over those two dead bodies.

ALL THE WORLD KNOWS

Job 32:8 “There is a spirit in man; and the inspiration of the Almighty gives them understanding.” In the next chapter, Job 33, it is then revealed as to when and how this information is given to man, and what this information is. This given to the spirit of all of mankind. Not one can say “I never knew.” All of mankind left on this earth are now given a choice as to whose image to be of.

It was stated here that God’s grace would be poured out at this time as probably never before. This is not just during the first three and a half, but the entire seven years. There could possibly be a greater harvest in the last three and a half, in which the two witnesses of God, and the rest of the believers who were affirming their words, abruptly depart. We will now examine this world and these last three and a half years.

WHY?

A question should be asked. Why, in the very last days just before the return of Jesus, would God send his two prophets to torment the world while testifying of Jesus... instead of showing his love, compassion, forgiveness, and mercy? There are no doubt many reasons. What comes to mind is the number of prophets who were killed. Luke 6:22-23 ‘Blessed are you, when men shall hate you, and when they separate you from their company, and shall reproach you, and cast out your name as evil, for the Son of man’s sake. - Rejoice you in that day, and leap for joy; for behold, your reward is great in heaven. For in like manner did their fathers unto the prophets.” Luke 11:46-48 “Woe onto you also, you lawyers (Interpreters of the law of the Bible)... Woe unto you; for you build the sepulchers of the prophets, and your fathers killed them. - Truly you bear witness that you allow the deeds of your fathers; for they indeed killed them, and you build their sepulchers.”

There was a constant effort to kill Elijah, but he was taken up to heaven, as was Enoch. And then the Savior himself came with a ministry of peace, compassion and righteousness. There were healings and miracles in which there were large eager crowds who had a desire to make him king. Then the Roman soldiers arrested him at the insistence of the Jewish leaders. And later, after examining him, Pontus Pilate asked, "What has he done? I find no fault in him at all." No one could answer what he was guilty of. They just wanted him dead. Pilate wanted to free Jesus, and the mob wanted to crucify him. And as he asked, "Why? What has he done?" they cried all the more, "Crucify him, crucify him!" Jesus preached love, peace, and forgiveness, and opened the eyes of the blind and ears of the deaf. He even raised the dead. He harmed no one. And the countless miracles that were done by him attested to his divine origin and compassion.

Yes, Jesus was embraced by all, except by most of the religious leaders. But as soon as the power of the government was exerted and revealed an apparent control over him, almost all of the people then rejected him. It became, and becomes, quite clear that the acceptance of Jesus has nothing to do with what defines who *he* is. But rather, what defines mankind are the benefits they will receive from him at the moment. And when that is taken away from them, there is anger. Not at the evil which was beating and about to kill Jesus, who is pure. Rather, anger that Jesus would not use his obvious power to rule, and that they would receive miraculous foods and healings and other benefits with him as their king. He has, in their minds, betrayed them, as now they are being denied their desires.

But the Lord wanted to give them far greater than that which fades away. He wanted to give *himself.* And those who understand this, receive it… for eternity. This is the understanding that the inspiration of the Almighty gives to all of mankind. Few receive the enormity of this special understanding. That explains why the preaching of the cross is foolishness to them that perish. But to us who are saved it is the power of God.

As we enter this special time of God's two witnesses, all on the earth will be well aware of this reality of the gospel and the promised coming rapture of the Church. They will soon be eyewitnesses to it. And as we explore Revelation chapter 13, what will be revealed is the heart of man being exposed, both the wise and the foolish.

This 13th chapter of Revelation covers the last seven years before Jesus returns to establish his everlasting kingdom. There will be an effort to identify symbolisms in as simple a fashion as possible, using scriptures and common sense. This is based on the assurance that the Bible will not, and cannot, contradict itself. Any apparent contradiction is specifically put there for the purpose to get the attention of those who know there can be no error in God's word. These end time words are not given for sensationalism, but to affirm the reliability and commonsense of the word of God. When no preconceived teachings or speculations are accepted, it is amazing how the Bible interprets itself. But only if it is believed that the word of God is exactly that; the Word of God.

CHAPTER 38

THE IMAGE OF THE BEAST

It is of utmost importance that there is a clear identification of who and what the beasts are. What is being identified, and for what purpose? There are two men in Revelation 13 that are identified as beasts. Both Daniel and Revelation use various animals and beasts to identify nations at different time periods. It is up to us to make any connection or conclusion. But the most important identification of the beast is Satan himself. This process is made easier, if it can be understood that Satan has many names. All are used to identify him. The identification as the Beast has greater ramifications for Christians than any other name that identifies him.

Revelation 13:1-3 "I stood on the sand of the sea, and saw a beast rise up out of the sea, having seven heads and ten horns, and upon his horns ten crowns, and upon his heads the name of blasphemy. - And the beast that I saw was like a leopard, and his feet were like the feet of a bear, and his mouth like the mouth of a lion; and the dragon gave him his power, and his throne, and great authority. - And I saw one of his heads as though it was wounded unto death; and his deadly wound was healed, and all the world wondered after the beast."

It is obvious that this beast (involved in this particular time in history) with the wound to the head is the central identifying theme of the beasts. So much can be understood if we knew, first of all, for what purpose was this wound inflicted? What kind of a wound was it? Where and when was it was inflicted, and by what means or weapon? And why is all the world wondering after this one particular beast?

The reading of this passage can be quite difficult unless a little common sense is used. And in particular, if the law of non-contradiction is used. Concerning living entities, there is one dragon and three beasts. The beasts are also identified as various animals and nations. And their power and authority are from the dragon. This power from the dragon is to all the beasts, nation, nations, or individuals, as these biblical beasts are identifying nations in different time frames, and two specific men. One from the Sea of men, and another from the earth (Israel). The first beast, Satan, appeared in the Garden of Eden as a serpent. This identifies and authenticates the first timeframe beast (serpent). Also, this timeframe was the fall of man. And this was the specific time when Satan was made the god of this world. (Adam and Eve were cast out of God's world, in which there was no death.)

These beasts have the name "blasphemy" written on their heads, revealing a united ten-part world. A world hindered until the Church is taken away. We will later examine Israel, which poses an unusual situation concerning this world. Israel, from the time of Abraham, has always been the apple of God's eye. And from the time God promised a specific land to Israel, this land has been set aside for her. Beyond that, the Lord specifically said this was his land, which he gave to Israel. Leviticus 25:23 "The land shall not be sold forever. For the land is mine; for you are strangers and sojourners with me." (Are not of this world.) There will shortly be given an unusual and far different position in which Israel will be regarded. This is the result of a certain prophesy that will be fulfilled before these last seven years.

Rev. 13:4-8 "And they worshiped the dragon who gave power unto the beast; and they worshiped the beast, saying, 'Who is like the beast? Who is able to make war with him?' - And there was given unto him a mouth speaking great things and blasphemies, and power was given unto him to continue forty and two months. - And he opened his mouth in blasphemy against God, to blasphemy his name, and his tabernacle, and them that dwell in heaven. - And it was given unto him to make war with the saints, and to overcome them; and power was given him over all kindreds, tongues and nations. - And all that dwell upon the earth shall worship him, whose names are not written in the book of life of the Lamb slain from the foundation of the world."

These verses, concerning this man from the sea, combine with this man from the earth. Both men are called beasts. Their actual reigns will be but for the last three and a half years. This man from the sea of man will apparently be a military man from this ten-part world government. It is stated he receives power from the dragon. "And they worship the dragon who gave power to the beast. And they worshiped the beast."

TWO DIVERSE SPIRITS

We have an interesting wording that reveals much. It is stated "there was given unto him a mouth speaking great things and blasphemies. And he opened his mouth in blasphemy against God, to blasphemy his name, and his tabernacle, and them that dwell in heaven." These are almost identical to the words of the apostle Paul. This when Paul was writing of spiritual battles, and then asked the church to pray for him. Ephesians 6:19 "And for me, that utterance may be given unto me, that I may open my mouth boldly to make known the mystery of the gospel." Colossians 4:3-4 "Praying also for us, that God would open unto us a door of utterance, to speak the mystery of Christ, for which I am also in bonds, - That I may make it manifest, as I ought to speak." This man spoken of in Revelation 13:5 blasphemed the Lord, unlike Paul, who wanted to speak the mysteries of God.

It is quite clear that Paul is praying that the Holy Spirit would give him the words so that the Lord would be in control of the words he speaks, that he may speak the mysteries of God. He was asking the Lord to control his very words; not to give complete control of his mind and body to the Lord, but that he would correctly repeat His words because of the fear that he may leave out or add a word that would diminish God's words in any way. Jesus is defined as the word of God. This should be the prayer of every Christian. Of course this is extremely rare, as the Lord does not control us. Quite the opposite. We must learn to control and carefully weigh the words that come out our mouths. However, there are times when the Lord does give utterances that are his, using man's mouth to speak the words of God.

Obviously, the Lord is not giving this man these words of blasphemy. It is another source, filled with anger, knowing he has but a short time. This is absolute control over this man's words. This is evidenced by words of blasphemy against whom this man should have no grievance or knowledge of. Rev. 13:4-5 "There was given unto him a mouth, speaking blasphemies… he opened his mouth in blasphemy." Satan has complete control of this man who is more than submissive. The world worships the dragon and the beast because the dragon possesses this man. (Rev. 13:4) Yes, it is obvious this man from the sea of man is blaspheming He whom he should have little knowledge of. But the fact that he blasphemies God, his name, his tabernacle and those that dwell in heaven affirms that old dragon is now using this tabernacle of flesh in frustration and anger. This man has become a reflection, or an image, of the beast.

Satan has just been cast out of heaven. And he no doubt knows who now dwells in his former world. A heaven now cleansed and made pure, fit to receive those who are now in the image of God. The absolute control that he demands and exhibits over these two images of himself will soon fill this world.

BEAST FROM THE LAND

Rev. 13:9-12 "If any man has an ear, let him hear. - He that leads into captivity shall go into captivity; he that kills with the sword must be killed by the sword. Here is the patience and faith of the saints. - And I beheld another beast coming up out of the earth; and he had two horns like a lamb, and he spoke like a dragon. - And he exercises all the power of the first beast before him, and causes the earth and them who dwell on it to worship the first beast, whose deadly wound was healed."

"Those that lead into captivity shall go into captivity, and he that kills with the sword must be killed by the sword." This means that all that lose their lives will save them. And all that save their lives will lose them. This may be confusing, but is talking about this actual time of the hunting down of Christians to kill them. (The mode of killing them is beheading.) But before the killing, the first part is more evil, involving those who lead into captivity. Those who lead into captivity are those who do grasp the uniqueness of the Judeo-Christian Bible.

All the world has been constantly hearing the gospel from God's two witnesses. Also, all the world has witnessed God's two prophets rise, after lying dead for three and a half days. (This is also believed here to be at the same time God takes away all of his Church.)

For three and a half years there has been a steady reminder that all must be completely washed and made pure. And that man is incapable of being fit to enter into eternal life. The only way possible is through the express image of God, his only begotten Son; through the cross. It is reasonable to assume that the final authentication of their gospel message would be the rapture of the Church. First the dead, and then the living, in the twinkling of an eye. This was witnessed by all. Which then caused much fear when these men that were dead became alive again. The world saw the two witnesses of God brought back to life, after being dead for three and a half days. Suddenly standing on their feet, followed by rising to meet the Lord in the air. This was at the same moment that, worldwide, the Christians rise to meet the Lord. Terrifying to some, and an uplifting affirmation and conviction to others, determined not to be left behind again.

This event will be the most profound and telling in human history. And it will continue into the great tribulation. It will reveal the heart of man and the justice of God. All of the world will have continually heard the uninterrupted gospel of Christ, and praises of God. All this in conjunction with miracles authenticating that these men – the two witnesses – were of God. With further affirmation being that every attempt to harm them resulted in the would-be harmer's death.

Does that mean those who are left behind have been abandoned? Until the acceptance of Jesus as Lord and Savior, none are Christians. The Holy Spirit that changes mortal to immortal is omnipresent, and has not left; as the arms of the Lord are always outstretched, and the Word of God never changes.

Then, even after witnessing these very events, those who "lead into captivity" become filled with resentment and anger. This is separate from those who were ashamed to testify to that which they knew to be pure, and are now filled with sorrow that they were left behind. But now they know that they must lose their lives to save them. This will not be a time of hiding and digging in garbage cans to survive, fearful of being found out as a believer. This, as never before, will be a time of finality in choosing which image to be of. Do they want to be in the image of the beast? Or in the image of God?

None can say "I was deceived and did not know". This is no different than now. There is a clear rejection or acceptance of the truth of the word of God, no matter how dramatic its proofs. This blindness is of the heart that knows exactly what they are rejecting. And those who lead into captivity are of no greater or lesser evil than those who are beheading these Christians. The former is increasingly identifying our government, laws, and schools. And, unfortunately, too many of our churches.

SPOKE LIKE A DRAGON

Rev. 13:11 describes the beast coming out of the earth, that has two horns as a lamb but speaks like a dragon. This is the man of sin, the son of perdition, defined in 2nd Thes 2:3-4 "Who opposes and exalts himself above all that is called God, or that is worshiped, so that he, as God, sits in the temple of God, showing himself that he is God." The obvious conclusion is that this man must be an Orthodox Jew who has rejected the risen Jesus, and is claiming to be the promised Messiah. The false Lamb of God. His speaking as a dragon reveals his true identity. There are many antichrists, but there is one specific anti-Christ into whom Satan himself will enter. Satan, having been cast out of heaven, is no longer an angel. But he is now is a demon, - the devil. As to what extent of power he will then have, other than through man, this writer can only speculate. 2nd Thes. 2:9 "Even him whose coming is after the working of Satan with all power and signs and lying wonders of falsehood." Rev. 13:13 "And he does great wonders, so that he makes fire come down from heaven on the earth in the sight of men." (Thessalonians calls them 'lying wonders'. This cannot be a contradiction, but rather perhaps two different observations of the same events through different eyes.)

Rev.13:12 "And he exercises all the power of the first beast before him, and causes the world and them who dwell on it to worship the first beast, whose deadly wound was healed." He exercises all the power of the first beast before him; both of these men receive their power from the dragon. Both are anti-Christ and images of the beast

(Dragon). He "causes the world to worship the first beast (dragon), whose deadly wound is healed."

Rev. 13:13-15 "And he does great wonders, so that he makes fire come down from heaven in the sight of men. - And deceives them that dwell on the earth by the means of those miracles which he had power to do in the sight of the beast, saying to them that dwell on the earth that they should make an image to the beast, that had the wound by the sword and did live. - And he had power to give life to the image of the beast, that the image of the beast should both speak, and cause as many that would not worship the image of the beast should be killed."

CHAPTER 39

IT IS FINISHED

As we are given more information, the key to unraveling this mystery (which is not really a mystery) is to embrace the Law of non-contradiction. And to understand the significance and power of this sword of the Lord, which is the word of God. And then completely accepting that this sword is the word of truth. There can be no wavering on this reality. There is something else that must be understood and completely grasped. The essence of man is his spirit, which is eternal. Our spirit occupies this body of flesh for a season, and is tried. 1st Thes. 5:23 "And the very God of peace sanctify you wholly; and I pray God your whole spirit and soul and body be preserved blameless unto the coming of our Lord Jesus Christ." Only the Lord Jesus can preserve body, soul and spirit.

There is a designed purpose behind this world that has control of our education system, to indoctrinate our children with the idea that there is no God and no spirits. With this brain of flesh having endless potential and power, prayer is made that our body, soul and spirit are preserved blameless unto the coming of our Lord Jesus Christ. These words are preceded in Thessalonians explaining the gathering of the saints to meet the Lord in the air. You must be washed by the blood of the Lamb.

These strings of events reveal that the spirit of man does not die. And as believers, those who desire the Lord's purpose are thankful, with an absolute awareness there is nothing they can contribute to their salvation other than to believe. The Father does not desire that man feel beholden to him with a debt to be paid; but thankful, and desiring the fruits of this new heart.

TWO IMAGES

Rev. 13:14 "He deceived them that dwell on the earth by the means of the miracles which he had power to do in the *sight* of the beast (in sight of the beast, because he is occupying this man), saying to them that dwell on the earth, that they should make an image to the beast, that had the wound by the sword, and did live." Just as God created man to be in the image of God, so this man, the son of perdition, is already an image of the beast, authenticating he is antichrist. Rev. 13:11 "And he had two horns like a lamb; but spoke as a dragon." He that leads into captivity will go into captivity.

This is at the time when all of the world heard the uninterrupted gospel for three and a half years. The following scripture reveals this last times world, a world that is not much different than this one... as all must decide of whose image is desired. 1st John 2:18-21 "Little children, it is the last time, and as you have heard that antichrist shall come, even now there are many antichrists, by which we know it is the last time. - They went out from us, but they were not of us, for had they been of us, they would no doubt have continued with us; but they went out, that they might be manifest that were not all of us. - But you have an unction from the Holy One, and you know all things. - I have not written unto you because you know not the truth, but because you know it, and no lie is of the truth."

This first beast is the dragon, and it is he who received this deadly wound from Jesus at the cross. This deadly wound was inflicted with these words of the Lord in John 19:30, "It is finished." That was when Jesus gave up the spirit, and physical death followed. Satan was defeated with this mortal wound by the sword (word) of the Lord. Hebrews 2:14-15 "For as much as the children are partakers of flesh and blood, he likewise took part of the same, that through death he might destroy him that had the power of death, that is the Devil, - And deliver them who, through the fear of death, were all their lifetime subject to bondage."

SWORD OF THE LORD

The exact moment these words came from Jesus, the sword of the Lord, it affirmed and accomplished that the judgment of the dragon was the death of Satan. Rev. 19:15 "And out of his mouth goes a sharp sword, that with it he shall judge the nations." These words that came from his mouth, the same Words that spoke the worlds into being. Words that cannot be altered. The words of life. John 19:30 "It is finished."

And then this man from the earth saying to the world "That they should make an image to the beast. - that had the wound by the sword." (Rev 13:14) Both the man from the sea of man and from the earth are images of the beast, as they are controlled by, and mirror, him. The world was not told to make a statue, robot, computer or android. But an image to the beast. Both of these men are images of the beast. To a degree, as Jesus is the image of God. The difference being the father, Son and Holy Spirit are one, while being completely separate, as all believers are. Those of the image of the beast are in complete submission and controlled by the beast.

This we can understand, as to how someone can be in complete submission to another. But the Bible is clear that no man can even conceive, or it has not even entered into the heart of man, what the Lord has for those who enter into the kingdom of heaven, being in the image of God. 1st Cor. 2:9 "It is written, Eye has not seen, nor ear heard, nor has entered into the heart of man, the things God has prepared for them that love him." How is it possible for vain man to comprehend these words of the Lord?

Luke 7:28 "Among those born of women there is not a greater prophet that John the Baptist; but he that is least in the kingdom of God is greater than he." What is being conveyed is a kingdom completely foreign to mankind. Before making this statement concerning John, Jesus asked "What went you out to see, a man clothed in soft raiment? Behold, they who are gorgeously appareled, and live delicately, are in king's courts." John told of the coming of Jesus the Lamb of God. What is then revealed is that there are none that could enter into life eternal were it not for his shed blood. Jesus is servant of all, and is the greatest in the kingdom. That is completely foreign to all of mankind. Or is it? This writer believes there are many that know this must be so. In reading and then believing the Gospels and the writers of the New Testament, there is absolute assurance and gratitude that these things are so. The world will not, cannot accept this.

This writer cannot comprehend what this new heaven will be like. But great insight is revealed by observing those who are offended at the preaching of the cross and gospel of the Lamb of God. Anyone who knows the Lord wants all religions to be openly compared with these words of life. But political correctness deems any comparing with the Bible as favoring the Bible. And for good reason. There *is* no comparison. Our founding fathers were also convinced of this, believing that this freedom to examine and compare the word of God with other religions would result in a stronger faith in the word of God. This is what freedom of religion is about. Our founding fathers had no doubt there is but one God, based on the Judeo-Christian Bible.

This nation was founded as a special nation. The most telling is the Constitution, which is clearly based on the Bible. But revisionists have even twisted this truth to unimaginable proportions. Mainly, that our founding fathers were composed of few real Bible-believing Christians. And in the last few years there has been a political religious fervor to render our Constitution useless, with an abnormal behavior to diminish and destroy this Constitution with a liberal Supreme Court.

GIVE LIFE?

Rev. 13:15 "And he had power to give life unto the image of the beast, that the image of the beast should both speak, and cause as many as would not worship the image of the beast should be killed." We must address two statements that are completely impossible to accept, unless properly understood. The first is giving life to the image of the beast. Now if you are addressing this man from the earth giving life to this image, or even the dragon, this cannot be accepted; as only God gives life. And the second being "He had power… that the image of the beast should both speak, and cause as many as would not worship the image of the beast should be killed." Now we have this image that has always being depicted as some inanimate statue, robot, computer or even android etc. Christians have no problem believing they are created in the image of God. Why is it so difficult to believe there will be an event in which all Christians are to be killed by those in the image of the beast? This image being living, speaking images of the dragon. As a matter of fact, most all evil done against Christians is done by antichrists of varying degree.

These events make sense if the proper word for life is used. The wording is interesting, and most importantly the translators missed a key word. And because of this, it should have brought special attention, and more thorough scrutiny of this passage. It is the belief of this writer that the Lord allowed this obvious error. He knew that those who have complete assurance in the word of God would examine this more completely, and that it would be in the latter days. Rev. 13:15 "He had power to give life to the image of the beast." The original Greek word translated life is Pneuma, and always means 'breath'. So, the wording is "He had power to give *breath* to the image of the beast, that the image of the beast should both speak, and cause that as many as would not worship the image of the beast should be killed."

That power or authority would have to be over mankind. As even if an inanimate object could speak, or come to life (which, of course, cannot be), there would still be no awareness or ability for it to do the will of he who has power over it. The term "power over inanimate objects" is never used. But now it makes sense. As Satan is the beast, giving breath to this living image of himself. This also reveals complete control over those foolish enough to be in his image. 2nd Thes. 2:4 "Who opposes and exalts himself above all that is called God, or that is worshiped as God." And of course, the worshiping of the image of the beast is worshiping that old dragon. As Satan occupies but one man, who is the image of the beast in a more personal and intimate way than the rest of the world? He is the antichrist.

WHO IS THIS HE?

It is the first beast that has the deadly wound by the sword. Having been cast out of heaven, he is no longer Lucifer the angel, but now chief of the demons – the devil. He is now occupying the body of this man from the earth. This same man who has been hindered by the

Lord from doing these lying signs and wonders in sight of the beast. Until God's two witnesses, along with the church, have finished their task and then been taken away to be with the Lord.

As we examine God's two witnesses and their ministry more completely, we see the grace and wisdom of God to an extraordinary degree. Rev. 11:7-9 "After they shall have finished their testimony, the beast that ascends out of the bottomless pit shall make war against them, and overcome them, and kill them. - And their dead bodies shall lie in the street of that great city, which is spiritually called Sodom and Egypt, where also our Lord was crucified. - And the people will not allow their dead bodies to be put in graves."

SATAN SHALL KILL THEM?

Now Satan has just killed these two prophets of God. But as he is now the devil who occupies this man, the son of perdition, it is by him that Satan kills them. Obviously, the world has witnessed the son of perdition doing what has been unsuccessfully attempted for three and a half years. As all the world knows, every attempt to kill these two men has resulted in the death of the attempter. In the mind of this world, whoever accomplishes this must be God or have the power of God. This man of sin receives worship as God in the temple of God.

Actually, this does not work out well for either. Satan had proclaimed himself to be God when he was Lucifer, the angel of light, and had indescribable beauty. But now, after being cast out of heaven, he occupies this mere man as the devil, and actually is a prisoner in this frail, corrupt human body. It is this body that will obtain all of this adoration. Oh, if only man could see him in all his glory and beauty! And this man being occupied is in terror, now knowing his fate.

This man of Sin who wanted adoration and worship as God has not only relinquished all control of his mind and body to Satan, but is now a prisoner, and is being treated by disgust by him who now occupies his body. And he now knows, as never before, an even greater terror awaiting him. The soon return of the Lord from the heavens… to be followed by the lake of fire.

But for now, the world is ecstatic, as they say "Who but God could do what we have just witnessed?" And they send gifts to one another, not allowing these two men's bodies to be put into graves. This is the time "That wicked one will be revealed; the son of perdition. And he sits in the temple of God, showing himself that he is God." (2nd Thes. 2:4) Yes, that wicked one will be revealed to the wise, and worshiped by the foolish. Both Rev. 11 and 2nd Thes. 2 are events leading to the rapture of the Church, and the antichrist no longer being hindered. Now he is demanding worship as God, and receiving it.

ALL THE WORLD KNOWS

Rev. 11:11-13 "And after three days and a half the spirit of life from God entered into them, and they stood upon their feet, and great fear fell upon them who saw them. - And they heard a great voice from heaven saying unto them, 'Come up here'. And they ascended up to heaven in a cloud, and their enemies beheld them. - And at that same time there was a great earthquake, and a tenth of the city fell, and in the earthquake, were slain seven thousand men. And the rest were terrified and gave glory to the God of heaven."

CHAPTER 40

ANTICHRIST KILLS GOD'S WITNESSES

What this world has just witnessed are these two men being killed. And by a very special Rabbi, with a reputation of peace and love. This is not presented as sarcasm. It is believed here that this man will be a Rebbe; a very special pious and devoted Rabbi. A man that has proven himself through his righteousness and a giving and loving nature. The Rebbes have been described as very special men who profess to love the Lord. "The Rebbe's sense of inner servitude to the Almighty was manifest even while he is immersed in the most complex subjects in Talmud, Jewish law, or the Kabbalah." (These Hasidic Jews or Hasid -Hasidim is a Jewish sect of the 2nd century devoted to strict observances of ritual Law.)

Intertwined within these ritualistic rites is the Kabbalah, which the Lord strictly forbids. This is referred to as rituals and observances of spiritual practices to contact spirits, angels, or the dead for the purpose of receiving extra knowledge of the Lord. And this extra knowledge, which has been used by many scientists, is also forbidden… and dangerous. The booklet "Rebbe" reveals the blatant use of the Kabbalah. When deception is mixed with truth, the final mix is deception. Rebbe p. 15 "Though the Torah is divided into the written Law (Bible) and the Oral Law; Midrash, Talmud, Kabbalah etc., in truth they are one." To even suggest that one of these special gentlemen will be the antichrist would be unthinkable. Would it be like suggesting Job could be a possible candidate to be the Messiah?

It would be wise to analyze what we are doing or thinking. The first is we do not, nor can we, possibly believe the word of God if we in any way entertain the thought that a man could possibly be the Savior. God calls none good, and then expands on this by stating man's greatest righteousness are as filthy rags. To believe that God is to anoint this Hasidic Jew to be the Savior of all of mankind, the promised Messiah; and then for this man to show himself to be God, to receive worship as God? This is rejecting the words of the prophets that were affirmed by the angels. This in itself rejects any comparison to being good, let alone righteous. As this denial of Jesus as Messiah is denying eternal life to any that are deceived by their teaching.

Acts 1:10-11 "And while they looked steadfastly toward heaven as he went up, behold, two men stood by them in white apparel; - Who said, 'You men of Galilee, why stand you gazing up into heaven? This same Jesus, who is taken up from you into heaven, shall so come in like manner as you have seen him go into heaven.'" Yes, the angels themselves attested that when our Messiah returns, it will be from the heavens.

All of Israel were aware of what the prophets wrote concerning the coming Messiah. Matt. 11:2-6 "When John had heard in prison the works of Christ, he sent two of his disciples. - And they said unto him, 'are you he that should come, or do we look for another?' - Jesus answered and said to them, 'Go and show John again those things which you do hear and see: - The blind receive their sight, the lame walk, the lepers are cleansed, and the deaf hear, the dead are raised up, and the poor have the gospel preached to them. - And blessed is he, whosoever shall not be offended in me.'"

This is a terrible indictment. "Whosoever shall not be offended in me." It is the shame of the cross that offends, but unto us who are saved it is the power of God. The world cannot understand how the cross can be the power of God. This is the heart of God; this is the covenant and gospel. Jesus came to die for the lost. The cross is the power that transforms men into the image God created them to be.

Yes, the Rebbe's righteousness could, in a way, be compared to Job's. However, there is a glaring difference. When this soon-coming man of sin sees the opportunity to be worshiped as God, he will take it. In comparison, when Job's eyes were opened and he saw God, he abhorred himself, and repented in dust and ashes. No man is in the image of God, nor will they be so until their corruption takes on incorruption, and their mortality takes on immortality. Shortly we will expand on God's covenant with man.

PAUL

Now Saul was a devout Jew, living as a Pharisee. He made havoc of the Christians; committing them, both men and women, to prisons because of their belief in Jesus as the promised Messiah. Acts. 9:1-2 "And Saul, yet breathing out threatenings and slaughter against the disciples of the Lord, went to the high priest, - And desired of him letters to Damascus to the synagogues, that if he found any Christians, men or women, he might bring them bound to Jerusalem." Saul had zeal for the Lord, believing he was pleasing God. His good works went beyond good works, to punishing in God's behalf those who would believe that this Jesus is the Son of God. This Messiah who was promised by the prophets.

Hebrews 7:19, 28 "For the law made nothing perfect, but the bringing in of a better hope did, by which we draw near unto God. - For the law makes men high priests who have infirmities, but the word of the oath (covenant), which was since the law, makes the Son, who is consecrated for evermore."

Acts 9:3-6 "Then as he came near to Damascus, suddenly there shone about him a light from heaven. - And he fell to the earth, and heard a voice saying unto him, 'Saul, Saul, why persecutes thou me?' - And he said, 'Who are thou, Lord?' And the Lord said, 'I am Jesus, whom thou persecutes; it is hard for you to kick against the pricks.' - And he, trembling and astonished, said, 'Lord, what will you have me do?'"

Saul then became Paul and received persecution as none other, because of his faith in Jesus as Lord. 2nd Cor. 11:23-26 "Are they ministers of Christ? (I speak as a fool) I am more. In labors more abundantly, in stripes above measure, in prisons more frequently, in deaths often. - Of the Jews five times received I forty stripes, save one." (Forty lashes with the whip was often enough to kill a man) – "Three times beaten with a rod. Once I was stoned." (Stoning was a form of execution) "Three times I was shipwrecked, a night and a day I have been in the deep." (In the deep is under the water) – "In journeying often, in perils of waters, in perils of robbers, in perils by my own countrymen, in perils by the Gentiles, in perils in the city, in perils in the wilderness, in perils in the sea, in perils among false brethren," etc.

Job had suffered to a degree that few others have. Because he did not waver in the God that his heart hungered after, as he would not settle for any other, God revealed himself to him. In the same way, Paul had dedicated his life in living a righteous life. However, as he was brought up as a Pharisee, he had rejected Jesus as the promised Messiah and was waiting for another. He believed that the one to come would be a righteous Jew, not one truly God and truly man. Isaiah 7:14 "Therefore the Lord himself will give you a sign; Behold, the virgin shall conceive, and bear a son, and shall call his name Emmanuel." (Emmanuel means 'God with us.')

And then Saul, as a Pharisee, imprisoned and killed those who believed the very words that the Bible clearly states. And what his own heart had revealed to him, which he proved by his actions, was that man can never be the Messiah. Oh, how those words from the Lord must have resonated in his heart. "It is hard to kick against the pricks." It was after Paul was covered in this light of the Lord that his heart also, as Job's, would settle for none other. No, Paul was not complaining concerning these trials he received. But rather, was revealing that because of these trials and tests (as Job), he was given greater revelations and understanding. In fact, he was thankful to be chosen to receive persecution for his faith. From a human standpoint, this is difficult to understand. As also is: how can this be, that my Savior would die for me?

SAUL SEPARATED

Saul separated himself by man's imposed religion. However, he was after the heart of God. Anyone so disposed will be accommodated by the Lord. The Judeo-Christian Bible stands out in complete contrast to the religions of man. It is simply the heart of God, reaching out to the heart of man. Then when man responds, there becomes such an awareness of love and truth that man becomes completely aware of his shortcomings. He then tries to comprehend the Lord's absolute love and truth. This has been programmed into the spirit (heart) of man from the first day the spirit of man became one with their body of flesh.

FLESH AND THE SPIRIT

Man is a prisoner in this body of flesh, and will remain so until this body of flesh returns to dust. Paul and Job received unusual revelations concerning these two worlds. And when Job's heart saw the heart of God, he said "Before, I heard of you. But now I see you, and abhor myself, and repent in dust and ashes." It was after seeing the heart of God that Job accepted and believed in the fullness of being in "the express image of God in his Son." And how do we know this to be so? Because if he did not believe this, it would have been impossible for Job to function in any normal capacity, with the realization and the knowledge that he would be judged by this same God who is perfect in all ways. This would have left him paralyzed with fear, as it should. But that isn't what happens when anyone believes on, and then accepts Jesus as Lord and Savior. Instead, there is a peace and the assurance of being completely loved.

What you are doing is allowing your Lord to take your sins. And what follows is a joy unspeakable and full of glory. Think on this: If any innocent man were to take the penalty for your sins, would you be full of joy and glory? Of course not. This would identify you as evil beyond description, to have this joy when an innocent man receives the punishment you deserve. But the innocent taking the sin of the guilty is not why Christianity is so offensive to this world. The reason the world is offended by Christianity (actually, it is a violent hatred) is because it exposes the heart of man alongside the heart of God.

"For God sent his Son into the world not to condemn the world, but that the world through him might be saved." (John 3:17) The word of God reveals Satan, and the reason he rejected the Father. Pride of self seems to be the major cause. All of this is recorded in Isaiah 14 and Ezekiel 28. And in Job 33:16-18, it is interesting when Elihu tells Job of this spirit in man that receives inspiration from the Almighty: "He opens the ears of men and seals their instructions, - That he may withdraw man from his purpose, and hide pride from man. - He keeps back his soul from the pit, and his life from perishing by the sword." A man *should* take pride in his accomplishments or work in the context of doing well and doing their best for others. This, however, is completely the opposite of self-centered pride.

This realization of the heart of the creator God completely overrides and overwhelms those who know that only he can purify and cleanse. What an incredible joy to be given the understanding to know this is so; to be so special that the Lord reveals this to us. Who then would desire an eternal soul that the Lord himself has cleansed? Yes, those that believe there is such a God, who sent his only begotten Son to wash our sins with his blood. And as a substitution, he takes our sins as his. All this, that we may be completely washed and pure. To the world this is foolishness, and brings on violent behavior. But to the hearts of those that are convicted of these truths, the cross is the power of God, and our hearts are completely overwhelmed with a desire to be as he is. The greater the understanding and truth of this that overtakes Christians, the greater the realization of their sinful nature. This does cause greater condemnation, but in turn magnifies what our Lord has done. With a far greater realization of the greater cost and love involved.

Paul's eyes were literally opened testifying of this certain man (obviously himself). 2nd Cor. 12:1-5 "It is not expedient for me, doubtless, to glory. I will come to visions and revelations of the Lord. - I knew a man in Christ above fourteen years ago (whether in or out of the body, I cannot tell; God knows) - How he was caught up into paradise, and heard unspeakable words, which it is not lawful for man to utter. - Of such a one will I glory; yet of myself will I not glory, but in mine infirmities."

What are these unspeakable words he heard which are not lawful to utter? It is assumed it is quite extensive. Along with 1st Cor. 2:9 "Eye has not seen, nor ear heard, neither has entered into the heart of man, the things which God has prepared for them that love him."

Any mention of himself that Paul spoke of, was never to exalt himself. Because he saw the Lord as few do. Romans 7:24-25; 8:1-4, 6-7 "Oh wretched man that I am! Who shall deliver me from the body of this death? - I thank God through Jesus Christ, our Lord. So then, with the mind I myself serve the law of God; but with the flesh, the law of sin. - There is therefore, now no condemnation to them who are in Christ Jesus, who walk not after the flesh, but after the spirit. - For the law of the spirit of life in Christ Jesus has made me free from the law of sin and death. - For what the law could not do, in that it was weak through the flesh, God sending his own Son, in the likeness of sinful flesh and for sin, condemned sin in the flesh, - That the righteousness of the law might be fulfilled in us, who walk not after the flesh, but after the Spirit. - For to be carnally minded is death, but to be spiritually minded is life and peace. - Because the carnal mind is enmity against God; for it is not subject to the law of God, neither, indeed, can be."

These scriptures can be quite confusing and condemning. Actually, they do not make any sense unless you believe there is a creator God that is presently and personally involved in the affairs of man. And all efforts to exalt one's self will diminish access of revelations of the Lord. The ultimate self-exaltation comes from professing atheism. The good news is there is no such thing as an atheist. The number of people that have even professed to be so are really quite small. The actual number is zero. The reason those words of Paul are quite confusing is because it is difficult to believe there could be such a God that would actually concern himself with man's problems. This is because man is flesh. "Because the carnal mind is enmity against God; for it is not subject to the law of God, neither, indeed, can be."

CHRISTIANS CALLED TO BE SEPARATE

Christians do not have the mind of the world; but we have the mind of Christ, because we are washed. At this time, what will be given are words from the Lord that offend this world. A world that has willingly received what the Lord calls a reprobate mind. This is contrary to what the Lord has instilled into all of his creation. It is what is called instinct to protect their young. This nature is programmed by our creator. But man, who is created in the image of God, has been given an extension of this instinct beyond physical protection for a season. Actually, this starts at conception.

Our life in the flesh is but for a moment. James 4:14 "What is your life? It is but a vapor that appears for a little time, and then vanishes away." The Lord God has programmed into us this protection and well-being for our and other's children. Unless we have a reprobate mind. This is the same as angels. "Are they not all ministering spirits, sent forth to minister for them who shall be heirs of salvation?" (Heb. 1:14) As can be seen, angels are all ministering spirits. This means they were *created* to be ministering spirits. Obviously, Satan and his angels rejected being ministering angels in favor of being adversaries to God and the believers.

God sent his only begotten Son to die for man. All man has to do is accept this. Accept that the Lord would do such a thing as to take their sins, that they may be pure. Logically, the only reason this would be seen as offensive would be the thought that God could even dare to suggest that man can be improved upon. This is the ultimate act of applying 'political correctness', that this behavior from God cannot be accepted.

As for angels, it seems there has already been this separation. As we are told, "Are they not all ministering spirits?" As said previously, this reveals to this writer that this is how they were created. Just as man, they have the same right to reject what they were created to be. We know one third of the stars in heaven were cast out by Satan to kill Jesus as soon as he was born. It is interesting to note that there is no effort to be made to interfere while Jesus was in Mary's womb.

ANGELS WITNESSING CREATION?

The Lord is speaking to Job and asked him, in Job 38:4a,7 "Where were you when I laid the foundations of the earth? - And the morning stars sang together, and all the sons of God shouted for joy?" It seems that at this time there was no rebellion. It came later, after Satan was observing Adam and Eve, and pride entered in. It would seem it was not difficult for Satan to gain followers in observing the conduct of man after being cast out of Eden, because Satan saw imperfection. A perfect man does not need ministering to. Or a constant reminder that they are sinners in need of redemption.

God does not have a different standard for man and angels. This was revealed in Satan, and those who followed him in rebellion against God. When cast out of heaven, they became demons. And Satan will become the Devil. This is basically the story of the rebellion of man against what they were created to be. No doubt God's two witnesses will speak of this. Now a man and his wife are to minister to their children and others so that they may become heirs of salvation. This is similar to the angels of God. The fullness of this is greater than man can fully grasp. In refusing this they, both angels and man, become an adversary, and are given to a rebellious mind.

AMERICA'S DECLINE

Iran's leaders continually proclaim they will soon destroy Israel, so that she will no longer be a nation. It would appear our president Obama has done all that he can to help Iran achieve this goal. This writer wants to believe this is not his intent, but the evidence suggests otherwise. The United States has been a very special nation. First, as sending missionaries out to all the world to proclaim Christ Jesus. Also, she is the leading nation by far in helping victims of disasters. And militarily, she is a stabilizing force in the world. But unless a dramatic change takes place in the White House from the last eight years, this nation will never recover from the direction she is taking.

Without this happening, this special blessing from the Lord will cease and we will become just another country. We are called to be a light upon a hill, and this is possible only if this nation has a dramatic hunger for the special truth that produces light. Gen. 12:3 "I will bless them that bless thee, (Israel) and curse them that curse thee. And in thee shall all families of the earth be blessed." This recognizing of Israel must be more than just vetoes to defend her against U.N. sanctions, but to cherish her as one chosen of God. With a constant gentle reminder that their promised Messiah did indeed rise from the dead, and will return from the heavens where he was seen departing to.

There would have to be a complete change of direction for the United States. And it seems that we have gone too far; making it an impossible task to turn around. And without help from the Lord it would indeed be impossible. However, if just a small percentage of Christians pray to the Lord for this nation, and refuse to compromise, this writer is convinced the Lord will give this nation a little reprieve. It will not be long though, as prophetic events are unfolding. This nation will soon be a part of the new one world order, of a soon coming ten nation world. This will happen. But even when it does, there is always an escape for those who refuse to be part of this world. Even for those who have waited until the last moment. And it will be but a small price to pay. As those who then lose their lives will save them... and those that save their lives will lose them.

(Note: Since this was originally written, our new president has reversed the direction this nation has taken for the last eight years. If this nation will continue in the direction our president Trump has taken, this nation will once again be blessed.)

GOG AND MAGOG

The event that precedes this soon coming one world government has already happened. It was the rebirth of God's nation Israel. This, after twenty-eight hundred and eighty years of not being a nation; and then being resurrected from the dead. This alone is an absolute declaration that the Bible indeed is the word of God. The happening of this resurrection was recorded by God's prophets, and it occurred on May 14, 1948. The significance and accuracy of this prophesy alone defies any odds. Therefore, it provides absolute proof that this is the word of God.

These prophesies were recorded by the prophet Ezekiel, about 585 B.C. (this was also recorded by many other prophets). This prophecy goes on to reveal exactly what will be the result of this present-day dream of Iran and her neighbors surrounding her. At the time of this writing, Iran is listed as the number one sponsor of terrorism and enemy of Israel. But this prophesy in Ezekiel lists Iran as just one of many nations that come against Israel to wipe her out. There is much more involved than a nation coming into being that calls herself Israel. But for this prophesy to be fulfilled, Israel must be the completely resurrected nation of Israel.

And at the time of this prophesy, Israel (the northern kingdom) had ceased to exist 135 years before. (She was not the whole house of Israel.) And that by Assyria. The *whole* house of Israel ceased to exist about 200 years before that, and that by herself. Israel became a divided nation, therefore ceasing to exist, as then she was not the full house of Israel. As we shall see, Ezekiel prophesied that Israel will be restored whole. That being, the whole house of Israel as one.

The nation of Israel was comprised of the family of Jacob (whom

God called Israel). They came out of Egypt with about two million people. They were ruled by judges, and the laws of God. Then the people wanted a king. The first king was Saul, then David, then his son Solomon. After Solomon died, this nation of twelve sons was divided. This was 931 B.C. The northern nation, called Israel, consisted of the descendants of ten of Israel's children and Levites, designated as priests. Their first King was Jeroboam. And the southern Kingdom, Judea, consisted of Benjamin, Judea and Levites. Their first King was Rehoboam. They then were two nations, actually engaging in warfare against each other at various times.

In 721 B.C. the northern nation of Israel was taken captive by Assyria, in which most of the citizens were removed and other peoples brought in. (This is a common practice that helps to eliminate rebellions.) 135 years later the southern nation of Judah was taken captive by Babylon. Some were left in Judah. Then later, most of the remaining returned to Judah.

SABBATH

Before Ezekiel prophesied concerning Israel returning to their land, he stated why they were taken from this land that is the Lord's land. Leviticus 25:23-24 "The land shall not be sold forever: for the land is mine; you are strangers and sojourners with me. - And in all the land of your possession you shall grant a redemption for the land." This chapter begins with the Lord speaking to Moses. In Lev. 25:2, he told Moses "Speak to the children of Israel and say to them, 'When you come to the land which I give you, then shall the land keep a Sabbath unto the Lord.'" The full meaning of Sabbath, or rest, was not comprehended then except, no doubt, by Moses. But it will be understood by a significant number in Israel as there becomes an effort to alter God's covenant to Israel to become of the Image of the beast.

THE ABOMINATION OF DESOLATION

Dan. 9:26b-27 "And the end of it shall be with a flood, and unto the end of the war desolations are determined. - And he shall confirm the covenant with many for one week, and in the midst of the week he shall cause the sacrifice and the oblation to cease. And for the overspreading of abominations he shall make it desolate, even unto the consummation, and that determined shall be poured upon the desolate." This is speaking of the last seven years, and this "he" is this man (antichrist) from the earth (a Jew) as defined in 2nd Thessalonians.

2nd Thes. 2:3-4 "Let no man deceive you by any means, for that day shall not come, except there come the falling away first, and that man of sin be revealed, the son of perdition, - Who opposes and exalts himself above all that is called God, or that is worshiped, so that he, as God, sitteth in the temple of God, showing himself that he is God." This is where we have left off, but what has not been addressed is the setting that will bring this world into what will be the final, or end, age. And why it is so called. The end of the age for everyone is what choice they have made before their death.

CHOICES

A situation is presented before mankind in the Bible. And it continually presents itself. You either believe the Bible is the word of God, or you do not. Very few emphatically believe that the Bible is completely the word of God. And unless you do, you are a part of the world pretending you are not. And the Lord does not make it easy to let go of this world; in fact, it is the Lord's will that we remain in the world. The Lord's intercessory prayer is the 17th Chapter of John, when Jesus prays to the Father concerning the saints. John 17:14-18 "I have given them thy word; and the world has hated them, because they are not of the world, even as I am not of the world. - I pray not that you should take them out of the world, but that you would keep them from the evil. - They are not of the world, even as I am not of the world. - Sanctify them through thy truth; thy word is truth. - As you have sent me into the world, even so have I also sent them into the world." For the believers, it is impossible to reject the word of the Lord, because of proofs that are undeniable. And the sanctifying of the word brings a heart that will settle for nothing but the heart of God.

Now addressing Israel's history in our near future, this lays the groundwork for God's two witnesses who are to testify of Christ Jesus for three and a half years in Jerusalem. This will be a far different world than this present one. In this present world, the religious beliefs are endless, along with professed atheism. The two major, dominant religions are Christianity and Islam. But in this soon to come world there will be the recognition of the creator God of the Judeo-Christian Bible. Because all the world will know this truth: the God of the Jews is God, and Israel is God's special chosen people.

There is a problem, however, as Israel is divided into two camps. One third believe that their Messiah is the Jesus who died on the cross and rose again, promising to return from the heavens that he ascended to. However, two thirds believe he has not yet come. And when he does come, he will establish his promised everlasting Kingdom over all of the world, as was promised by the prophets. Satan is still, and until Jesus returns from the heavens, the god of this world.

CHAPTER 41

PROPHESY AGAINST GOG

That most of Israel's neighbors want her destroyed is evidenced by the number of nations that come against her in this prophesy. Ezekiel 38:1-6 "And the word of the Lord came unto me, saying, - 'Son of man, set your face against Gog, of the land of Magog, the chief prince of Meshech and Tubal, and prophesy against him, - And say, "Thus says the Lord God: Behold, I am against you, O Gog, the chief prince of Meshech and Tubal, - And I will turn thee back, and I will put hooks in your jaws, and I will bring thee forth, and all your army… - Persia, Cush, and Put with them; - Gomer and all its hordes; the house of Togarmah of the north quarters, and all its hordes; and many peoples with thee."

Most, if not all, Bible scholars state that modern day Russia is the leader of this huge army that will come against Israel, and several modern Muslim nations can be identified. However, the scope of these nations is enormous. If careful attention is paid to the wording of verse four, then many answers are given to events that otherwise would make no sense.

Ezek. 38:4 "I will turn thee back, and put hooks into thy jaws, and bring thee forth." The Lord says "I will turn you back". Turn them back from their invasion into Israel. They must have entered into Israel. The question is, why did they leave? And then it is stated the Lord himself will draw them back (into Israel) by putting hooks in their jaws. What happened that caused them to leave, as their purpose was to completely wipe Israel out?

Ezekiel 38 and 39 cover a vast time frame, and not always in chronological order. Prophesy cannot be understood unless there is complete confidence there are no contradictions in God's word. And all prophesy centers around Jesus the Son of God, in order to reveal him. Rev. 19:10b says "Worship God; for the testimony of Jesus is the spirit of prophesy." Common sense helps to align these events. We know there are events transpiring to bring about a simple choice in the last days for all the world to either accept the Christ of the Judeo-Christian Bible or not. Man's countless religious views will come down to two: either accepting or rejecting the Lamb of God. The latter is being of the image of the beast, who demands worship as God.

But why is it then necessary to put hooks in the jaws of these nations to draw them back? There is not given a time between when they left and when the Lord draws them back. However, there is clear reason as to why they left. Ezek. 38:9-12 "Thou shall ascend and come like a storm; thou shall be like a cloud to cover the land, thou and all thy hordes, and many people with thee. Thus saith the Lord God: 'It shall come to pass that at the same time shall things come to your mind, and you will think an evil thought. - And you shall say, I will go up to the land of unwalled villages; I will go to those who are at rest, who dwell safely, all of them dwelling without walls, and having neither bars nor gates, - To take a spoil... from the people (Israel) who were gathered out of the nations.'"

UNWALLED CITIES

What could possibly happen that Israel would become a nation of unwalled cities, which means that the cities, and the nation, would cease to protect themselves? There is only one possibility, which would answer why they are not protecting themselves and why it would be necessary for the Lord himself to draw Gog and Magog back. The next few verses reveal an unseen wall of protection surpassing any wall man could build. And also, a blindness that only the Lord could cause to make them come back to what they had fled from.

Ezek.38:18,21-23 "And it shall come to pass at the same time that Gog shall come against Israel, says the Lord, that my fury shall come up in my face. - And I will call for a sword against him throughout all my mountains, says the Lord God; every man's sword shall be against his brother. - And I will enter into judgment against him with pestilence and with blood; and I will rain upon him, and upon his hordes, and upon the many peoples that are with him, an overflowing rain, and great hailstones, fire and brimstone. - Thus I will magnify myself, and sanctify myself, and I will be known in the eyes of many nations, and they shall know that I am the Lord."

The only thing that is reasonable is this combined mass of armies came against Israel to overwhelm her with sheer force with which she could not respond. But then unmistakably the Lord himself causes these vast armies to turn on themselves. And as with Sodom and Gomorrah, fire and brimstone from heaven will target only this army. The Lord will magnify himself and these nations will, with complete conviction, know this is the hand of the Lord God of Israel.

This is why these nations fled Israel. When they first attacked her, Israel was armed and then God intervened. And these nations were well aware of what was happening. How much later it was when the Lord drew them back would be speculation. But the only way they would attack Israel again could be explained by the Lord putting hooks in their jaws and drawing them back.

The drawing back would involve Muslim nations, and Russia, if properly identified as the chief prince Meshech and Tubal. This writer is not qualified to accurately name these nations. But believes Turkey will be involved, and also Germany, if Germany is Gomer.

Chapter 39:1 repeats the words of 38:2-3. This often done to reveal two different events. This time, invasions. The complete prophesy seems to bear this out. Ezek. 39:1-2 "Therefore, thou son of man, prophesy against Gog, and say, 'Thus says the Lord God: Behold, I am against thee, O Gog, the chief prince of Meshach and Tubal.' (This writer believes this Tubal has a connection with Baal, which involved spiritual wickedness in high places) - 'And I will turn thee back, and leave but a sixth part of thee, and will cause thee to come up from the north parts, and will bring thee upon the mountains of Israel.'"

Leaving but a sixth part expands beyond this army who comes against Israel, to the nations themselves. Ezek. 39:6-7 "And I will send a fire on Magog, and among those who dwell securely in the coastlands; and they shall know that I am the Lord. - So, I will make

my holy name known in the midst of my people, Israel, and I will not let them pollute my holy name any more; and the nations shall know that I am the Lord, the Holy One in Israel."
So not only Israel knows the reality of the Lord God, but the nations also will know of the reality, and also the hand, of this God.

LET US REASON

The Lord says 'Let us reason together'. It is up to us to reasonably interpret these words the Lord has given us. Israel was armed to the teeth, but without the supernatural intervention from the Lord she would not survive. Imagine a people knowing their lives, children and entire nation would have but hours to exist as these hordes of armies come upon Israel in such numbers that in order to kill them, you would need to kill scores of your own. And then to witness this invading army turn on themselves, completely ignoring the Israeli army and her citizens. And then fire and brimstone coming from heaven, with supernatural precision killing only those who would harm her citizens.

It would not take long to figure out what has just happened. And what effect would this have on the people of Israel? The Lord has revealed, or will bring back to mind, the covenant he has made with her. Gen. 12:2-3 "And I will make of thee a great nation, and I will bless thee, and make thy name great, and thou shall be a blessing. - And I will bless them that bless thee, and curse them that curse thee. And in you all the families of the earth will be blessed." Would not these words come to mind to those who were spared?

Israel is challenged with the reality of what just happened. How could they not believe the word of the Lord? Would they then continue to arm themselves, or trust in the Lord? Knowing that without the Lord's intervention all would be lost, could they do anything but then trust completely in the Lord? This is the reason Israel will become a nation of unwalled cities. It is reasonable to assume that when the Lord puts hooks in the jaws of Gog and Magog, drawing them back, that is the time that he will then leave but a sixth part. More than likely a small part of this army that will be spared would be silent believers in Jesus, or at least have completely rejected the teachings of the Koran.

At his time, all of the world will know there is one God, and he is the God of Israel. This world is now aware of this one God, and his power. However, the real power of God is the cross. This is impossible to understand apart from knowing God. As the cross is still foolishness to the world.

Israel's borders will possibly be enlarged, making way for all of her people to return. That is, if they had not done so already. And then with Muslim nations, along with any that allied themselves with Islam against Israel, being decimated, this would make Islam a non-factor in these last days. But this would be immaterial, as all the world will know there is but one God, and specifically who his people are. Then a question comes up. Why is this not the end of the story? All of the world will know the Lord God is the God of Israel, but Israel is composed of Messianic Jews and Orthodox Jews. This plays out in revealing who will be this coming *antichrist.*

CHAPTER 42

AFTER GOD'S HEART

It is not enough to know there is but one God. Everyone already knows this now. Even the demons know, and tremble. What has just happened in Israel will reveal to many the God of the Bible, who has shown himself to the world in a dramatic and violent way. An argument could be made: Why does not God reveal himself to mankind by just showing himself? This argument is constantly being made by those who already know the Lord has revealed himself. That is why many devote a good part of their life to forbid the very words of God to be heard and adhered to by anyone. Yes, they know, but are blinded.

There is only one thing God wants from man. His heart. This is the most precious and valuable thing that man has to offer. Jeremiah 17:9 "The heart is deceitful above all things, and desperately wicked, who can know it?" (Who can know the heart of man?) What God wants for man is a changed heart. Now as for God revealing himself to man and telling him what he wants from him; God *has* revealed himself to man, he revealed his heart. Then what did man do with the heart of God? He hung the Lord on a cross. This ultimate evil is the rejection of God's only begotten Son. This act brought about the event when the Son of God took all the evil of man as his. Of course, this is foolishness to the world. But to those who want the heart of God more than anything, this indeed is the power of God. What God wants man to have is so special that it cannot be earned, so it is presented as a gift. But to receive this gift, you must treasure it more than life itself. Then, for you to believe there is such a God confirms and affirms this special covenant the Lord has made with man.

It is a free gift that cannot be bought. 2,000 years ago, the Lord revealed himself and his power and love to mankind in the express image of himself, in his only begotten Son. And when man then saw the power and heard the wisdom of Jesus, born of a virgin in the village of Bethlehem as proclaimed by the prophets, they wanted to make him a king. This was after witnessing his words. The same words that spoke healing and life into being, and with miracles, opening the eyes and ears of the blind and deaf and even raising the dead. And signs and wonders to behold. The Lord desires to reign *in* the heart of man, not *over* him.

THE HEART OF MAN

After affirming by signs and wonders that he indeed was Messiah the redeemer, then the Lord revealed the heart of man. John 6:1-2, 5-6 "After those things Jesus went over to the sea of Galilee - And a great multitude followed him, because they saw his miracles which he did on those who were diseased. - And when a great company came unto him he said to Philip, 'Where shall we buy bread, that these may eat?' - This he said to test him, for he knew what he would do." It was then that the miracle of the feeding of the five thousand men, plus the women and children, took place. And this was from five barley loves and two small fishes. And there were twelve baskets full of uneaten food left over.

John 6:14-15 "Then these men, when they had seen the miracle that Jesus had done, said, 'This of a truth is that prophet that should come into the world.' - When Jesus perceived that they would come and take him by force, to make him a king, he departed again into a mountain himself alone." It is noteworthy that Jesus perceived they wanted to make him a king. Not their King. This mindset prepares us to understand this dilemma that not only Israel must come to grips with, but also all the world. Using the word "their" is very personal and special and is why Jesus is referred to as the bridegroom, with each individual believer separate from all others as the bride. This, also, the world cannot understand.

As discussed earlier, the Lord will draw the nations back into an Israel of undefended cities. And all the world will witness divine supernatural protection. This supernatural protection was the reason the nations fled, but then with the drawing of them back again, with the second incursion leaving but a sixth part? There will be no mistake as to what has taken place in all the world. As no doubt Israel had revealed to the world their intention of trusting in the Lord completely.

THE WORD OF GOD

We have now reached the point where all of this world knows there is but one God, the One defined in the Judeo-Christian Bible. But there is a problem that has always plagued mankind. When the Philippian jailer asked "What must I do to be saved?" he was told to just believe. Believe what? This jailer and his family were then told the gospel, as it is the way to salvation. Very few people actually just believe the simplicity of the pure gospel message, and do not realize it. When you believe something, it is because there is absolute assurance not only in your heart and mind but all your being. You know it is right. That is why it is said that the Church is built on the blood of the martyrs.

Believing is being assured there is no deception or errors involved. This really is quite involved. There can be no contradictions. But man has a problem with this, because how can it be that a document written by man can have no contradiction? The answer is, it cannot. The original Hebrew and Greek is inspired of God, not man. 2nd Timothy 3:16-17 "All scripture is given by inspiration of God, and is profitable for doctrine, for reproof, for correction, for instruction in righteousness, - That the man of God may be perfect, thoroughly furnished unto all good works." As we know, there are none that are good or righteous except God. Jesus, as truly man and truly God, is called the Word of God. As none are perfect, there has to be a means to make a man perfect beyond man's ability to do so.

The translators of the King James Bible were actually terrified for fear of making even one mistake. It is this understanding of knowing the fallibility of man that brought about Hebrew (Old Testament) and Greek (New Testament) concordances. This is so the average Christians would have access to the original writings. So, when something looks out of place they can check it out. Christians are tested as to if they believe the Word of truth. If this were not possible, the Bible itself could be the ultimate deception perpetrated by God himself.

WHO TO BELIEVE?

This brings us to whom the Lord has supernaturally revealed himself to: Israel, and all the world. So once again the statement is presented to Israel and all the world, "Just believe and you will be saved." All of the world at this time has absolute assurance that the God of Israel is the Lord God. This time is recorded in Zechariah, pertaining to this future event that will soon take place. Zech. 8:13,21-23. "And it shall come to pass that, as you were a curse among the nations, oh house of Judah and house of Israel, so I will save you, and you shall be a blessing. Fear not, but let your hands be strong." (This reveals a fearful time to be coming, but be strong.) - "And the inhabitants of one city shall go to another, saying, 'Let us go to speedily to pray before the Lord, and to seek the Lord of hosts; I will go also.' - Yes, many peoples and strong nations shall come to seek the Lord of hosts in Jerusalem, and to pray before the Lord. - In those days, it shall come to pass that ten men shall take hold out of all languages of the nations, even shall take hold of the skirt of him that is a Jew, saying, 'We will go with you; for we have heard that God is with you.'"

Now at this time there are not even professing atheists. And all of the religions of man have been rejected because of the events that have taken place in Israel. All because of these two incursions by these nations into the holy land. So now, all the nations and peoples have abandoned their religions. This, with absolute assurance that the Lord God of Israel alone is God; by miracles and wonders to behold. Surely God will now establish his everlasting kingdom! This is also what Jesus' disciples themselves believed for a season. That is, that Jesus would establish his kingdom, at this time of his visitation. As a matter of fact, he did. But it was not of this world; rather, he reigns in the hearts of his people.

2,000 years ago, there were creative miracles that revealed the presence of the Lord God of Israel. These miracles, with the addition of teachings, also authenticated that this indeed was the promised Messiah of the Hebrew prophets. Then, after many miracles by the promised Messiah, Jesus perceived they wanted to make him a king. (These miracles included returning life to those that had died. There is no reference to anyone having been brought back to life in Ezekiel or Zechariah.)

2,000 years ago, we know what eventually happened to this man (Jesus) that the people wanted to make a king. Jesus was taken by the authorities and beaten to the point of being unrecognizable as even a man. And with the religious leaders wanting him killed, he was then turned over to the governor, Pontus Pilate, for trial after they had finished beating him.

In John 18:33-38 Pilate then asked Jesus "'Are you king of the Jews? - And what have you done?' - Jesus answered, 'My kingdom is not of this world; if my kingdom were of this world my servants would fight that I should not be delivered unto the Jews. But now my kingdom is not from here.' - Pilate said, 'Are you a king, then?' Jesus answered, 'You say I am a king. To this end was I born, and for this cause came I into this world, that I should bear witness unto the truth. Every one that is of the truth hears my voice.' - Pilate said to him, 'What is truth?' And when he had said this, he went out again unto the Jews, and said unto them, 'I find in him no fault at all.'"

TRUTH

What is quite telling is that when Pilate asked the Lord "What is truth?" this followed Jesus' words "Every one that is of the truth hears my voice." There was no more conversation, and Pilate went out immediately to the Jews and stated "I find in him no fault at all." This revealed and affirmed Jesus' words "Every one that that is of truth hears my voice." Pilate did not enter into any more conversation, then immediately proclaimed to the Jews that he found no fault in the only one of whom there is no fault. Pilate heard the Lord's voice and, being of truth, immediately proclaimed it. This is not to be taken lightly, as is revealed in what takes place next.

CHOOSE

Pilate, after stating "I find no fault in him at all", then wished to release Jesus. In John 18:39-40 he said "You have a custom, that I should release unto you one at the Passover. Will you that I should release unto you the King of the Jews?" - They cried out again, saying 'Not this man, but Barabbas.' Now Barabbas was a robber." What is interesting is what follows. Pilate had the authority to release Jesus. But he doesn't do so. In fact, he does something that seems contrary. He has Jesus scourged (whipped). Then he presents this beaten and scourged Jesus to the mob. John 19:4 "Pilate, therefore, went forth again and said unto them, 'Behold, I bring him to you, that you may know that I find no fault in him.'"

Reason would say that if Pilate found no fault in Jesus, why would he have him scourged, and then crucified when he had the power to release him? Instead, he gave this decision to the people to judge themselves. Why did this happen? Because of these words: "Everyone that is of truth hears my words". The prophets and the Lord himself affirmed Jesus as the Passover Lamb, and he had to be scourged, beaten and crucified to fulfill the scriptures on that very day. Jesus *had* to die on the cross. Pontus Pilate could not do anything to alter the word of truth.

This word of truth is what defines our creator. How can this be, that my Lord would die for me? In this world, our Lord is mainly ignored. Except for a rather constant using of his name in profanity. Then, of course, there are the intellectual arguments of the foolishness of a God dying for his creation. And this is foolishness to the world. But to the believers wanting the heart of God more than life itself, it is the power of God. But thoughtful contemplation reveals something very special. Our creator has revealed something so special and personal. A love beyond comprehension; even greater than the love a mother has for her child. Then this expands from "what kind of a God is this?" to the realization that my Lord wants believers to have such a heart.

That is why God created man in his image. It is amazing and logical, that only God can create mankind in his image. As God is spirit and eternal, so is all of mankind created to be; each completely diverse one from all others. Man must spend a season in these bodies of flesh. This diverseness is evident in that each, as individuals, have the right to have their names taken out of the book of life. Rev. 22:19 "And if any man shall take away from the words of the book of this prophesy, God will take away his part from the tree of life. And out of the holy city, and from the things that are written in this book."

And now 2,000 years later we have entered this time of incredible grace where the Lord has dramatically brought mankind to this reality that there is but one God, which they reject or accept, the God of Israel. As even the demons believe there is one God, and tremble. What has happened now is that man must decide: does he want the heart of God? From the beginning, this choice has always been this simple. And of course, the heart of God is his only begotten Son; the express image of the Father. The waiting for another, or a better, deal has been going on for centuries. And soon he is about to appear. He who will soon be revealed in Jerusalem. The coming promised Messiah of Orthodoxy. This is because they have already rejected the word of God in favor of the writings of man. John the Baptist's disciples came to Jesus and asked if he were the one? Or should they should look for another? Jesus directed them to the word of God, and those things that were said of him, and were then done by him.

We will now address an important combination of events transpiring at the same time period as this invasion of Israel. We have revealed this amazing event, in soon to come history of this world. This is recorded in Ezekiel 38 and 39, involving Gog and Magog. This huge armada of nations around and north of Israel that will come against her, in order to destroy Israel completely. Then we are informed the Lord puts hooks in their jaws and draws them back. Logically assuming they left off their intent to destroy Israel, because something happened in which they could not destroy her. And that something, revealed in Ezekiel, is the Lord himself. Israel then disarms themselves, completely trusting in the Lord. Then the Lord puts hooks in the jaws of the nations, drawing them back.

Ezek. 38:9-11 "Thou shall ascend and come like a storm. Thou shall be like a cloud to cover the land, thou and all of your hordes, and many people with thee. - It also shall come to pass at the same time shall things come into your mind, and you shall think an evil thought. - And you shall say, 'I will go up to the land of unwalled villages; I will go to those who are at rest, who dwell safely, all of them dwelling without walls, and having neither bars nor gates.'" This evil thought that comes to their mind is the hook in their jaws to draw them back.

They left Israel quickly, without accomplishing their purpose. And then, after witnessing God miraculously defending them, Israel disarmed themselves. Israel has decided to now trust the Lord completely, because they realize there is no way they could defend themselves against any such future armada of nations. They are such a small nation, and should Israel try any atomic retaliation it would cause unacceptable causalities of her own citizens. But now any and every attempt to harm God's people will result in their enemy's death, by whatever means was their intent to harm them.

Ezek. 39:2a,7a "I will turn you back and leave but a sixth part; I will make my holy name known in the midst of my people, Israel." This is so there will be absolutely no doubt to all of the world that it is the Lord God of Israel who is responsible. This second time is in order to decimate them; extending to the nations' homelands that send their armies. Thus, leaving no doubt to all the world that Israel indeed is the apple of God's eye.

It is assumed here it will be but a short time before God's two witnesses will appear. The Lord's protection is that whatever evil intent this invading force has for Israel, they shall likewise be killed... this very same thing will be in place with God's two witnesses. Rev. 11:5b "If any man will hurt them, he must in this manner be killed." These two witnesses will not appear until after the man of sin starts establishing his kingdom. He will be hindered by them for three and a half years.

When trying to discern prophesy, it is often left up to us to recognize that the Lord wants us to reason and fill in events that are affirmed by other scriptures. Not only to check if we are paying attention, but also to extend our conversations (prayer) with the Lord. As the more understanding we receive, the more conversation with God that ensues. The Bible is the most reliable and complete book ever written. This extends to events that will take place often hundreds and thousands of years in the future, with absolute accuracy. It is in this effort to want not only to know the Lord, but to know him to an intimate degree, that actual dialog ensues.

It is amazing how often the Lord answers when believers search the word of God *for* the word of God. But it will be a still small voice, mainly centering on knowing his heart. This in itself reveals the most desirable and valuable gift, and the greatest joy of all. All other truths follow. There is but one criterion: You must believe *all* the Bible is the word of God. And apparent contradictions reveal greater insight, along with a greater assurance concerning the reliability of the Word of God.

OVERSTEPPED AUTHORITY

The world knows that the Lord God is the Lord of Israel. This will leave only two choices. Shortly after the Lord's intervention in Israel, the temple will be built in which antichrist will appear. Satan will overstep the authority that God has allowed him. He will enter this man of sin in the temple of God as God. This will be seven years before the return of Jesus and his angels from the heavens. Because Satan does this, he and his angels will be cast out of heaven. This casting out of heaven will be the preparing of a place to receive those who will be raptured.

2 Thes. 2:1-4 "We beseech you, brethren, by the coming of the Lord Jesus Christ, and by our gathering together unto him, - That you be not soon shaken in mind, nor troubled, neither by word, nor spirit, nor letter from us, as the day of Christ is at hand. – Let no man deceive you by any means, for that day shall not come, except there come a falling away first, and that man of sin be revealed, the son of perdition, – Who opposes and exalts himself above all that is called God, or that is worshiped; so that he, as God, sits in the temple of God, showing himself that he is God."

This is a clear declaration that this event must take place before Jesus comes to gather the saints into himself. The rapture will not occur until after this man of sin appears in the temple of God, and then demands worship as God. This is the start of the last week, or seven years, before Jesus returns to start his thousand-year reign. When, during these last seven years, will the rapture occur? We are assured it can't, until two things happen first. A falling away, and "that man of sin, the son of perdition", is revealed. There has always been many people falling away. However this second part; the man of sin, the son of perdition, reveals a specific onetime event that reveals with absolute clarity this falling away.

At this time all the world and Israel will know that the Lord God is the God of Israel. There will be two belief systems in Israel at this time: the Orthodox Jew and the Messianic Jew. This man of sin will be Orthodox, as Christians are assured they are the temple of God and the risen Christ will soon return from the heavens. The temple to be built in Jerusalem is where antichrist will proclaim himself the promised Messiah. This is the ultimate falling away. This name "son of perdition" gives further authenticity to these events.

Antichrist will be hindered three times before he can reign in the last three and a half years. The first hindering will be God's two witnesses for three and a half years. The second will be for a short time when God's two witnesses raise from the dead, three and a half days after Satan kills them. Then the third time, this writer inserts a plague that affects every person on this world. This event that reveals the Love of God that is wrath. How can this be? This is not adding to nor taking from scripture. But inserting scripture to verify scripture and the very heart of God.

During this three and a half years' time of God's two witnesses, they called plagues upon the earth, and for withholding of rain. Why were not the wonderful works of God exhibited during the time of their testimony? Would not this win souls for the Lord? This is to affirm of whom they are testifying of, and to reveal to the people this giving, loving God. And then to reveal the rewards if they just accept Jesus, and testify of him.

The answer to this involves the heart. And this can never be explained to a world that believes the preaching of the cross is foolishness. People are won over by promises that fulfill the desires of their heart. The Lord came to change the heart of man. And the only way this is possible is to desire and hunger after the heart of God. And that is why the preaching of the cross is the power of God.

Two thousand years ago, the world witnessed the express image of God. And they crucified him. And through the centuries, many who believed on him fared no better. Right now, what is being addressed is this final event, encapsulating 6,000 years of lifetimes into three and a half years of testimony by these two witnesses of God. And mankind has been making choices all of these years in accepting or denying the Lord. Jesus told Nicodemus he must be born of the water and Spirit to enter the Kingdom of God. This is the promise of God in his covenant to mankind. "The promise of the Spirit through faith." (Gal. 3:14)

The finalization is the rapture. This born-again event is man's real birth, when mankind will embark on their eternal journey. An eternity that we are told, in 1 Cor. 2:9-10, "Eye has not seen nor ear heard, neither has entered into the heart of man, the things that God has prepared for them who love him. - But God has revealed them unto us by his Spirit. For the spirit searches all things, yea, the deep things of God." How can it be that what has entered into the heart of man cannot be seen nor heard, but is revealed by His Spirit?

This is answered in the covenant God has made *to* man. And those who receive it as a covenant *with* man, are those who do not realize this is a living covenant in the person of the Son of God. Man can reject this covenant. No one can break it; this covenant can only be rejected. Yes, God did create man in his image. And it appears evident their names are written in the Lamb's book of life. This spirit, which is the essence of man, indwells this body of flesh for a season. This when they are tested and tried, and some are refined as gold. But few receive this. Rev. 13:8 "And all that dwell on the earth shall worship him, whose names are not written in the book of life of the Lamb slain from the foundation of the world." Rev. 22:17-19 "And the Spirit and the bride say, Come. And let him that heareth say, Come. And let him that is athirst come. And whosoever will, let him take of the water of life (Word of God) freely. - For I testify unto every man that hears the words of the prophesy of this book, If any man shall add unto these things, God shall add unto him the plagues that are written in this book; - And if any man should shall take away from the words of the book of this prophesy, God shall take away his part of the tree of life, and out of the holy city, and from the things which are written in this book."

It seems there is a consistent rejection of what God has established. God cannot, and will not, break this covenant with man. However, if man involves himself to make a new covenant, this new covenant has rejected the will and Word of God. Let us examine not only these words of life, but an event that will take place that clearly defines this separation of choice.

CHAPTER 43

COVENANT

This covenant is a promise from God to man. He gave it to Abraham. A covenant is an agreement between two or more. And as the Lord cannot lie, deceive, or break this promise, this then is an everlasting unbreakable promise made to man, and affirmed by Himself. Man cannot break this promise, only reject it for himself. The only part man has is that he must want this promise more than life itself. And what is this promise that is offered to man? It is the heart of God. This is clearly revealed in Jesus, the express image of God. Hebrews 1:1-3 "God, who at sundry times and in diverse manners spoke in times past unto the fathers by the prophets, - Has in these last days spoken to us by his Son, whom he has appointed heir to all things, by whom also made the worlds; - Who, being the brightness of his glory, and the express image of his person, and upholding all things by the word of his power, when he had by himself purged our sins, sat down on the right hand of the Majesty on high."

So, as God made this covenant, it had to be affirmed and agreed upon with another, which neither Abraham, nor could any other man could qualify to keep this everlasting covenant. Hebrews 6:13,18a "For when God made this promise to Abraham, because he could swear by no greater, he swore by himself, - That by two immutable things, in which it impossible for God to lie, we might have a strong consolation." (The Father and the Son, whom are one.)

This covenant given to Abraham from God includes all of

mankind. Israel is involved because of faithful Abraham. Satan is the god of this world because man has made him so. But the Son, and those who believe on God, are not of the world. In John 17:13-17, when Jesus is praying to the Father, he says: "And now I come to you, and these things I speak in the world, that they might have my joy fulfilled in themselves. - I have given them thy word, and the world has hated them, because they are not of the world, even as I am not of the world. - I pray not that you should take them out of the world, but that you would keep them from the evil. - They are not of the world, even as I am not of the world. - Sanctify them through thy word. Thy word is truth."

There is something else that is not of this world, and is part of this covenant. The land of Israel. The USA, its leaders, its people, the world, and Israel would be wise to heed these words concerning this special land of Israel. Lev. 25:23 "The land shall not be sold forever. For the land is my land, for you are strangers and sojourners with me." (Not of this world.) Keep in mind what is being conveyed in these words: "You are strangers and sojourners with me." There is no great mystery. It means exactly what is said. This home (land) and those who are of the seed of Abraham are here but for a short time as sojourners.

And then on May 14, 1948 this world witnessed the truth of the word of God in a miraculous event only exceeded by the creation, and the birth of Jesus. This miracle is the word of God that was proclaimed, and assured all of this event that would happen: The resurrected Israel, as foretold by their prophets. But this clearly defined and articulated prophesy given in words to the world in Ezekiel chapters 36-37... this pure word of God... was dismissed or ignored by a world in which truth is not just ignored, but *rejected* as their enemy. But soon this world will not be able to deny or ignore the Lord of Truth.

That is when the Lord himself intervenes, by defending Israel against man's attempt to wipe her from the face of the earth. This will affect and reveal to the world beyond any doubt the hand of the Lord. This soon coming event is recorded in chapters 38-39 of Ezekiel. Then all of the world will profess that the God of Israel is the Lord alone. Man is now moving into the final chapter of what has always been, but cleverly presented in multiple choices; having to reject Jesus, the express image of God, or accept him. You either accept the Word of the Lord or you do not. But then the Lord eliminates this multitude of excuses of rejecting his word, and brings it down to two choices. You either believe, and choose the risen Messiah, the Son of God, who will establish his everlasting kingdom with his return from the heavens with the saints; or you choose this man. "This man of sin to be revealed, the son of perdition. - Who opposes and exalts himself above all that is called God. Or is worshiped, so that he, as God, sits in the temple of God, showing himself that he is God."

THE REBBE

A small booklet of only 46 pages, The Rebbe, just begins to define the qualities and attributes of these special Rabbis and their compassion to others. And this goes beyond just their fellow Jews, but to all of humanity. When thinking of the righteousness of Job, these special Rabbis come to mind. Just a small passage is taken from this booklet The Rebbe. Page 5 - "What is it about the Rebbe that exudes so much love? What is it about the Rebbe that makes him so present even now - binding so many to him so deeply? - The following is an attempt to express personal appreciation of the Rebbe by exploring some of the manner in which he expresses himself in his discourses, correspondences, personal conduct, and modus operandi."

It is also written in this booklet of these special dedicated men: "This essay does not and cannot adequately render the Rebbe's personality and conduct. Nor is it capable of touching upon the Rebbe's immense scholarship. It is instead a humble endeavor to capture some sense of what the Rebbe means to so many – and what his uniqueness means to many - and his uniqueness and contribution to world Jewry. It is an effort to record and share a little bit of the Rebbe's consuming passion in the service of G-d, his love, his study of the Torah, and his vision of a world perfected." It is also stated of the Rebbe: "This was not a man who was interested in creating followers; this was a man who was passionate about creating leaders." It is obvious these men that are waiting for the coming Messiah are not evil. Quite the contrary.

This was given to reveal that even man's greatest praises to their best, compared to God and what he desires for man, exceeds our comprehension. Our greatest righteousness are as filthy rags. There is none good, no, not one. These are kind and gentle people, but they have rejected the Son of God looking for another.

CHAPTER 44

ROMAN CHURCH

Christianity started with the cross, in which Jesus gave up his life and took the sins of whomever would accept his sacrifice for them. Immediately afterward there was persecution. First by the Jews, and then by Rome. This persecution by Rome was quite extensive at the time of the emperor Constantine.

Constantine was quite different than any of the rulers of Rome, or for that manner most pagan rulers. In that he, being a pagan himself, observed this continual persecution of the Christian church and said it did not make sense, nor was it reasonable. He observed how the Christians paid their taxes, were hard working and honest with high moral standards; in fact, observed that the Christians were the very best citizens in his kingdom. And he believed this persecution was unreasonable and counterproductive. This mindless hatred toward Christians is sadly analyzed only by a few, as did Constantine. Yes, very few leaders are concerned with anything but their position of authority.

Constantine had separated himself from what could be termed 'mob psychology'. This is a constant attack of negative and false accusations and unreasonable hatred, which produces acceptance of lies. The fact that this only works against a specific truth should reveal there is such a thing as spiritual warfare going on. But we will not paint a picture of Constantine as a special man of God just because he recognized what actually all of mankind can see, but most reject.

We will not judge the mind of this man, but only state what he did. The most positive and important contribution was that the Bible was actually accepted in this church. For no matter how perverted a church may become, if the Bible is retained, anyone searching for truth can find it.

This is the start, or beginning, of this "woman who rides the beast" which all of the world gets caught up with, and then expands to all facets of life. The emperor of Rome is recognized as the head of Rome not only politically, but religiously. Some emperors claimed Godhood. He accepted Christianity, and proclaimed it as the official religion of Rome in 313 A.D. But he continued to head the pagan priesthoods. And he officiated at pagan celebrations, all the while building Christian churches. This reveals that he was not a Christian. This is proven because the only avenue to eternal life, through Jesus Christ, was rejected by him. And then in A.D. 325 he, as the de facto head of, convened over the first ecumenical council. (The combining of several churches as one for the sake of unity. In this case, to install the Roman church to be the head.) However, these pagan churches could keep their deities and practices. This further separated it from being Christian.

The Christians that received him honored him as Bishop of Bishops. And Constantine called himself Vicarious Christi (Vicar of Christ, or another Christ. Or, acting in the place of Christ.) In the middle ages, the Bishops of Rome began to claim they were the sole representatives of Christ on the earth. Demanding that the entire church worldwide must be subject to their rule, they forbade any other Bishops to be called Papa or Pope and took to themselves the three titles of Constantine: Pontifex Maximus, Vicar of Christ, Bishop of Bishops. They retain this to this day. They also claimed infallibility for any official pronouncement of their Pope, who is voted on by man to be receiving this title. And should their pronouncements be contradicted by the Bible, the Bible would be in error.

The Christian church has always existed from the time of Christ, to the time of the Roman Catholic church that appeared almost three hundred years after the beginning of the Church. It has always affirmed there is but one Christ, the Son of God, the Redeemer and only mediator. 1st Tim. 2:5-6 "For there is one God, and one mediator between God and men, the man, Jesus Christ, - Who gave himself a ransom for all, to be testified in due time."

It is not the purpose here to argue or debate religion, but only to present and analyze this world during these last days. With the assumption that the Bible has a proven record of absolute accuracy, what has been and will be presented are documentations from but a few of the many prophets... Ezekiel, Daniel, Zechariah and the prophesies of Revelation... at the point in this specific coming time when all of the world will have absolute assurance there is but one God. And that he is the God of Israel. What is to be given now are events to take place in these last few years. It is during these last few years that God himself will intervene to narrow this down to receiving a very clear choice. At this time, none can say anyone deceived them. There is but one choice: To believe and receive the risen Christ, conceived of the Holy Spirit; or choose an anointed, or self-anointed, man.

CONCEIVED OF THE HOLY SPIRIT

Those who reject Jesus are rejecting the only way to enter into life; that is, entering the Kingdom of God. Luke 1:28, 31-32, 34-35: "The angel Gabriel greeted Mary, saying, 'You are highly favored; the Lord is with you. Blessed are you among women. You shall conceive in thy womb and shall bring forth a Son, and shall call him Jesus. - He shall be great and shall be called the Son of the Highest. And the Lord shall give unto him the throne of his father.' Then said Mary unto the angel, 'How shall this be, seeing I know not a man?' - And the angel said, 'The Holy Spirit shall come upon you, and the power of the Highest shall overshadow you. Therefore also that holy thing which shall be born of thee shall be called the Son of God.'" The birth of Jesus, the Christ, was because he was conceived of the Holy Spirit and was the express image of God. Now, for man to be in the image of God and enter into the kingdom of God, he must be born again. He must be first born of water, then of the Spirit. A new birth, as Jesus explained to Nicodemus (John 3:5). This was already established as recorded in the very first chapter of the Bible. But man, after a season in the flesh, has the right to reject what God has done.

The essence of man is his spirit. This spirit is a prisoner in this body of flesh until its death. It can be explained as a programmer of the brain. And when the brain goes the way of this body, the spirit of man goes the way it has chosen.

CHAPTER 45

GENESIS TO REVELATION

Gen. 1:26a, 27 "And God said, 'Let us make man in our image, after our likeness.' - So God created man in his own image, in the image of God created he him; male and female created he them. Gen. 2:7 "And the Lord God formed man of the dust of the ground and breathed into his nostrils the breath of life; and man became a living soul." Unless you know all of the narrative, there are obvious, glaring contradictions. And only if you are completely convinced the Bible is the word of God, will you know these two scriptures give insight. In these two creations, the first depicts mankind, male and female, without sin and in the image of God. In the second, man was formed out of the dust of the ground. The first is spiritual and eternal. The second shows that mankind returns to dust after a season. The first involves man, with the Father, Son, and Holy Spirit. The second involves the creator of all things, Jesus the Son of God.

Anyone who believes that they are made in the image of God cannot become in the image of God. A whole book was written addressing this. This book was about the most righteous man on the earth, Job. When Job was given eyes to see the Lord he cried out, "I had heard of you by the hearing of the ear, but now my eyes see you. Therefore I abhor myself, and repent in dust and ashes." (Job 39:5-6) As new Christians recognize their need for a savior, it is not so dramatic as that. But there must be an *absolute conviction* of this need.

THE TEMPLE

Just before the last seven years, there will be a temple built in Jerusalem. This has been in planning for years. And it will take only one year to complete. As all the world has witnessed the miraculous intervention of the Lord in behalf of Israel, this same world will know the Lord God of Israel is, indeed, the Lord God. But they will not all *know* him. As in Israel, there will be Christians worldwide who have received the living, resurrected Jesus as Lord. With the assurance that he will soon return from the heavens with his saints.

The Christians in Israel will not be involved in the building of this temple, as they are told and know that *they* are the temple of God. 1st Cor. 3:16 "Know you not that ye are the temple of God, and the Spirit of God dwells in you?" This temple will be built by the Orthodox Jews who have rejected the risen Christ.

When this temple is built in Jerusalem, an Orthodox Jew will present himself as this promised Messiah. This will happen along with "power and signs and lying wonders of falsehoods." (2nd Thes. 2:9) Now, since these are lying wonders, that means they are an illusion. When Satan first enters this man, there will very likely be many miraculous signs. But because of Satan doing this without God's permission, Satan and his angels will be cast out of heaven. Then will come the lying signs and wonders.

It is at this time that God's two witnesses will appear. This, after the man of perdition has revealed himself as the promised Messiah. Not only will they appear, but they will completely hinder any of these lying wonders to continue. Now this man of sin will be silenced. Satan and the rest of his angels are now demons, having lost their angelic powers. But because Satan has entered into this man, then he alone of all those cast out of heaven possessed him, having had complete control of this man. Satan and his angels are now hindered by the Spirit of God, and must remain silent for three and a half years. This includes an inability to influence or possess. 2nd Thess. 2:7 "For the mystery of iniquity does already work. Only he who now hinders will continue to hinder until he is taken away." This taking away is when there will be the gathering of the saints to meet the Lord in the air, commonly called the rapture.

CHAPTER 46

SEARCHING THE HEART OF GOD

We are admonished not to add to or take from the word of God. We are also told to reason together, and prove all things, and hold fast to that which is good. Many scriptures appear to be incomplete; and they are, for the purpose of encouraging us to inquire or reason continually with the Lord. He wishes for us to have conversations with him, and to search his heart. The Lord wants us to reason and think on his word. An example of this will be given concerning these last seven years. There will be no taking from or adding to the word of God. But we will be using different scriptures, which taken by themselves causes one to wonder, why is the Lord doing this? And when is it taking place?

It is not unreasonable for us to believe the Creator of all that there is. He created this from nothing. And through his very existence, the world and all there is exists. And it continues to do so, only because of his presence. Every word and action from God has a purpose. And nothing can be withheld from him. There is, however, one exception as to what he cannot do, but only because to do it would undermine the very heart of God. *He will not force his will upon man.* For to do so would eliminate both his justice and love. Even man knows you cannot demand love. And as for justice, can any man define perfect justice? Both love and justice will be administered; but not now. All of mankind has been given the freedom to reject the word of God, or to be as they were created to be. That is, to be in the image of God. Man was created, not cloned.

And now we will endeavor to make sense of what appear to be random unconnected prophesies, in order to give greater completeness to other scriptures. Satan enters into this man of sin. This man presents himself as God, as he is now being possessed, completely controlled by Satan. Satan has overstepped what the Lord has allowed. This causes a war in heaven where he and his angels are cast out. After being cast out, he is now the Devil, and his angels are demons. But these demons are hindered from entering into any man. The reason for this will be made clear shortly, as there cannot be any contradiction in scripture.

The two prophets will prophesy for three and a half years, along with affirmation from the Christians in this world. But those of the world will hate these two men because of the plagues from them, along with the word of God. All this time this world has been trying to kill these messengers of the Lord. The world has rejected their words, and are angered by these plagues that accompany the word. But the Christians are convicted, and affirm that these plagues are what man deserves. They, as Job, are convicted of the righteousness of God and the depravity of man. As Job did, they understand; and seeing God, they abhor themselves, and repent in dust and ashes. The world cannot understand this. But they are filled with joy and peace, as they embrace the words of these two men. They are washed clean. But unless they knew there was a *need* to be washed, there would be no repentance. And they are thankful for being constantly reminded. This overwhelms them to the point that each reminder of sin multiplies what has been forgiven. How can this be? It is this indescribable love, the heart of God that overwhelms.

Then after three and a half years, as they finish their testimony, the world witnesses this man of sin. The son of perdition who has claimed Godhood. This man who has remained silent for all of these years. He does what no man could do. He kills these two prophets of God. Now the Bible does not specifically state this. However, what the Bible does state is Rev. 11:7,10 "And when they have finished their testimony, the beast that ascends out of the bottomless pit shall make war with them, and shall overcome them, and kill them. - And they that dwell on the earth shall rejoice over them, and make merry, and send gifts one to another, because those prophets tormented them that dwelled on the earth."

And then three and a half days later, these two men stand on their feet and are called up to meet the Lord. (This is the rapture, or gathering of the saints to meet the Lord in the air.) Rev. 11:11 "...and great fear fell upon those who saw them." And now there will be few to dispute the man of sin's words. But he again is interrupted. This time for five months. However, at this time, this world is engulfed in unimaginable terror.

CHAPTER 47

LEFT BEHIND

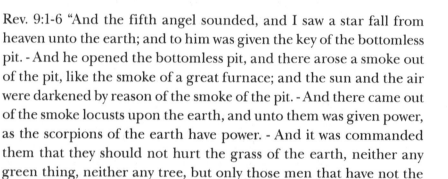

Rev. 9:1-6 "And the fifth angel sounded, and I saw a star fall from heaven unto the earth; and to him was given the key of the bottomless pit. - And he opened the bottomless pit, and there arose a smoke out of the pit, like the smoke of a great furnace; and the sun and the air were darkened by reason of the smoke of the pit. - And there came out of the smoke locusts upon the earth, and unto them was given power, as the scorpions of the earth have power. - And it was commanded them that they should not hurt the grass of the earth, neither any green thing, neither any tree, but only those men that have not the seal of God in their foreheads. - And to them it was given that they should not kill them, but that they should torment them five months; and their torment was like the torment of a scorpion, when he strikes a man. - And in those days shall men seek death, and shall not find it; and shall desire to die, and death shall flee from them."

Rev. 9:11 "And they had a king over them, who is the angel of the bottomless pit, whose name in the Hebrew tongue is Abaddon, but in the Greek tongue Apollyon."

All of man will be tormented except those who have the seal of God. This would also include this man, the son of perdition who has proclaimed himself God. The epistle Jude speaks of these evil Angels, and how they ended up in chains, under darkness in this bottomless pit. Jude 6 "And the angels that kept not their first estate, but left their own habitation, he has reserved in everlasting chains under darkness unto the judgment of the great day." There is given a physical appearance as locusts. Then they are further described in Rev. 9:7-11 "And the shape of the locusts were like horses prepared for battle. And on their heads were, as it were, crowns like gold, and their faces were like the faces of men. - And they had hair like the hair of women, and their teeth were like the teeth of lions. - And they had breastplates of iron; and the sound of their wings was like the sounds of chariots of many horses running to battle. - And they had tails like scorpions, and there were stings in their tails; and their power was to hurt men five months. - And they had a king over them, who is the angel of the bottomless pit, whose name in the Hebrew tongue is Abaddon, but in the Greek tongue is Apollyon."

These were angels that left their first estate. They were not cast down, but left on their own. And that was because they would not adhere to the Lord's rules. They had to then be locked up in chains of darkness, and later released by this angel of God at this specific time. Always keep in mind that the Lord does not control man or angels, but he is in complete control over them and events that will fulfill his purpose. Men and angels have the freedom to align themselves where they will. Though it is God's will that none would perish, it is man and angels that will establish with whom they will align. Revelation 9:3 states "They were given power, as the scorpions of the earth have power."

Jude identifies these disruptive creatures as those angels that left their first estate. As to how or if they are different from these other types of angels identified in the Bible, it doesn't say. Cherubim have two wings. Another type of angel is called seraphim, having six wings (Isaiah 6:2). There is no identifications of the number of their wings from these angels except they have wings. Nor are they given a name or names. Only that they left, and were not cast out, of heaven. And though a description is given of them, it is most likely in the same manner as Satan. He was described in Isaiah 14 and to a greater extent in Ezekiel 28:12-19. Satan was described as fit to be in Eden, the garden of God, and then described as "The anointed cherub that covered, and I (God) set you so; you were upon the holy mountain of God..." (Ezekiel 28:13-14) His beauty and magnificence was as one to be in God's presence, but then he fell, only to at a later time to be brought down to the pit. Isaiah 14:15 "Yet thou shall be brought down to hell, to the sides of the pit."

These demons, however, are described as dreadful, probably befitting them and their present abode and purpose. Also, the description is of them when they are coming from the pit. They wanted to leave God's kingdom, whereas Satan and his angels did not. And these seemed to only want to torment and destroy. We know this because they had to be told not to destroy any plant life when they were released for a season. The key given to this angel of God is for a very specific purpose; to release these evil sadistic demons upon this earth at this particular time. Every person on the earth will be directly affected.

This also affects those who missed the rapture, and then later became Christians who have the seal of God. This writer has involved them in what could be called a special mission field of extraordinary circumstances. And like all mission fields, they are called by God to be involved in an important part of his will. God can do anything, but he will not present in his word a situation where doubters can point it out as an obvious error or contradiction. In such situations, it is up to the Christians to read the Scriptures to reveal special truths. This writer incorporated what Christians wish to do to show gratitude and thankfulness, desiring to mirror their Savior.

Those having missed the rapture, and knowing *why* they did, now completely believe. The rapture is a special event. After it occurs, new believers are raptured at the time they believe. These demons can't torment these new Christians, as they have the seal of God. They should have entered the kingdom of God immediately after believing. This writer believes they did not wish to leave yet. Why? Because they knew the torment inflicted by these demons was so horrific, those stung would wish to die. But *if there were no one to care for them, none could live*; as this torment would last five months.

These new Christians are now caregivers for all the world. This is because their hearts are on what they want for others. These new Christians are not Christians because of the promises of the reward of heaven, but what has always been promised and engraved on the heart of man. That is, to be in the Image of God. And the reward is the eternal presence of God. Rev. 21:22-23 "And I saw no temple in it (the City of the New Jerusalem). For the Lord God Almighty and the Lamb are the temple of it. - And the city had no need of the sun, neither of the moon, to shine in it, for the glory of God did light it, and the Lamb is the lamp of it."

The normal reaction would be to separate themselves from these who are afflicted, since they had already begun to show their hostility toward them before they became tormented by these demons. Then suddenly, like divine providence, those who would likely kill them are completely incapacitated. But instead of rejoicing over the hand of God on their enemies, their thoughts and concerns are on those who do not yet have the seal of God.

And this is precisely *why* they have the seal of God. It is imperative that they act quickly. There is so much to be done, and by so few. The power grid, the facilities to care for them, the handling and distribution of food and medical needs, etc. This would need to be an immediately coordinated, worldwide effort that could not be successful without the Lord. Yes, the only possibility would be divine intervention. This would be the greatest humanitarian and evangelistic worldwide event ever. The world is divided into those who have the seal of God and those who do not. Those who are not of the Lord are completely incapacitated. And without these Christians, there is no possibility of any of those without the seal of God coming through this ordeal alive. And if not for the presence and hand of the Lord, this effort would fail. Those with the seal of God are continually thankful for His presence.

For five months, these Christians would care for these people that were tormented so horrifically and continually that they wanted to die. To stay alive for all this time they would need constant care. There would no doubt be many of those being tormented that would be thankful, and aware that the Christians were both unaffected and the ones giving this care. And after the five months are over, there would still be a need for them. It is during this time, as they regained their health, that the gospel message could be more easily given and comprehended. (We now have about three years until the Lord returns from the heavens.)

The Lord has given five months of continual pain and torment to all of mankind that have rejected him. And with this, the continual presence of saints. These saints became servants caring for their every need, and then stayed with them until they were whole. And they asked for nothing. Also, it can be assumed they never spoke of what they had done. But, with joy, spoke of what the Lord had done for those whom they are caring for. That he sent his Son to die for them, and they only need to believe there is such a God.

So now the Lord is finally giving this man, who has proclaimed himself as God, a full opportunity to addresses this world without interruption. He is addressing a world in which every individual has been tormented by these demonic forces for five months. And the Christian caregivers suddenly disappeared from their midst, as now the Lord pours out his wrath upon a world in antichrist control. A world which receives continual devastation. This writer has refrained from writing of these events that affect the whole world, in which varying accounts are given as to how many people could survive. When referring to his return with his angels and saints, Jesus stated that *if those days were not shortened, there would be no flesh saved alive.*

Before this outpouring of the wrath of God, all of the world has witnessed firsthand the heart of God. So now we can understand how this, the wrath of God, can and does reveal the mercy and love of the Lord. It also authenticates these words: God so loves the world and wants that none be lost. Satan wins nothing in what is often described as a contest for the soul of man. This is not a contest, but a lifetime of trials and testing. The Lord calls this a time of refining of men as fine gold and silver is refined; with fire. This, as the spirit of man is captive in this temporal body of flesh with full opportunity to choose. Will it be the image of the beast? Or as we were created to be; in the image of God? This choosing is simply an acceptance or rejection of what we have been created to be.

So how can man understand what it means to be in the image of God, or the heart of God? As we are told, "Eye has not seen, nor ear heard, nor entered into the heart of man, the things that God has prepared for those who love him." And then we are told "But God has revealed them to us by his Spirit; for the Spirit searches all things, yea, the deep things of God." (1st Cor. 2:9-10) The word of God answers most of our questions. And most importantly, it teaches us the heart of God. There are many scriptures that jump out, revealing apparent contradictions. But as we know, there is no contradiction in the word of God. So, we do not ignore these scriptures that appear to contradict other scriptures. Often it is these scriptures that we are drawn to because of our complete assurance that there can be no error. And if we search and inquire of the Lord, He will reveal his heart. If we did not have this assurance and belief in God and his word, and if we refused to inquire, we would not receive this understanding.

SAVED IN CHILD BEARING?

One such "mysterious" scripture that reveals the heart of God as it is understood is 1st Timothy 2:15. This concerns salvation: "Notwithstanding, she shall be saved in childbearing, if they continue in faith and charity and holiness with sobriety." Now without carefully reading this scripture it would seem that every mother would be saved. This is what could be called an attention getter. It is stated they will be saved "If they continue in faith." What is the Lord revealing concerning child bearing? All female animals are born with an instinct to protect their offspring, sometimes even against their own mate. Often they sacrifice their own lives. Had not the Lord given this instinct, not only to protect but care for their offspring until they are able to fend for themselves, there would be no continuation of their kind.

This protection is revealed in a mother bear. When sensing danger, she will smack her cubs, sending them up a tree for protection until the danger passes. And then later she will call them down. And when the cubs are well grown enough to fend for themselves, she will once again smack them, and again they scurry up a tree. But this time she does not call them down. It is time for the mother and her cubs to go their separate ways. There is no way anyone could believe in the evolution of man and God's creatures, if they have any kind of knowledge of either.

This is also what the Lord has instilled in all of mankind in their spirits, or essence of being which is eternal. Our spirit is not programmed to function just to exist. But all are given the freedom to choose their destiny. The key word is the *freedom*. God is neither a despot nor a manipulator. In fact, it goes beyond wanting the heart to wanting, more than life itself, the heart of God. There is a natural instinct to protect our children. But for Christians, there is an added dimension of wanting to give them the knowledge of a creator God, and with this an even greater concern for their offspring's soul, or spirit. (Of which the Lord commands the husband is to take the lead role.) This concern for their eternal souls is of far greater value, but cannot come about without a great love for their child. And this is perhaps an even greater mystery. Why does not the Lord instill an even greater overwhelming love that mankind would bring their children, and others, to know and receive the Lord? The answer to this is… he does. But there is a hindrance called self.

Jesus gave of himself completely. And God so loves the world that he gave his only begotten Son. And all man has to do is believe in him. It is impossible to hear or read the gospel message without understanding this. But to completely believe there is such a God as this is easily dissuaded. So, what it comes down to is quite simple. Do you want more than anything to have such a heart as this, the heart of God? This seems an impossible desire, because of man's fallen nature. But to long for and then to receive such a God is what separates the world's religions from Christianity. The more you are forgiven, the more clearly you can understand the righteousness of God. And the greater this becomes thankfulness and love. How can it be that my Savior would die for me?

CHAPTER 48

JESUS RETURNS

Rev. 19:20 "And the beast was taken, and with him the false prophet (the one claiming to be God) that did signs before him, with which he deceived them that had received the mark of the beast, and them that worshiped his image. These both were cast alive into a lake of fire burning with brimstone."

Those who are raptured at the gathering of the church, both living and dead, will be joined by these new Christians as part of his army. And they will reign with Jesus for 1,000 years. Rev. 5:10 "And has made us unto our God kings and priests, and we will reign on the earth." It is stated the Christians will reign with Christ as kings and priests. Combining scriptures, it seems the saints are identified as a royal priesthood, or kingly priests. Violence and wars will not be allowed. Much will be answered in that it is stated Jesus will rule them with a rod of iron. As the saints are washed and made pure, and the angels are of God, we know that they are not to be among those ruled with a rod of iron.

As Christians, we are told we are in this world, but not of it. Jesus has not established his everlasting kingdom to be occupied by a decimated world in which none are born again Christians, and must be ruled by rod of iron. The Bible continues to have surprises right to the end. As priests, there will only be taught the words of life. This is obvious, as there will be no deception. And there will be a clear precise rendering of the scriptures, as all the world will know of the

Lord. They may have their own gods. But only the true God and his words will be presented, as there can be no false teaching.

Rev. 2:26-27 "He that overcomes and keeps my works unto the end, to him will I give power over the nations; - And he shall rule over them with a rod of iron; as the vessels of a potter shall they be broken." This group that will reign with Jesus will include God's angels, who were ministering spirits to the heirs of salvation. The question is: how will the resurrected saints rule this coming world with a rod of iron? Ruling with a rod of iron does not align with God's past relationship with man. Mankind was created with complete freedom to obey or reject God. Now at this time there will be no wars, hurting, lies, or evil permitted in all of this kingdom of God. This is not possible in man's present state. So there has to be put in place an unusual situation or controlling factor without the actual control of the minds and hearts of man.

All of God's saints now have become as they were created to be: in the image of God, after his likeness. This no doubt would include these new Christians that refused to take the name and number of the beast. They would then become of the image of God after they are martyred, and return with the Lord as kings and priests or kingly priests. But they will not control. How do you rule with a rod of iron, and not have complete control? And how many saints and angels will return with the Lord? Jude 14 says "And Enoch, the seventh from Adam, prophesied of these, saying, 'Behold, the Lord comes with ten thousands of his saints.'" This is but one of many descriptions, with others giving numbers that appear much larger. This is not a contradiction, as no exact number is given.

SERVANTS REIGN AS SERVANTS

Ruling with a rod of iron as a servant does not seem to make sense. But God has stated, "My ways are not your ways." It seems that the greater the servant one is, the greater he will be in the kingdom of heaven. A mother or father that rules their house with a rod of iron, but doing so as a Christian, is a servant of God. They are ruling as such, and this is for the love and benefit of their children. Matt. 11:11 "Verily I say to you, among those born of women there has not risen a greater than John the Baptist. Notwithstanding, he that is the least in the kingdom of heaven is greater than he." Men with new eyes and hearts can then clearly understand why the cross is the power of God.

Isaiah 11:6-9 has a description of this new world. As to how the wolf will lay down with the lamb is not that difficult to understand. Animals will not rebel when the Lord programs this new behavior in them, as there will be no wars, violence or hurt in all this world. It appears that this world will be unable to misbehave. There will be some way to do this without controlling man, as an absolute hindering would reduce him to a robot. This problem has been resolved in principle, as recorded in Rev. 11 with God's two prophets. In which, if any man would hurt them, they would in like manner be killed. Logically this same principle will be used at this time, except they will not be killed. During this time, they would be hurt as they desired to hurt, but in a way that would cause no harm to anyone. This could be defined as the ultimate, just, rod of Iron. Very much as an all-knowing, just, and caring father when correcting his children, if he loved them. There is another element that will be looked into later.

For those left to repopulate the earth, it would be much like your conscience, in that any bad behavior on your part would be revealed to you before you could implement it; to the point of achieving its purpose. It could cause a problem, however. Would this now forced corrected behavior result in self-righteousness in some? Therefore, diminishing their awareness that they need a savior? That is why the gospel, and the history of man right up to the return of Jesus and his army, is taught. And none of man's religions, or revised history, or evolution will be taught. God does not change. He wants to change the heart of man for a new heart. This can only be achieved through mankind who want, more than life itself, the heart of God. This last 1,000 years the Lord will be giving man a world in which there will be no deception allowed which could hinder man from becoming what God created him to be.

As these resurrected saints are Priests and Kings of God, there will be a constant revealing and education of the Lord and his words. And no doubt a clear revelation of prophetic scriptures foretelling events as they were fulfilled; and their purpose. There will be no lies or deception allowed in all of Christ's kingdom. The only lies and deceptions allowed are those fermenting in the heart of man. Nothing has changed. As in this new world they also need a redeemer, and to be born of the water and the Spirit to enter the kingdom of God. At this time, they are *in* Jesus' everlasting kingdom, but not *of* it. It is expedient for this world to comprehend this. *They still must be born again.* They are told that this is the everlasting kingdom, and this will be followed by a new heaven and earth.

SEEING JESUS AS HE IS

1st John 3:2 "Beloved, now we are the sons of God, and it does not yet appear what we shall be. But we know that when he shall appear we shall be like him, for we shall see him as he is." What does this mean? This is speaking of the rapture of the church when they meet the Lord Jesus in the air. The Christians will then see the Lord as he is, because they will be like him. Because when raptured, they will be changed. This mortal must take on immortality, and this corruption must take on incorruption. Having a new heart and eyes, they will then see him as he is. This will also apply to those on the earth during the millennial reign. Jesus is now reigning on the earth, and the rapture has taken place. So now when they see him as he is (Lord and Savior), they will then be as he is. Now born of the Spirit. They will be changed, completely and instantly. As God is spirit, so the saints on the earth will become as he is; Spirit. They will vanish from the sight of those present. They will just disappear. More clarity will be given on this later.

CHAPTER 49

A NEW WORLD

The new world will be changed to be completely different from this one. With a much larger land mass, much like the earth before the flood. The mountains will be brought low. And as there is no mention of death, it appears the world will be much like the Garden of Eden. It also will be populated by the few survivors from a world gone mad. This with a very large number of angels and Christians that came with the Lord, as his army, to be kings and priests. This presents an unusual situation, as there is a vast gulf between them. The Lord has separated them into two camps: those being ruled by a rod of iron, and those ruling, being kings and priests. Any speculation as to this world needs to focus on those being ruled with a rod of iron, as there is absolutely no hint of oppression. And there is peace, and a clear picture of freedom.

So what form does this ruling with a rod of iron take? This rod of iron cannot be control, to impose God's will over man in a dictatorial manner. Rather, it would be a clear and absolute assurance these people will conduct and govern themselves by God's standards. God wants that none should be lost. As nothing changes as far as becoming a Christian, and all of this world has full access of the sinful nature of man that brought about the need for a savior to take their sins and wash them that they may be pure, this brings a question. The Bible is clear that there are none that are good. No, not one. And that our greatest righteousness are as filthy rags. It is obvious the greater the evil, the greater the longing for that which is pure. In this new world, restriction on evil itself hinders this urgency for that which is pure. So the question: Is it not reasonable that man is being tested to see if his heart desires absolute love and purity, rather than just removing the evil that offends? With anything else being unthinkable; simply wanting the heart of God. And His heart is seen in the express image of Himself; His only begotten Son.

We have apparently gone full circle. From God removing man from the garden of Eden because of disobeying him, and now back to what appears similar to Eden, with the plus that now that old serpent that tempted Eve is locked up, and God's role models, his countless angels and resurrected saints, are here instead. This is directly following a world that, had Jesus delayed his coming, there would be no flesh saved. Yes, this world of peace with no deception or wars has taken the place of a world that had gone completely mad. And there is the actual presence of the Lord, in which he reigns in his kingdom.

However, an event takes place that seems unthinkable. This is seldom, if ever, mentioned as it doesn't seem to fit into this Garden of Eden world. But this event reveals, as none other (except in the book of Job), that the Lord is after the heart of man. And it is those who are after the heart of God. This is the last event that takes place before the Lord creates a new heaven and earth, and it more clearly brings to mind the compromising and the perverting of Christianity... to the point where it is no longer Christianity. This is revealed in Rev. 20:7-9 "And when the thousand years have expired, Satan will be loosed out of his prison, - And shall deceive the nations which are in the four quarters of the earth, Gog and Magog, to gather them to battle; the number of whom is as the sand of the sea. - And they went up on the breadth of the earth, and compassed the camp of the saints about, and the beloved city. And fire came down from God out of heaven and devoured them all."

CHAPTER 50

QUESTIONS

In this present world, it is not difficult to understand the necessity of man needing his sins to be washed clean before he can enter God's kingdom. But in this coming last world kingdom of peace and gentleness, this need to be washed becomes more involved. Man must become as Job and not just hear of, but see, God. And when you see God, your heart sees a righteousness and love that should cause you to abhor yourself and repent in dust and ashes. This contrast between the righteousness of the most righteous man on the earth and God cannot be conceived.

This writer is aware of the ministries that teach self-esteem. When it is accepted with assurance that the Lord indeed has taken your sins, and you are washed, you then have esteem. Not self-esteem, but your esteem and thankful thoughts are on he who washed you. Yes, it is your very thoughts on *who* makes you pure that gives you peace and joy. There is a noticeable difference between Christians and the world. Your thoughts are not on being good, but on he who loves you. And your thoughts concerning yourself diminish.

What is difficult to understand is, why would the creator of all there is take man's sins if they only would believe on him? Well, it really goes beyond that. It's believing the creator God would have such love that he would die for man, and take their sins so that they would be made pure. Developing a heart that would want such a heart as God's. This will be a difficult time in this world as never before, as the Lord is ruling with a rod of iron and will not allow evil. When the fire is removed, it is difficult to be refined.

THE HEART OF MAN

God will rule with a rod of iron, and the fear of the Lord. But God will not control the heart of man. The prophet Jeremiah spoke of the heart of man, and this reveals why he will not control it. Jer. 17:9-10 "The heart is deceitful above all things, and desperately wicked; who can know it (the heart)? - I, the Lord, search the heart, I try the reins, to give every man according to his ways, and according to the fruit of his doings." The heart is the soul and eternal man; the flesh is but for a moment. God tests man, giving him free rein. Man is given the freedom to choose the direction of his soul.

It would not appear to be so in this last world kingdom, as God is forcing peace and order because of the fear of the Lord. But God is seeking the heart of man. Man, who is conducting himself honorably, will be constantly reminded of his hypocrisy because of his heart. Some will recognize this and abhor themselves, repenting in dust and ashes. Their heart will be longing for a God that will wash them. With all their being, they will desire to be in his presence and image. They have access to the unaltered word of God as no others have had. Full knowledge that the creator God sent his only begotten Son to not only wash clean; but, as a sinless man, to take our sins as if it were he that committed them. Because neither he nor the Father want anyone to perish.

To help understand this, we will go to the words of Paul the apostle, whom after receiving Jesus as Lord and Savior spoke of his own heart in the flesh. Romans 7:19 "For the good that I would, I do not. But the evil I would not, that I do." It is the belief here that Paul's outside, natural behavior exceeded most, if not all, of the inhabitants of this world. But that did not satisfy; as the Lord spoke to his heart.

MEETING THE LORD

The natural man is quite illogical. Self-centered, embracing self, and susceptible to mob psychology; as when all the world follows Satan to their death. This is completely different from those that receive Jesus as Lord and Savior, which is an individual and personal commitment called a marriage. Each believer is the bride; and Jesus, the groom. As all of this new world knows of God, there is the natural wish to identify him. This is not a difficult task, as this generation has knowledge of fulfilled prophesy leading up to this last 1,000 years when Jesus will reign from Jerusalem with a rod of iron for the entire time. A time when there will be no war and the predatory animals will live peacefully, becoming vegetarians. Everything, including this utopian paradise, will affirm this.

All of these things will happen as prophesied. This leaves a question: where are Jesus and all of these angels and resurrected Saints? The Bible clearly states that when Jesus returns, he will establish his everlasting kingdom, the Kingdom of God, and reign from Jerusalem. At this time, there will be a gathering of intellectuals to answer this mystery. The answer is in the Bible; and in the very chapter where God has proclaimed his love for mankind. And the rest of the New Testament reveals that the means God chose for the path for man to become sinless, in the image of God, was the cross.

Yes, God did create man in his image. But man is given the right to either reject this, or to want, more than life itself, for this to be so. The Bible affirmed this when Jesus spoke to Nicodemus, and stated the second and then third birth that must take place. Man was created in the image of God. This was recorded in the very first chapter of the Bible. But yet, this cannot be. For if this were true, man would have no need for a Savior. These occupants of this last world government will have many questions and mysteries. All of which can be answered. And there is a special blessing for those who read the book of Revelation.

As Jesus had explained to Nicodemus, there are multiple births. The first is the natural birth from the womb. The last results from the gathering of the Saints to meet the Lord in the air. But before this third birth can take place, the second must occur… the believing and accepting of Jesus as Redeemer. This results in a problem for the residents of this last generation in this final 1,000 years. They know by the scriptures that Jesus has now established his everlasting kingdom after descending from the heavens with his army of angels and risen saints to rule from Jerusalem.

But where are they? Not one of these survivors of this world gone mad can enter this Kingdom of God. Because not one is a born again Christian. And yet they have gone from a world at the brink of destruction, to a world like the Garden of Eden. Who would not believe they have entered the kingdom of God? The Bible has stated that Jesus will reign over this kingdom. It also states this Garden of Eden does not end with mankind being expelled, but by being destroyed, along with Satan, by fire from heaven. And after that will come a new heaven and earth. Yes, Jesus will reign over them. But with a rod of iron. This is the only way for fallen man to live for any length of time without violence and war.

He reigns in this thousand-year kingdom which is as the Garden of Eden. At the same time, he is reigning in his everlasting Kingdom as the light of it. Rev. 22:5 "And there shall be no night there, for the Lord God giveth them light and they shall reign forever." As we are told, man cannot even conceive what God has prepared for those who love him. Therefore, there will be no attempt to do so. It is not the purpose here to, with pride, reveal extra knowledge or wisdom. As anyone reading this manuscript can readily see, this author does not possess writing skills. But he has noticed, through the years, Christians that are so very thankful that the creator God would have such love for them. And then they are bombarded on all sides, being told that science has proven there is no God. And the many Christian churches that completely contradict each other and will outright reject so much of the Bible.

As the years go by, because of listening to others supposedly more educated and knowledgeable than themselves explain away the truth of the Bible, doubt and unbelief can take hold. And faith and assurance can be lost because of allowing man to take away what God has placed in their hearts. But God will allow only one person to remove your name from the book of life. And that is yourself. Mob psychology, wishing not to offend mankind, plays the greater part in this. But it still comes down to whom it is easier to offend... God, or man.

God has made us diverse to such an extent that he sent his Son to die, singularly, for each one of us. Likewise, the Bible is a personal love letter to each of us. When you see what seems to be an error, because you know it is the word of God, you know it is true and that the Lord is trying to get your attention. If you do not believe it is true, it will not get your attention. This results in trying to explain it away if confronted by the enemies of God, instead of searching these words of truth to help not only yourself, but perhaps also them. Christianity is the ultimate truth to a very special people that recognize the heart of God, who is testing and trying the hearts of his people.

Jesus has established his everlasting kingdom at the start of this millennial kingdom of man. This is only the first 1,000 years of God's everlasting kingdom. Of which are, to our knowledge, only Christ, the angels, and the resurrected Saints who returned from the heavens with him. There is a camp of the saints that the world makes battle with. And as they will no longer know war, it is obviously a different battle, perhaps a personal battle or war of the heart.

Of the people that will occupy this new earth, not one is a Christian. They are in this world, but not of it. They can't be of this world until they are born of the Spirit, which is the third birth. None are able to enter into his everlasting kingdom until they are born again of the Spirit. And because the Bible is the word of truth, it would not be truth if both of these kingdoms combined as one. It is impossible to understand the Bible by believing what cannot be. If you truly believe, you will continue trying to understand these words, and not ignore what is difficult to understand. There are two governments. One lasting for one thousand years, the other everlasting.

Nothing has changed as far as salvation. All must be born again. Jesus rules this world with a rod of iron, which is the fear of the Lord. Thus, it causes man to behave as never before. God is seeking the heart of man, and this cannot be by controlling it. The only way for man to enter this kingdom is for man to want, more than anything, the heart of God in exchange for his. This exchange is made possible in the most remarkable way. The Son of God takes our wicked hearts. Jer. 17:9 "The heart of man is desperately wicked. Who can know it?" And then, he gives a new heart to those who desire the heart of God.

MINISTERING SPIRITS

This writer does not completely understand the fullness of ministering spirits (angels), which are involved quite extensively in the salvation of man. The magnitude of this varies, and the Lord has withheld this for a reason. If man knew, he would make an extensive effort to search them out personally. And this is strictly forbidden. We do know, however, the Holy Spirit's role in continually revealing the Gospel message to the heart of man during sleep. Also it must be assumed that since all of this new world will know of the Lord, there will be many diverse churches. And as the Lord will not allow any perversion of scriptures, all the correct scriptures will be presented, much more so than now. Even though the pastors will not be Christians. The only thing that would stop belief in the truth would be their own heart.

As has been pointed out, as soon as someone realizes the truth of salvation, and receives Jesus as Lord and Savior, they are born again. Their second and third birth are simultaneous. They would then immediately leave this world, and appear in the kingdom of God. This should be a clue, again dividing the people. Questions will come up. Is God intervening by removing those who are inquiring of him, being displeased with them? What kind of a God is this, who would remove these people from this now paradise for inquiring of, or wanting to know him? Or what kind of people could possibly find such a God acceptable that does not want anyone searching him out?

It is amazing how clever unreasonable man can be. Communist nations forbade Christianity. As a result of persecution, the Christians started small underground house churches, and it grew even more. After the communist nations realized they could not destroy Christianity by forbidding it, they then founded State-run churches, being Christian in name only. They selectively watered down Christianity. This is more effective in destroying the church than forbidding its teachings; as it results in lukewarm Christianity that is not *true* Christianity.

During this millennial period, God will not allow any perversion or altering of scripture. This will leave personal blindness the only hindrance to salvation. And should a pastor come to the knowledge and conviction of being a Christian while preparing his message, he would then disappear, immediately entering the kingdom of God. This would eliminate anyone from coming to know the way of salvation except from a personal searching of the word. (This is really not that unusual now, as many come to the truth in spite of misguided pastors.)

During this millennial period, people will be living in a virtual paradise. There will be those who were fascinated with this God in the previous world of sin and violence. Who took the sin of those who believed in him? There is something else that all of mankind will know. Were there not the fear of the Lord, man would be quite evil. Each individual knows what is in their hearts. It is a desire to have this, a servant heart. There will be churches in abundance at this time, and all Christian, but in name only. It is interesting to speculate; what would they speak of? The conversation would probably be quite diverse, as now. During this time, there will be people who suddenly disappear. And this would be paramount in all conversations, being a continual occurrence in all of the world. This mystery would be the constant overriding conversation for this 1,000 years. And if these questions are asked to the Lord, the answer will be found. This is the same as now.

It will be more difficult to hate evil and love that which is good in a virtual paradise. But this world will have an advantage. No deceit and no lies will be allowed, and there will be access to true history. This history will center on the Bible and God, not man.

At the end of the 1,000 years, why would all the nations follow Satan to battle against the Lord after He releases Satan from the pit? Perhaps the question should be asked: why is there anyone left that has *not* entered into the kingdom of God? The answer to that is, no doubt, the heart of man. This world has neither recognized nor understood the cross. We know Satan will not be allowed to speak, as no lies will be allowed and he is a liar, with no truth in him. Why, then, would they follow him? This writer believes Satan will appear as an angel of light. 2nd Cor. 11:14 "And no marvel; Satan himself is transformed into an angel of light."

We know that not one of these people have received the Lord. For had they done so, they would have immediately left this world and entered into the Kingdom of God. So now they see this angel of light and follow him. They are following their eyes, and not their hearts. If they were following their hearts they would be following an old, rugged, bloodstained cross. The Bible states that the world is then gathered with Satan to battle, and they encompass the camp of the saints. And of course, this also is no physical battle against the saints.

It is obvious this battle is about becoming in the image of God… or the image of the beast.

These people know there is to be a new heaven and earth after this 1,000 years. And this battle, in which they are gathered with Satan? This is aligning with or being of the image of the beast. You do not come as a mass into the kingdom of God. It is an individual and personal eternal unity with he who loves you. Rev. 2:17 "To him that overcomes I will give a white stone, and in the stone a new name written, which no man knows except he that receives it."

Those following this angel of light will be following what they wanted. Those following the cross will receive what God wants for them.

ALL THINGS ARE NEW

When fire from God comes from heaven and destroys them all, this is now the beginning of the new heaven and earth. This is also the continuation of God's everlasting kingdom. This narrative will finish with the beginning. As this is the beginning of man's fantastic journey of the purpose for his creation, of which there will be no end. And all because of wanting to be as they were created to be. Created with the desire to know their creator, and with a heart that understands it is not about themselves and what they do for God. But simply believing what God has done and wants for them.

All praise be to our gracious Lord and God forever and ever, to the glory of His name. Amen.

Printed in the United States
By Bookmasters